Global Leadership Perspectives

Sara Miller McCune founded SAGE Publishing in 1965 to support the dissemination of usable knowledge and educate a global community. SAGE publishes more than 1000 journals and over 800 new books each year, spanning a wide range of subject areas. Our growing selection of library products includes archives, data, case studies and video. SAGE remains majority owned by our founder and after her lifetime will become owned by a charitable trust that secures the company's continued independence.

Los Angeles | London | New Delhi | Singapore | Washington DC | Melbourne

Global Leadership Perspectives

Insights and Analysis

Simon Western
Éric-Jean Garcia

Los Angeles | London | New Delhi
Singapore | Washington DC | Melbourne

Los Angeles | London | New Delhi
Singapore | Washington DC | Melbourne

SAGE Publications Ltd
1 Oliver's Yard
55 City Road
London EC1Y 1SP

SAGE Publications Inc.
2455 Teller Road
Thousand Oaks, California 91320

SAGE Publications India Pvt Ltd
B 1/I 1 Mohan Cooperative Industrial Area
Mathura Road
New Delhi 110 044

SAGE Publications Asia-Pacific Pte Ltd
3 Church Street
#10-04 Samsung Hub
Singapore 049483

Editor: Kirsty Smy
Assistant editor: Lyndsay Aitken
Production editor: Sarah Cooke
Marketing manager: Alison Borg
Cover design: Shaun Mercier
Typeset by: C&M Digitals (P) Ltd, Chennai, India
Printed in the UK

First published 2018

Library of Congress Control Number: 2017955500

British Library Cataloguing in Publication data

A catalogue record for this book is available from the British Library

ISBN 978-1-47395-343-7
ISBN 978-1-47395-344-4 (pbk)

At SAGE we take sustainability seriously. Most of our products are printed in the UK using responsibly sourced papers and boards. When we print overseas we ensure sustainable papers are used as measured by the PREPS grading system. We undertake an annual audit to monitor our sustainability.

PRAISE FOR *GLOBAL LEADERSHIP PERSPECTIVES*

'In our global world this book by Simon Western and Eric-Jean Garcia is highly overdue. They make quite clear – similar to the observation that there is no baby without a mother – that there is no leader without a context. The authors have made a heroic effort to point out to people interested in the subject of leadership that its essence can only be understood in a contextual, cultural way. This book is a required reading for anyone who truly wants to understand what leadership is all about.'

Manfred F. R. Kets de Vries, Distinguished Clinical Professor of Leadership Development and Organizational Change, INSEAD, France

'Thoughtful essays by local experts, brilliantly brought together by two analyses – the first categorising and correlating what they say; the second drawing out what they *don't* say, and thereby revealing more about leadership than anything else I have seen in the past few years. And who can resist a book that starts off with asking "What drives the libidinal economy of leadership and followership dynamics?", then goes on to "bring into the picture past echoes of war, freedom struggles, authoritarianism, trauma and of rich relational and kinship networks ... how culturally informed ways-of-being-in-the-world shape leadership and followership expectations and practices." Definitely a must-read for scholars and leaders alike, and sure to spark debate and further studies.'

Jonathan Gosling, Emeritus Professor of Leadership, University of Exeter; Lead Faculty, Forward Institute; Visiting Professor, Renmin University, China; CBS, Denmark and IEDC, Slovenia.

'This is a must-have book for both practitioners and scholars of leadership since both can enhance their awareness of leadership perspectives in an international context.'

Dr Alexandros Psychogios, Professor of International Human Resource Management, Birmingham City University

'This new book on leadership is most welcome indeed. In its descriptive section it allows the reader to confront and compare a wide array of approaches to leadership, demonstrating how different traditions and cultures shape leadership theory and practice. In its analytical section, it proposes a fresh and critical perspective on the different themes of the leadership literature, highlighting its achievements as well as its gaps, contradictions and remaining questions.'

Erhard Friedberg, Professor Emeritus of Sociology, SciencesPo Paris

'Leadership is a relationship in a context. Someone can be a leader in one context but not in another. This valuable book includes essays on the cultural context of leadership in 20 countries. The enlightening analysis shows how in much of the world traditional paternalistic and controlling leadership models are being challenged by a more adaptive and progressive global model.'

Michael Maccoby, author of The Leaders We Need, Strategic Intelligence, *and* Narcissistic Leaders

'As practitioners, academics, consultants and trainers working to make leadership development effective through times of chaos, *Global Leadership Perspectives* strengthens our capacity for action. Identity, community and context shape leadership in ways that require more listening at the margins. This book opens us to more inclusive leadership development for local and global resilience.'

Eliane Ubalijoro, PhD. Executive Director of C.L.E.A.R. International Development Inc. and Professor of Practice at McGill's Institute for the Study of International Development.

'The ASEAN story is a compelling one. In its five decades it has made considerable strides towards economic integration. However, its narrative is really about a varied group of countries being challenged to define themselves as one community, one people. A people in search of an identity. A collective in pursuit of leadership to take it to the next level. This publication serves to shed light on these challenges. A must read for students, business leaders and policy makers.'

Excellency Tan Sri Rebecca Sta Maria

'Very inspiring piece of original research work. The Arab and Middle East chapter identifies cultural and management issues, with "surgical" capabilities of knowledge and practical experience.'

Dr Ahmed Aljanahi, Deputy Group CEO of the Noor Bank, Dubai, UAE

'This truly unique book offers a fascinating collection of insights on cross-cultural leadership.'

Alexey Volokhov, Learning and Coaching Development Manager, 3M Global Academy for Innovative Development

'The chapter on Japan gives an easy-to-understand overview of the atmosphere one finds in a typical Japanese organization and how a leader navigates within it. At the same time, the chapter lays out the challenges faced by such a leadership style for companies competing in global markets. The chapter and others like it in this volume will help the reader understand what makes good leaders in the different organizational styles found around the world.'

Kentaro Iijima, Former Corporate Senior Vice President of Fujitsu Marketing

'This new collective book on leadership is very inspiring as I have been wondering, for my ten years' experience in a Leader position of an international organization and thirty-five year career, whether Leadership is a strongly typed concept or not. This book convinced me to admit the universal principles of leadership.'

Abel Didier Tella, Directeur Général, APUA/ASEA

CONTENTS

ABOUT THE AUTHORS

SIMON WESTERN

Dr Simon Western is CEO and founder of Analytic-Network Coaching Ltd, an avant-garde coaching company whose purpose is to 'coach leaders to act in good faith to create the good society' www.analyticnetwork.com. He is an internationally recognized thought leader on coaching and leadership; a consultant, coach, keynote speaker, academic and author of two acclaimed books: *Leadership: A Critical Text* (Sage, 2013) and *Coaching and Mentoring: A Critical Text* (Sage, 2012). Simon works with senior leaders on strategy, organizational change and their personal leadership challenges. Bringing critical theory, networked theory and psychoanalytic thinking to help leaders develop new insights, act ethically and create change in organizational life is key to his work.

He currently holds positions as President and CEO of ISPSO (the International Society for the Psychoanalytic Study of Organizations), Adjunct Professor of University College Dublin and is Honorary Professor, Higher School of Economics, Moscow.

ÉRIC-JEAN GARCIA

Dr Éric-Jean Garcia received a PhD in Higher Education & Leadership Development from the Institute of Education, University College London (UCL) and holds an MBA from the University of Dallas (Texas, USA). Éric-Jean is Affiliate Professor of Leadership at Sciences Po, Paris (France), where he leads several leadership programmes in Executive Education. He is also an international keynote speaker, and advisor in leadership for business and public organizations and author of two award-winning books: *Leadership* (De Boeck, 2011) and *Le génie du leadership* (Dunod, 2013). Through his work Éric-Jean seeks to foster critical thinking, challenge taken-for-granted assumptions and beliefs, reveal dilemmas of leadership and advocate the development of contextually and ethically relevant organizational strategies.

ABOUT THE CONTRIBUTORS

Fernando Sandoval Arzaga holds a PhD in Management from ESADE Business School in Barcelona, Spain. He is a Postdoctoral Researcher at London Business School.

Gabriela Barrial holds a MA Psychology from UBA, University of Buenos Aires, Argentina. She is a Certified Ontological Coach by Newfield Consulting; Value Drivers Consultant by Horwath International; has a P3C Practitioner Certificate in Consulting and Change from The Tavistock Institute of Human Relations and is Certified in Intensive Balint Leadership by the American Balint Society.

Asha Bhandarker holds a PhD in Management from Osmania University, India. She is a distinguished Professor of Organizational Behaviour at IMI Delhi and Senior Fulbright Fellow. She is also a well-known consultant in the Indian corporate sector and a noted researcher with many publications in the domain of leadership and management education to her credit.

Richard Bolden (PhD, Leadership Studies, University of Exeter, UK) is Director of the Bristol Leadership and Change Centre at the University of the West of England. His research interests include distributed and shared leadership; place-based leadership; leadership and identity; and evaluating leadership and organization development in complex environments.

Jane Chapman has been a member of ISPSO since 2003 and an organizational and marketing consultant until her recent retirement. She now acts professionally as an Anglican priest. Her main work in the ISPSO tradition has been the article 'Hatred and Corruption of Task' published in *Organisational and Social Dynamics* (2003; 3 (1): 40–60).

Chao C. Chen is professor of management and global business, Rutgers University. His current research interests include behavioural ethics, group harmony, and cross-cultural management. He has published numerous articles in leading management journals and a book on Chinese management and leadership philosophies.

Cheryl Getz holds an EdD, Leadership Studies from University of San Diego, USA; MA in Athletic Administration from Central Michigan University, USA; BS in Education from University of Cincinnati, USA.

Johan Grant PhD is a certified psychologist. Johan is a consultant and part-time assistant professor at the Department of Psychology, Lund University, Sweden. Johan has 20 years' experience as a consultant working with C-suite executives in Europe, the USA and Latin America, focusing on coaching, executive team development and strategy implementation.

Zachary Gabriel Green holds a PhD in Clinical and Community Psychology from Boston University, USA; MEd in Counseling, Cleveland State University, USA; BA in Psychology – Minors in English and Education, from Case Western Reserve University, USA.

Firoz Abdul Hamid is specialized in speech writing, crisis and media communications, organizational transformation, human resources development, branding and governance for the public and private sectors, universities and think-tanks. She holds an MBA and BEng (Hons), ACGI, Civil Engineering from Imperial College London, UK.

Yasuhiro Hattori was born in Kanagawa, Japan. He received his PhD from Kobe University and researches Japanese human resource management and organizational behaviour. Recently, he is also interested in the global HRM of Japanese companies.

Daniel Arturo Heller was born in Colombia, raised in Massachusetts, and has lived in Japan for more than 20 years. He received his PhD from the University of Tokyo and researches Japanese management practices in the world automobile industry and interorganizational learning in strategic alliances.

Irena Izotova holds an MA in Business Psychology from Higher School of Economics (Moscow). Her extensive professional experience covers executive and leadership team coaching and organizational consulting for multinational and Russian business organizations (e.g. Johnson & Johnson, 3M, Unilever, Severstal). She is currently a researcher and lecturer at Higher School of Economics.

Beata Jałocha holds a PhD in Management Science from Jagiellonian University, Kracow, Poland. She also gained education through programmes offered by Kedge Business School, France and City University of New York, USA.

Serdar Karabatı holds a PhD in Management and Organization from Bogazici University, Istanbul, Turkey. He is currently Associate Professor of Management at Istanbul Bilgi University, Turkey.

Jeff de Kleijn is a Sinologist with a Master's degree from Leiden University, The Netherlands, specialized in contemporary China. He has lived, studied, and worked in China and Asia for most of the past 20 years. He also holds a postgraduate Master of Marketing degree from TIAS Business School, The Netherlan.

Jeremias J. De Klerk is a professor in leadership and human capital management, and a research director at the University of Stellenbosch Business School, South Africa. His research interests include leadership, behavioural ethics, system psychodynamics, engagement and workplace spirituality.

Konstantin Korotov holds a PhD in Management (Organizational Behaviour) from INSEAD (France, Singapore and Abu-Dhabi). His previous professional experience includes being a Director with Ernst & Young, a researcher and an executive coach at INSEAD, and research assistantship at New York University, USA.

Nai-keung Lau is a Member of Basic Law Committee of the National People's Congress Standing Committee, Visiting Professor of Jinan University and Beijing Business Management College, China. He served as Adviser to Shanghai Academy of Social Sciences Exchanges Office for Taiwan, Hong Kong and Macau Affairs, and as a Member of Commission for Strategic Development of HKSARG.

Jian Liang is a management professor at the Advanced Institution of Business Research at the Tongji University. He got his Ph.D. from Hong Kong University of Science and Technology and his research interests includes employee proactivity, leadership effectiveness, cross-cultural management and business ethics.

Susan Long is a socioanalytic consultant, author and director of Research and Scholarship at the National Institute for Organisation Dynamics Australia (NIODA). She teaches at the University of Melbourne Executive Programs, INSEAD in Singapore, MIECAT and the University of Divinity, Australia. She is also General Editor of the journal *Socioanalysis*.

Fentahun Mengistu has served as a policy analyst at the Ethiopian Higher Education Strategy Centre. He earned his MA in 2009 in Educational Leadership and Management at Addis Ababa University.

Ekaterina Belokoskova-Mikhaylova holds a PhD in Philosophy from Moscow State University, Russia and is continuing studying at The White Institute, USA. Previously, she has been HR director for Japanese companies in Moscow as well as Vice-President of the National Federation of Psychoanalysis in Russia.

Vachel Miller taught at Bahir Dar University in Ethiopia as a Fulbright Scholar. He holds an EdD in Educational Policy and Leadership from the University of Massachusetts Amherst, USA.

Peliwe Mnguni obtained her PhD in Leadership and Organisation Dynamics from Swinburne University of Technology in Australia. Her research, teaching and consulting practice is grounded in systems psychodynamics. Peliwe's research and teaching areas include leadership, change and transformation, as well as executive coaching.

Oscar Muiño, until 2014, was professor in the Master in Journalism and Media – National University of La Plata, Argentina. He is a Member of the Argentine Political Club. His publications include *Alfonsín* (Aguilar, 2014). He was Undersecretary of Public Information and Executive Secretary of the EFSUR.

Claudia Nagel holds a PhD in Organizational Psychology, a Master's in Business Administration from Cologne University, Germany, and a postgraduate diploma in Psychoanalysis from ISAP, Zurich, Switzerland. She is visiting professor at Hull University Business School, UK, research fellow at Zeppelin University, Germany and visiting scholar at Vrije Universiteit Amsterdam, The Netherlands. In her own consulting firm, she focuses on 'behavioural strategy'.

Déo M. Nyamusenge holds a Master in Leadership from the University of Exeter, UK. He is General Director of International Space Consulting (Abidjan) and African Leadership Alliance (Kinshasa). All over Africa he works as facilitator, trainer, coach and social researcher in leadership, strategic and organizational development.

Beyza Oba holds a PhD Degree in Management and Organization from Istanbul University. She is currently Professor of Management and Organization at Istanbul Bilgi University, Turkey.

Maria Fonseca Paredes has a PhD in Industrial Relations from University of Toronto, Canada and an MBA and Master of Science in Computer Systems from ITESM, Mexico. She is a founding researcher of the STEP Project for Family Enterprising. Her research interests are in the areas of strategic management, entrepreneurial family and contribution of workplace innovations to organizational effectiveness and performance.

Valérie Petit: From 2003 to 2017, Valérie was an associate professor of Management at EDHEC Business School, France, and the director of the Open Leadership Research Centre on leadership and diversity. She holds a PhD in Management and three Master's, in political sciences, communication and social-psychology. She teaches, writes, trains and does research on leadership, ethics and diversity. In 2017, she became a member of the French Parliament.

Vaseehar Hassan Bin Abdul Razack is the former CEO of the Dallah Al Baraka Group in Malaysia and Chairman of RHB Islamic Bank Berhad. He has an MA in Organizational Psychology from INSEAD; a PhD in Leadership from Vrije Universiteit Amsterdam, The Netherlands; an MSc in Organizational Psychology from HEC Paris, France; and an MBA from Aston University, UK.

Girma Shimelis is a lecturer at Jigjiga University in Ethiopia. He earned his MA in 2011 in Educational Leadership and Management at Addis Ababa University. He is now a PhD student in Educational Policy and Leadership at Bahir Dar University, Ethiopia.

Pritam Singh holds a PhD from BHU, India and an MBA from Indiana University Bloomington, USA. He is known as a corporate guru, thought leader and turnaround CEO of business schools like IIM-L and MDI-Gurgaon. He has a distinguished career record and has been honoured with numerous awards, including the Padmashree (one of India's highest civilian honours).

Maria José Tonelli is a psychologist and has a PhD in Social Psychology. She is full Professor at FGV-EAESP, Brazil, where she was the Deputy Dean from 2007 to 2014. Currently she is director of the Research Centre on Organization and People. She is Editor-in-Chief of RAE – Revista de Administração de Empresas.

Yngve Magnus Ulsrød is an Executive Master in Consulting and Coaching for Change (INSEAD). He is a Norwegian executive with multiple leadership roles in Europe, Asia and the USA for more than 30 years. Until April 2016 he was CHRO and Executive Vice President for a global logistics company. The majority of Yngve´s professional life is in the global arena.

Dimitrios Vonofakos holds a PhD, Psychoanalytic Studies, and Master's degree, Psychoanalytic Studies from the University of Essex, UK, and a Bachelor's degree, Psychology, from the American College of Thessaloniki, Greece.

David Weir is Professor of Intercultural Management at York St John University, UK, and has for several decades been researching and writing on distinctive patterns of management, leadership and management in the MENA world. He has worked in many countries in the region and in the recent past has been involved in organizational development projects in UAE, Jordan and Palestine.

Morgen Witzel (MA, History, University of Victoria, Canada) is a Fellow of the Centre for Leadership Studies at the University of Exeter, UK, former Editor of *Corporate Finance Review* and part-time lecturer at the London Business School. He is the author of more than 20 books on management, management history and leadership.

Michał Zawadzki holds a PhD in management (Jagiellonian University, Krakow, Poland), MA in sociology and philosophy (Nicolaus Copernicus University in Toruń, Poland), is Associate Editor for the *European Management Journal* and a reviewer for JCR journals. He was working as a postdoctoral researcher in the Gothenburg Research Institute (Visby Programme, 2015), Sweden.

ACKNOWLEDGEMENTS

Simon Western

To my wonderful family Agata, Lily and Albert, thank you for your love, inspiration, support and patience to allow this work to emerge through the long process of research and writing. Also I acknowledge those loved ones I have lost, yet are still with me and inspire me. My brother Mark, Mum, Dad, my beautiful son Fynn and my brother Stephen. Living with grief has become a part of my everyday being. Living with loss and with joy at the same time is a tribute to the transcendent power of love. I dedicate this book to all those mentioned above. Thank you all so much.

Finally, I wish to thank all friends and colleagues who support my work in so many ways; there is not such a thing as individual authors, we all write carrying others with us. Thanks to the chapter authors who worked generously and closely with us to edit and shape these wonderful contributions, to SAGE editors Lyndsay Aitken and Kirsty Smy who are a delight to work with, offering timely advice, wisdom, consideration and support and finally to my co-editor, Éric-Jean for his initial contact and suggestion that we work together on this project, and especially for his support and help to improve the Analysis section of this book.

Éric-Jean Garcia

First and foremost, I would like to express my whole hearted thanks to my wife Laure for her love, support and wise advice.

I also would like to thank my son Alexandre. Although he lives far away from us, his cheerful professional attitude and intellectual openness inspire me beyond being his father.

Great thanks are due to each of the chapter authors from across the globe for their trustworthy and effective cooperation through so many emails.

My thanks are also due to my friends and colleagues from IOE, University College London and Sciences Po Paris as well as the CEOs and several members of their Leadership teams from a wide variety of companies based in Europe, United States and Asia.

Finally, I wish to thank our Publisher, SAGE who wisely encouraged us to achieve our objectives both quantitatively and qualitatively as well as my co-author Simon who continuously worked hard with determination and inspiration throughout the journey.

INTRODUCTION

Simon Western and Éric-Jean Garcia

This book sets out to 'allow leadership to speak with different voices', to liberate leadership from how it is portrayed in the dominant academic and popular literature, and to discover local and regional variations of leadership thinking and practice.

The contents of this book reveal a much richer, contextualized, diverse and culturally informed set of leadership themes and approaches that challenge the limits of the dominant 'insider-leadership' discourses. We share 10 important findings from this book:

1. There are very rich differences in leadership across all 20 regions. The analysis found unique culturally informed examples of leadership themes and approaches that open new possibilities for understanding and developing emergent leadership practice and theory.
2. Leadership research and practices need to find new research approaches to work with historically and culturally embedded practices that inform how leadership and followership is understood and practised.
3. Working with gaps and lacks, rather than seeking empirical knowledge, offers an important additional way into discovering new outsider-leadership influences that can provide vital insights beyond the normative findings.
4. Eco-leadership (Western, 2013) emerges as a potential container, a meta-discourse that is able to embrace diversity within the wider eco-systems, enabling development of theory and practices that embrace all forms of insider- and outsider-leadership approaches.
5. Leadership cannot be reduced to a universal norm, nor can it be reduced to a set of skills and competencies. It is shaped by the wider culture in which it resides. This wider influence is internalized at individual, group, organizational and network levels which in turn contributes to shape the wider culture. A mutually influential process takes place between wider culture and the self/selves. What is important here is not to generalize that process but seek its subjective truth in local and specific contexts.
6. Political leadership and organizational leadership are connected and mutually influential.
7. In search of the leadership symptom: the experimental methodology that utilized psychoanalytic insights from Lacan, alongside cultural and historical approaches, critical theory and discourse analysis, revealed to us the potential of developing this new approach further. It revealed an understanding of leadership beyond rational and structural approaches. It offers a way into realizing what drives the libidinal economy of leadership and followership dynamics, which offers insights that can transform situations that repetitively get stuck in patterns of dysfunction.
8. These findings can inspire and encourage leadership practitioners, academics, consultants and trainers to be more aware of indigenous and culturally informed leadership approaches, enabling them to work in more sensitive, appropriate and pragmatic ways.
9. New leadership themes and practices also provide a counter-point, a short-circuiting (Žižek, 2003) that takes from the local and informs leadership thinking and practice beyond the country in which it is first identified; beyond or in a blended way, a 'creolization'

between dominant discourse that borrows and discards before melting it with local traditions, economic and legal realities.

10. Leadership studies is a complex field that requires daring enquiries and humility: daring to explore new territories and humility in front of the diversity, complexity and provisory truths about leadership.

Our impetus for writing this book is derived from working with leaders across the globe, and realizing that two large gaps exist in the literature. These gaps we believe have led to a failure to grasp and account for the diversity in how leadership manifests itself and is practised across the globe, influenced by local and regional histories, traditions and cultures in different regions of the world.

Firstly, the gap between theory and practice has been far too wide for far too long. The rhetoric and performative leadership that is displayed to match performance targets, versus 'what-is-really-going-on' in practice is a big gap. The leadership that goes unseen or is seen but not acknowledged, requires deeper, more textured and nuanced exploration. This gap is exacerbated in local and regional contexts outside of Westernized contexts, where culturally informed local practices and perceptions of leadership are largely ignored in the mainstream literature. 'In effect, the many authors who have persistently tried to elucidate leadership from a universal perspective have only contributed to making its meaning significantly more confusing and ethereal' (Garcia, 2008). For Collinson and Grint (2005) mainstream leadership researches are 'rather objectivist, essentialist and functionalist, frequently abstracted from specific contexts'. Lesley (2005) claims that 'objectivist' perspectives are typical of Western conceptions of leadership that divorce leaders (treated as subjects) from context and from 'followers' (treated as passive objects).

The second gap that also informs the first is between the mainstream existing methodologies used for researching leadership and the potential for different research methods that would or could produce much more diverse and applicable findings. Current leadership research focuses on individualism, behaviourism and 'organizationalism', reflecting the Westernized pervasive ideas as to what a leader is, i.e. an individual actor who influences others through their behaviours from their hierarchical roles within organizations. The mainstream research is designed to fit with the leadership and management journals. It grants awarding bodies that demand empirical and reductionist findings, reproducing the same conformist knowledge base that presently exists. The most common form focuses on searching for the holy grail of leadership behaviours and competencies that produce a 'good' leader (transformational leadership research: Bass, 1985, 1998; Burns, 2003). There is a marginal body of critical theory that challenges this work, but by its own admissions it often produces elitist knowledge that gets circulated in self-referential networks and has little impact on leadership practices (Parker, 2002). For instance, Critical Management Studies (CMS) has been criticized for having 'an excessively narrow conception of emerging social problems it can deal with. It often focuses on strictly organizational issues and seldom explores broader societal issues ... CMS has had little to say about the animal rights, militarization and war, (neo)colonialism, anti-globalization movements, the financial crisis, global warming, the rise of the populist alt-right and so on. In this way, CMS can be seen as parasitical to management' (Huault et al., 2017).

WHAT ELSE SHAPES LEADERSHIP?

This creates a gap, a blind spot as to 'what else' shapes leadership. The 'what else' we are interested in is the unacknowledged regional histories, cultures, tensions, traumas, religions, economics, technologies, emotional landscapes and the social changes that shape everyday leadership practices and leadership–followership dynamics. These sociocultural factors are interwoven with the powerful global forces that export leadership discourses and practices. The gap between studying the individual actor and their behaviours and the sociocultural influences on leadership are huge.

This book sets about working towards exploring these gaps. To achieve this, we carefully selected and invited authors from 20 diverse countries and regions to 'unravel leadership'. They accepted to deliver short chapters offering culturally informed leadership insights into their local contexts.

Our aim in Part One of the book is to allow these 20 chapters to speak for themselves. In our author guidelines[1] we asked authors to focus on 'sociocultural and historical influences', stating:

> Consideration must be given to historic, social, political and economic influences that shape leadership perceptions and practices. For example, monarchies and religion have a particular influence, as do democratizing revolutions and dictatorships, the question is how do these influences continue to shape contemporary leadership today? Are key individuals symbolic to leadership thinking in the past or present?

We urged authors to write courageously, and asked them to try to capture an essence of leadership that spoke through their particular culture and context. The results have been outstanding. The richness of the chapters made the analysis in Part Two of the book a great challenge to do justice to the depth and wealth of insights of the data and material available.

We will now briefly guide you through the book, before hoping that you become absorbed and enjoy the rich chapters, and become as intrigued in the analysis of these chapters as much as we did.

[1]The author guidelines are set out in full in the Appendix.

SIGNPOSTING THE WAY

Part One – Insights: 20 chapters from diverse countries and regions

In Part One, entitled 'Insights', we invited authors from 20 countries and regions to 'unravel leadership' and to write courageously, delivering short chapters that offered leadership insights into their local contexts. Part One of the book allows leadership to speak through these chapters without analysis or comment from the editors. We invite the reader to make sense of what these chapters are in their own way; to bring their own experience to the readings in order to gain insights into (a) leadership in the regional context in which they are written, and (b) to reflect on leadership more generally, and how each chapter might offer new insights into the reader's own leadership perceptions, beliefs, practices and context.

Part Two – Analysis: Using the 20 chapters as research data for analysis

The research design and methodology for this book are set out in Chapter 21. This research takes place in two parts, an *insider-analysis* and an *outsider-analysis*. The former seeks to understand which 'insider-leadership' discourses are present in each chapter, and how they are enacted and how they interplay with each other. This insider discourse analysis then looks for commonalities, i.e. how the insider-leadership discourses reveal themselves as patterns across the whole 20 chapters. To achieve this a discourse analysis was undertaken, based on previously published research, which identified the four dominant discourses of leadership that appeared in the West over the past century (Western, 2005, 2008, 2013). These four discourses defined what we termed as 'insider-leadership' approaches.

The second part of the analysis is called outsider-analysis and used a novel methodology to search for the gaps, the lack and the remainder that is left outside of the first discourse analysis. This analysis draws on Lacanian psychoanalytic theory, searching for 'symptoms' of leadership in each country/region, an essence that points to the 'Real' of leadership. This Lacanian 'Real' is beyond language and normative understandings, and offers a glimpse of what unconscious dynamics determine and shape leadership. Therefore, a symptom is something that points to leadership beyond rational knowledge and empirical findings. Our 'outsider-leadership' methodology produced very exciting and rich findings beyond our expectations.

Conclusion and discussion

Our conclusion–discussion reflects on what we have discovered about leadership and what gaps remain.

Through this process we have:

a. Uncovered leadership patterns, discourses, assumptions and practices that will help to fill the gaps in the dominant, contemporary leadership literature.
b. Identified new leadership themes and approaches that are either emergent innovations, or which have been held in traditions without being widely recognized or acknowledged.

This process fills gaps in the literature and also provides new data to disrupt normative leadership approaches, thereby opening a space for new leadership possibilities to develop.

FINALLY

Petriglieri and Petriglieri (2015) enquire if business schools can humanize leadership, identifying how leadership has been narrowed to 'to a goal-focused activity that can be broken down into a set of skills, on the one hand, or an expansion of it into a virtue' on the other. They continue, saying this 'dehumanizes leadership by disembodying and disembedding it, that is by severing its ties to identity, community, and context'.

Our research and analysis support this view and build on the notion of identity, community and context, taking it beyond the present day to specifically include the weight of history, tradition, religion, economic transitions and indigenous cultures that impacts much more on leaders and leadership dynamics than is recognized. What is important is to expand the context in which we 'imagine leadership'. It is to bring into the picture the past echoes of war, freedom struggles, authoritarianism, trauma and of rich relational and kinship networks and ties that differ in each region and place. It is to search for the symptoms of leadership that resist being reduced to knowledge and reside in affective and emotional networks of experience. This book sets out to explore how culturally informed ways-of-being-in-the-world, shape leadership and followership expectations, perceptions and practices.

REFERENCES

Bass, Bernard. (1985) *Leadership and Performance Beyond Expectations*. New York: Free Press.

Bass, Bernard. M. (1998) *Transformational Leadership: Industrial, Military, and Educational Impact*. Mahwah, NJ: Lawrence Erlbaum Associates.

Burns, James MacGregor (2003) *Transforming Leadership: A New Pursuit of Happiness*. New York: Grove/Atlantic.

Collinson, D. and Grint, K. (2005) 'Editorial: The leadership agenda', *Leadership*, 1, 5–9.

Garcia, E-J. (2008) 'Leadership in MBA programmes: an inquiry into lecturers' curriculum interests'. PhD thesis, UCL Institute of Education, London, UK.

Huault, Isabelle, Kärreman, Dan, Perret, Véronique and Spicer, André (2017) 'Introduction to the special issue: The evolving debate about critical performativity', *M@n@gement*, 20 (1): 1–8.

Lesley, P. (2005) 'Eating the menu rather than the dinner: Tao and leadership', *Leadership*, 1, 105–26.

Parker, Martin (2002) *Against Management: Organization in the Age of Managerialism*. Cambridge: Polity Press.

Petriglieri, Gianpiero and Petriglieri, Jennifer Louise (2015) 'Can business schools humanize leadership?', *Academy of Management Learning & Education*, 14 (4): 625–47.

Western, S. (2005) 'A critical analysis of leadership: overcoming fundamentalist tendencies'. Doctoral Dissertation: Lancaster University Management School.

Western, S. (2008) 'Democratising strategy', in D. Campbell and D. Huffington (eds), *Organizations Connected: A Handbook of Systemic Consultation*. London: Karnac. pp. 173–96.

Western, Simon (2013) *Leadership: A Critical Text*, 2nd edn. London: Sage.

Žižek, S. (2003) *The Puppet and the Dwarf: The Perverse Core of Christianity*. Cambridge, MA: MIT Press.

PART ONE

Insights

Twenty Individual Country/Regional Chapters

1
ARAB MIDDLE EAST
Diwan, Ummah and Wasta: The Pillars of Arab Leadership

David Weir: Professor of Intercultural Management at York St John University, UK and Chairman of Fourth Paradigm Consulting Ltd

This chapter is based on long years of attempting to study and understand what is distinctive and valuable in the approaches to leadership that exist in this region, and on a strong and evolving respect for its people and institutions. What is meritorious in the analysis undoubtedly derives from what I have learned over a very long period from students, friends and colleagues; what is mistaken may be ascribed to honest error.

LEADERSHIP IN ARAB CULTURE

For the purposes of this chapter we can define the Arab Middle East as those countries that lie between the Atlantic Ocean and the Arabian Gulf, often described as the MENA region (MENA stands for Middle East and North Africa), although there are clearly geographical inclusions that do not entirely fit this 'Arab' profile. Egypt is not entirely 'Arab' and yet shares many cultural features.

Leadership in Arab organizations in this region is *sui generis,* not a failed attempt to copy Western models nor a hangover from a decaying traditionalism, and in many ways constitutes a distinctive paradigm of organization (Weir, 1998). But the styles of leadership in this region are still not widely appreciated and their strengths not always accepted, even by those who live and work in the region. One of the reasons for a lack of appreciation of how leadership operates in these milieux is that, compared to some other approaches, much less is known about them, for in general multicultural bases for leadership are rare (Mangaliso, 1991). This situation is changing but only slowly, so this book with its global, comparative perspective is timely and welcome.

Three features of society are key to understanding leadership in the Arab world: first, overall this is a Muslim region; second, there are specific histories of the various nation-states in the region; and third, organizations in this region operate in distinct and identifiably different ways to those that form the framings of the patterns of organization typically taught in Western universities and business schools.

Islam is rather more than a religion, that claims in principle universal provenance and, unusually in terms of Western understandings of religion, is based on practice rather than dogma. It is, like Christianity but unlike Judaism, a unitizing religion. This word is not, as is sometimes claimed, a neologism, but has a precise connotation in this context. The OED gives the definition of 'unicity' as 'the fact of being or consisting of one, or of being united as a whole' and this is a very good characterization of the intrinsic nature of Islam as a cultural force (Weir, 2005). This is not the place for a theological discourse but it is impossible to understand the concepts of Tawhid or of Ummah, for example, without comprehending that in Islam there is a strongly integrative meme around the one-ness of all creation. 'Tawhid is the realization that God is One, is the Creator and Master of creation. He alone is the ultimate cause of all that is, as well as the ultimate end of all that was, is or will be' (Al-Faruqui, 1985). A good leader is one who creates the condition for collective unity.

In principle, Islam represents a pattern of behaviours and beliefs that affect the whole of human life, no segment being exempt (Tripp, 2006). Thus, to a believer, economic and business life are governed by precepts that can be known and must be followed. Neither leadership in general nor organizational leadership in particular and business and management as a sector are regarded as exempt domains within which normal communal obligations need not be maintained. Economic activity is subject to the same moral frameworks as those that regulate society at large. The practical obligations of the five pillars of Islam (Testimony of Faith, Duty of Prayer, Provision of Zakat, Self-modification and Purification – including Duty of Fasting during Ramadan, and Obligation to make the Hajj to Mecca) contain the structural foundations of the ethical basis of all behaviour for a believer, including the beliefs and practices of organizational leadership. Of these Pillars of Islam, Zakat is perhaps the hardest to grasp for non-Muslims because it relates to the giving from those who have to those who have not under the general prescriptions of Sharia. The term does not precisely translate as 'charity' or 'alms giving' and no fixed quantity or percentage is determined, but the failure to give Zakat appropriately is generally considered to be a source of shame for those who could give but choose not to.

Education is a central virtue in Islam and an often-quoted hadith of the Prophet enjoins that one should 'study knowledge from everywhere, even from China'. Thus, managers are enthusiastic to become qualified: MBA programmes are well subscribed and to be well educated is a source of honour and influence. Leadership behaviours that are incompatible with these understandings are Haram or unworthy and it is understood that they will not survive.

The ethical core of management and business in this world is thus founded on Islamic regulation, which is a continually evolving set of principles, interpreted in the light of contemporary experience, not a fixed and unalterable set of dogmas (Weir, 2005). The community of believers, the Ummah, represents the totality of those who accept the principles of Islam and to whom, therefore, this regulation applies. The Ummah also represents a massive internal market for goods and services of all kinds. Business and management leaders have to satisfy the demands of this huge constituency. Leadership in the MENA region is rooted in Islamic principle.

It is not uncommon to characterize the economies of the Muslim world in such terms as 'conservative' or 'traditional' but this is far from accurate and may often mislead the Western mind. These in reality are dynamic societies which have known much change in the past 50 years but here, above all else, the framings of 'leadership' are coterminous with the fundamentals of Islam. Within this paradigm, leadership has been framed as a largely masculine domain and one in which seniority represents a cardinal virtue.

There is no space to detail the micro-histories of the region even over the last century but some factors are undeniable. This remains fiercely contested terrain in which a post-colonialist narrative has co-dominated with one of emerging nationalisms uneasily seeking the legitimacy to supervene strong ethnic and belief constituencies. The emergence of the 'so-called' Islamic State or Isis/Daesh represents in some senses a recrudescence of the wider narratives of Pan-Arabism and Caliphate-based unicity of earlier periods. The discourses of leadership are positioned in wider disputations about the nature of society.

This often means that it is normal to construe 'leadership' as resting on the clear credentials of figures like Saddam Hussain and Muammar Gaddafi, who are by no means universally demonized, but respected also for their achievements. The legitimacy of a leader does not necessarily derive from the democratic credentials of the process of choice but rather more from their performative strength and the perceived justice and efficacy of their decision-making; so Haroun al Rashid, King Hussein of Jordan and Gamal Abdel Nasser and Shaykh Zayed of Abu Dhabi may be cited as exemplars of 'the just leader' (Sachedina, 1988). Business and organizational leaders are apt to be judged in terms of these wider frameworks.

DISTRIBUTED AND NETWORK LEADERSHIP

Westerners who do business in the MENA region typically come into contact with the all-pervasive nature of business networking, 'wasta'. This is an aspect of leadership that sometimes affronts them when they start to do business in this region. Like the 'guanxi' which operates in the Chinese world, wasta involves a social network of interpersonal connections rooted in family and kinship ties that surround and frame specific leadership situations. Wasta involves the exercise of power, influence and information-sharing through social and politico-business networks and is intrinsic to the operation of leadership, central to the transmission of knowledge and the creation of opportunity. But just as guanxi has positive connotations of networking and negative connotations of corruption, so too does wasta.

Many younger professional managers in the Arab countries are in fact very critical of wasta, but nonetheless believe that it will continue to form the basis of business for the foreseeable future for them and for their children. In an opinion poll carried out by the Arab Archives Institute in 2001, 87% of respondents stressed the need to eradicate wasta, viewing it as divisive and symptomatic of corruption, even though more than 90% also responded that they believed they would be using it at some point in their lives. This ambivalence is typical. Young managers typically share the aspiration to move upward in the organizational hierarchy and claim leadership positions (Abu-Doleh and Weir, 1997).

The impact on 'leadership' is that it is often difficult to separate the agency of individuals from that of wider collectives. Traditionally, the head of the family in Arab nations performed wasta services by obtaining for the supplicant what is assumed to be otherwise unattainable. In recent years, the term has also come to mean the seeking of benefits from government. Though wasta pervades the culture of all Arab countries and is a force in all significant decision-making, it is not usually mentioned by most academic writers nor is it often openly discussed by Arabs themselves. But one cannot understand how leadership operates without comprehending the reality of wasta.

Wasta has changed over time and its main goal has shifted from conflict resolution as a means of survival to intercession, and the term 'Wasit' denotes the person who mediates/intercedes as well as the act of mediation/intercession (Cunningham and Sarayah, 1993). Intermediary wasta endeavours to resolve interpersonal or intergroup conflict and a 'jaha' ('wajaha', mediation group of notable emissaries sent by the perpetrator's family to the victim's family) acts to inhibit revenge being taken following an incident involving personal injury. A good leader must be a Wasit to be a shaykh.

Wasta can therefore also imply mediation and binds families and communities for peace and well-being in a hostile environment and this benefits society as a whole, as well as the parties involved. Intercessory wasta involves a protagonist intervening on behalf of a client to obtain an advantage for the client, such as a job, a government document, a tax reduction, or admission to a prestigious university. In instances where there are many equally well-qualified seekers of the same benefit, those with the strongest wasta ties are usually successful. Whatever the perceived ethics of this system, it is hard to see a definition of leadership that does not imply that a leader should be one who has strong wasta and can exercise it wisely.

The third master dimension of leadership in the Arab world is that of the family for family models and structures form the basis of business organization. The family in the Arab world is the primary wasta channel. The traditional tribal leader, the Shaykh, was regarded as a man of honour, whose word was his bond and who would assume responsibility for his act, and although originally based upon family loyalty, wasta relationships expand to encompass the broader community of friends and acquaintance because wasta-based recruitment and allocation of benefits reinforce family ties, thereby connecting the individual to the economy and polity (Hutchings and Weir, 2005). Where a close family member appears at the office of a senior leader it is regarded as improper for the demands of organizational hierarchy to take precedence over the obligations due to family. The role models of business leadership are found in family structures.

FAMILIAL DISCOURSE OF LEADERSHIP

In the Arab world, leaders often derive seniority and thus legitimacy from age and experience rather than from qualifications, and employees will take their cues from leaders accordingly. But this does not mean that these leaders lack legitimacy.

The formalities of social, family and political life are coded similarly and hospitality and respect towards outsiders are expected leadership performances because these are the duties of the senior person of the family towards guests including prospective business partners. The head of an organization may be defined by familial terms as 'Abu Mazen' or a visiting leader of long-standing relationship termed as 'Amo' or 'Uncle' without condescension. Thus, it is impossible to undertake any kind of meeting in an Arab organization without the ubiquitous coffee or tea rituals and appeals to 'hurry up!' and to adhere to business timescales that make obvious sense in a Western business context here are regarded as affronts to family honour.

The diwan is a room with low seats around the walls, circumscribing a space that is empty of furniture, uncluttered and available for the movement of people within it; it is found in one guise or other in every Arab home and office, for it is a place of decision as well as of social intercourse (Weir, 2008). In the diwan, decisions are the outcome of processes of information exchange, practised listening, questioning and the interpretation and confirmation of informal as well as formal meanings. Decisions of the diwan may be enacted by the shaykh, but they are owned by all (Weir, 2011). This ensures commitment based on respect for both position and process. Seniority and effectiveness are significant, but to be powerful, the concurrent consent of those involved has to be sought, and symbolized in the process of the diwan. In the swirl of the diwan, leaders are visible and available and they have the opportunity to listen attentively to information, including soft signals as well as formal data and financial summaries: leaders who lose the ability to read the informal temper of the times also stand to lose legitimacy and become vulnerable. The use of decision-making space in this way is therefore distinctly different from the barrier of the executive desk or the rigidity of the boardroom table.

It is undoubtedly true that most leadership positions in the MENA regions in both the private economic and public governmental sectors are, as in the West, largely occupied by male leaders but in principle Islam preaches equality of the genders and the position of women leaders is distinctly nuanced (Moghadam, 2004). In some countries, notably in Palestine and Jordan, women leaders are prominent in politics for instance, and the influence of the queens in Jordan has been pronounced and significant in promoting the public role of women. Empirical research concludes that in Jordan senior managers are positive towards women as leaders (Al Kharouf and Weir, 2008). One of the leading investment and asset management groups in Qatar, Amwal, was founded as the Qatar Ladies Investment Company in 1998 as a small, family-focused investment bank. (Aguirre et al., 2011). In the emerging knowledge-based economies of the Gulf region, women possess some clear advantages of education and qualification (Sultan et al., 2011a, 2011b).

Globalization has impacted this region immensely over the past half century (Cogburn, 2003), but this has not necessarily destroyed the existing frameworks of organization and leadership by exposing organizations to globalizing influences such as multiculturalism and expatriation (Butler, 2009). In some ways providing more economic success to societies like the oil-rich Gulf states and offering wider opportunities for influence over economic contexts, markets and terrains of contestation has also re-enforced indigenous paradigms and role models and facilitated reverse-flows like Islamic Banking into the global organizational mix (Ariff, 1988; Zaher and Hassan, 2001). The perceived weakening of Europe and the USA as sources of economic power contributes to this process. Young Western-educated MBA graduates, for example, are not universally seen as the natural beneficiaries of improved organizational management, nor the liberal market paradigm as the uncontested framework for economic activity.

But these societies are dynamic, evolving and radically contested. Leadership in the Arab world is an evolving phenomenon but its roots are deeply located in the social structures and belief patterns of the region and its ways of life. This is not to elevate 'traditionalism' and 'conservatism' as the only master explanatory categories. This region evidences some of the strongest support for a new ideational liquidity based on knowledge (Bauman, 2005) and is not impervious to rapid advances in technology (Weir and Hutchings, 2006; Sultan et al., 2011b). This is a fast-changing landscape in which in terms of new leadership styles, this region and these organizational cultures may offer surprising advantages.

REFERENCES

Abu-Doleh, J and Weir, D.T.H. (1997) 'Management development and training needs in Jordanian companies', *Middle East Business Review*, January.

Aguirre, D., Cavenagh, M.M. and Sabbagh, K. (2011) 'The future of women leaders in the Middle East', *Global Perspective*, Issue 63 (Summer) (originally published by Booz & Company), 24 May 2011. Available at www.strategy-business.com/article/11209?gko=dc8bf (accessed 16 March 2016).

Al-Faruqhi, I. (1985) 'Tawhid: the quintessence of Islam', *Journal of South Asian and Middle Eastern Studies*, VIII (Summer).

Al Kharouf, A. and Weir, D.T.H (2008) 'Women and work in a Jordanian context: beyond neo-patriarchy', *Critical Perspectives on International Business*, 4 (2/3): 307–19.

Ariff, M. (1988) 'Islamic banking', *Asia-Pacific Economic Literature*, 2 (2): 48–64.

Bauman, Zygmunt (2005) *Liquid Life*. London: Polity Press.

Butler, C. (2009) 'Leadership in a multicultural Arab organisation', *Leadership & Organization Development Journal*, 30 (2): 139–51.

Cogburn, D.L. (2003) *Globalization, Knowledge, Education and Training in the Information Age*. Paris: UNESCO.

Cunningham, Robert B. and Sarayrah, Yasin K. (1993) *Wasta: The Hidden Force in Middle Eastern Society*. Westport, CT: Praeger.

Hutchings, K. and Weir, D.T.H. (2005) 'Cultural embeddedness and contextual constraints: knowledge sharing in Chinese and Arab cultures', *Journal of Knowledge and Process Management*, (2): 89–98.

Mangaliso, M.P. (1991) 'Whose knowledge matters? The case for developing multicultural theories of management', in Jonathan D. Jansen (ed.), *Knowledge and Power in South Africa: Critical Perspectives across the Disciplines*. Johannesburg: Skotaville.

Moghadam, V.M. (2004) 'Patriarchy in transition: women and the changing family in the Middle East', *Journal of Comparative Family Studies*, 35 (2): 137–62.

Sachedina, A.A. (1988) 'The Just Ruler (al-sultan al-adil)', in Abdulaziz A. Sachedina (ed.), *Shiite Islam: The Comprehensive Authority of the Jurist in Imamite Jurisprudence*. New York: Oxford University Press.

Sultan, N., Metcalfe, B.D. and Weir, D.T.H. (2011a) 'The "Future" cities of the Arabian Gulf: realities and aspirations,' in Nabil Sultan David T.H. Weir (eds), *The New Post-Oil Arab Gulf: Managing People and Wealth*. London: Al-Saqi.

Sultan, N., Metcalfe, B.D. and Weir, D.T.H. (2011b) 'Dealing with post-oil economies: towards knowledge-based economies: Some examples from the Arab Middle East', in Nabil Sultan and David T.H. Weir (eds), *The New Post-Oil Arab Gulf: Managing People and Wealth*. London: Al-Saqi. pp. 133–55.

Tripp, Charles (2006) *Islam and the Moral Economy*. London: Cambridge University Press.

Weir, D.T.H. (1998) 'The fourth paradigm', in Ali A. Shamali and John Denton (eds), *Management in the Middle East*. Kuwait: Gulf Management Centre.

Weir, David T.H. (2005) 'Some sociological, philosophical and ethical underpinnings of an Islamic management model', *Journal of Management, Philosophy and Spirituality*, 1 (2).

Weir, David T.H. (2008) 'Cultural theory and the diwan', *Innovation: the European Journal of Social Science Research*, 21 (3): 253–65.

Weir, David T.H. (2011) 'Space as context and content: diwan as a frame and a structure for decision-making', in Dvora Yanow and Alfons Van Marrewijk (eds), *Space and Social Organization*. New York: Sage.

Weir, David T.H. and Hutchings, K. (2006) 'Cultural filtering in the Arab world and China: exploring the interrelationship of the technological knowledge age, traditional cultural networking and interpersonal connections', in Sylvia Van De Bunt-Kokhuis (ed.), *World Wide Work: Filtering of Online Content in a Globalized World*. Amsterdam: VU University Press. pp. 129–42.

Zaher, T.S. and Hassan, M.K. (2001) 'A comparative literature survey of Islamic finance and banking', *Financial Markets, Institutions and Instruments*, 10 (4): 155–9.

2
ARGENTINA
Gauchos, Rebels and Dictators: Leadership in Argentina

Gabriela Barrial: Professional Associate at the Tavistock Institute of Human Relations, Professional Associate of International Balint Association, Leader of the Group Relations Argentina Think Tank and Managing Director for B&K Consulting and Change, Argentina and Chile; Associate Consultant to the Government of Buenos Aires and the Ministry of Health

Oscar Muiño: lawyer, teacher and writer working today with Nuevos Papeles.com as a journalist

Dimitrios Vonofakos: social researcher and organizational consultant, visiting Fellow at the University of Essex, member of OPUS (Organization Promoting the Understanding of Society) and Associate Editor at the *Journal of Organizational and Social Dynamics*

INTRODUCTION

Argentina is a country of immigrants. It received more immigrants between 1880 and 1914 than any other Latin American country. The basic characteristics of European emigration were young men of economically active age groups. Italians outnumbered the Spaniards overwhelmingly, in a proportion of 14 to 1. It is estimated that up to 28 million Argentines are wholly or partially of Italian descent and/or Spanish first or second generation, that is, 70% of the general population of Argentina. The second largest group are Lebanese, estimated at 3.5 million people, and third, the Syrian influx of immigrants.

There are also large communities of Jews and Armenians who entered the country during the great wave of European immigration. The Jewish community (300,000) is the third largest on the continent and the world's seventh. The Armenian community numbers 125,000.

The name Argentina comes from the Latin *argentum*, which means 'silver' but the word is popularly used as a synonym for 'money'. Similarly, leadership in Argentina is associated with economic power and/or social power. A national leader becomes known to a large mass of people either due to having a good financial standing or because that person has got a significant following (due to their political, social, sporting character, artistic or organizational traits).

But there is another significant layer associated with the leadership role in Argentina, and that is corruption. Corruption in Argentina appears in various forms breaking the legitimacy of institutions at their point of interaction with citizens and organizations.

THE GAUCHO – AN ARCHETYPE OF ARGENTINIAN LEADERSHIP

The origin of the leadership archetype – still very present in current political and organizational leadership – can be traced to the book *Martín Fierro* (1872),[1] which is widely considered a seminal work in the country's national literary output. To study the society of Martin Fierro is one of many ways to study the current Argentina society. There, the imagery of the gaucho is described and explored in fine detail as is its profound contribution to the formation of Argentine national identity. In that sense, pride, strength, nobility, violence, loyalty, insubordination as well as friendliness and empathy define the 'gaucho'.

But most importantly, the gaucho is particularly known for his solitude and single-mindedness. As Salaverría (1934) highlights in his travel chronicles, the gaucho always

[1]*Martín Fierro* is the title of a book written in 1872 by the Argentinian Jose Hernandez; the original title is *El Gaucho Martín Fierro*. In 1967, an English version was published by the State University of New York Press.

goes alone, in contrast to other ethnic groups such as the gypsies, who always travel in groups. Actually, the word 'gaucho' is derived from *güacho*, whose literal meaning is: a person without origin. In fact, 'orphan' is the Quechua language definition of the word 'gaucho'. (Quechua is an indigenous language family spoken primarily in the Andes of South America. Derived from an ancestral language, it is the most widely spoken language family of indigenous peoples of the Americas.) While in *Martín Fierro* (1872) the gaucho's condemnation is to 'put down roots', in this image of an idealized, predominantly insular, male leadership is where the essence of Argentine leadership resides.

The 1971 Nobel Laureate in Economics Simon Kuznets* is alleged to have described the countries of the world as divided into four groups: developed countries, undeveloped countries, Japan and Argentina (Petrella, 2015). These two did not fit into any systematization; they were particular and unpredictable. Such reasoning describes something inherent in the Argentine DNA, which is 'individualism'. And in that sense, the way in which Argentines consider themselves 'special' and 'unique' – even in their faults and shortcomings.

The gaucho identity is an introjected archetype that explains how Argentinian society built individual and social behaviour internalizing mental images and events in our lives that have strong emotions and feelings attached to them. They influence identity formation, belief and value systems and in turn lead to the construction of attitudes and behaviours. While the gaucho was going alone, there were no rules to stick to.

EARLY HISTORY

Between 1852 and 1930, Argentina had developed an amazing cultural and educational system, and a steady economic, productive and financial growth. Its elite – despite fierce and sometimes bloody confrontations – converged in a chosen model. Argentinian leadership had reached an agreement about the essence of its project, which was: to create a European state in the extreme West with capital wealth, immigrants and technicians (Cortéz Conde and Gallo, 1972; Botana, 1994; Halperin Donghi, 1994). Workers arrived from all of Europe, primarily from Italy and Spain, but also from Poland, Ukraine, Russia, Armenia and the wider Middle East. In fact, during that time the Argentine population was formed by such a high percentage of immigrants that they would often describe themselves as having descended 'from the ships'.

But it is particularly interesting to note that unlike the USA during the same time period, immigrants to Argentina resisted becoming officially naturalized. That took place

*NB: Cristina Fernández de Kirchner wrongly attributed the idea to Paul Samuelson (La Política On Line, 19 June 2009).

through the country's public education system, which became the means of 'becoming Argentinean' for the children of the recently arrived, with particular success (Romero, 2004); to such an extent that the vast majority of tango composers were first-generation Argentinians.

Nevertheless, this inherent resistance of the immigrants to 'put down roots' and integrate has through the decades manifested itself in this type of 'insular individualism' which is central to the modern Argentine national identity. And as such, leadership in Argentina is a practice influenced by a tendency among Argentines not to think of themselves as a nation, but to keep an individual-based perspective and, almost always, prioritize the segment of the society to which they belong.

Essentially, when the time comes to lead a business, an organization or a country, the gaucho is still very much embedded in the Argentine identity, the 'solo' style, playing new strategies in the middle of nothing and having no clarity about one's origins.

A WAY OF LIVING AND LEADING: THE RISE AND ESTABLISHMENT OF PERONISM

The other main centre of influence in Argentine leadership, namely financial power and a popular following, can be mainly traced in the modern political history of the country in the second half of the twentieth century starting with the age of *Peronismo* practising the populism strategy and seeking to focus on the leadership of 'popularity' and 'idealization of the Messiah' of this type of gaucho leader.

In 1943, for reasons still under debate, a nationalistic lodge of officials began a regime whose secret figurehead was Coronel Juan Domingo Perón, who had spent a long time in Italy during the era of Mussolini. Since mostly foreign trade from World War II had enriched the state, Perón promoted very favourable labour legislation for the working class in exchange for the unions' support. The unions that rebuffed his programmes were repressed (Godio, 1991; Mercado, 2015).

Political opposition was denied access to radio broadcasting, which was wholly or partially controlled by governmental agencies. There emerged a division between those who defended civil and political rights and those who supported the persecution of the opposition, who were deemed as a threat to recently acquired social rights. Argentinian society was divided for decades between social justice and civil freedom. *Peronismo* prevailed overwhelmingly in all the elections between 1946 and 1955, but after the death of Eva Perón in 1952, it turned into an increasingly authoritarian regime like others in the region (Stroessner in Paraguay, Rojas Pinilla in Colombia, Pérez Jiménez in Venezuela). When Perón broke ties with the Church, a faction within the Armed Forces began to plot and in 1955 he was removed from power by a military coup.

For 18 years the party was banned from presidential elections, but it retained the vote of millions who cast blank votes for the elections to show their support for *the leader*.

By the end of the 1970s, many thought the world would live to see the triumph of socialism (Sarlo, 2007). The USA had failed in Vietnam and Afro-Americans were demanding their civil rights. The events of May 1968 in France had an effect on Argentina, but Che Guevara´s execution caused a much louder commotion. In a famous letter lamenting the death of the guerrilla fighter, 'The best one of us has fallen', Perón proclaimed his conviction that the world would become socialist. This drove thousands of university students to identify Perón with Che Guevara and to organize guerrilla forces to take power (Baschetti, 1996; Anguita and Caparrós, 1997).

The Argentinians expected yet another coup d'état, like those that had taken place in 1930, 1943, 1955, 1962 and 1966. It did not happen. The military regime of that period (1976–83) produced a systematic annihilation plan against political opponents with clandestine operations and no justice protection which resulted in the brutal torture and killing of all potential and actual political opponents (the 30,000 *desaparecidos* or 'disappeared'). In terms of social and economic policy, the regime cancelled labour advances, dissolved the welfare state, dismantled Argentinian industry and favoured indiscriminate foreign low-quality and low-cost goods. This resulted in an annual inflation higher than 100% throughout the entire administration. Alarmed by continued deterioration, a segment of the Armed Forces sought for an external enemy to reinforce its internal position. On this occasion, this purpose was served by fuelling a long-standing dispute over the sovereignty of three remote islands in the Argentinian South Atlantic. Following the unsuccessful end to a short but bloody armed conflicted with the United Kingdom, there was now an increasing social demand for democratic elections, which eventually took place in October 1983. A wave of enthusiasm stirred the country. One out of three Argentinians was affiliated to a political party.

Overall, since 1930, *Peronismo* has governed for 38 years; the Armed Forces for 22; radicals for 14 and conservatives for 11. Nevertheless, Argentina has low institutional quality (Gambini, 1999). The relationship between political power and money is usually not clear, as campaigns cost more than parties can pay. Additionally, the entrepreneurs' leadership went off track a long time ago. Many industrialists lobby the state to obtain credit, tax relief or other benefits instead of improving their productivity levels.

ENTREPRENEURSHIP AND ECONOMIC INDIVIDUALISM

Today Argentina stands apart from other countries in two occupations in particular: entrepreneurs and psychologists. Research carried out by the Global Entrepreneurship

Monitor (GEM) in 2008 ranked Argentina as the most entrepreneurial country among the members of the G-20, followed by Mexico and Brazil. Capital is risk-averse and has largely avoided Argentina, thanks to its history of left-leaning politics, unstable economic policies including the largest debt default in modern history, and corruption at all levels of government. Private sector jobs are few. Age and gender discrimination, among others, are legal and widely accepted as a means to select employees. A large percentage of the population has little choice but to develop their own means of earning a living through entrepreneurial initiatives. Entrepreneurs themselves are focused on their individual profit and that of their peers, demonstrating little responsibility as to how their actions affect the economic development of their country.

Entrepreneurs and small businesses, often family businesses, dominate in almost every economic sector. Consulting and contracting relationships are more common than employment relationships and the tax system strongly favours such relationships. The self-employed 'sole contributor' is the preferred taxpayer status, which pays a fraction of the taxes paid in an employer/employee relationship. Again, the entrepreneur mirrors the gaucho-leadership archetype.

ORGANIZATIONAL LEADERSHIP: IMPORTING TECHNIQUES, IGNORING LOCAL CULTURE

The management consultancy field also lacks a responsible allegiance to the national identity. Like any other service offered for the improvement of organizations it relates particularly to the political context.

During the 1990s, when the political–economic privatization model had its boom, Argentina and the other countries of Latin America were rocked by surging economic growth. Mergers and acquisitions destabilized organizations and brought about rapid transformations, both internal and external. Invited foreign investors were richly rewarded. Organizations changed rapidly in response to the promise of leaving the old state of stagnation behind. New technologies, both hard and soft, were incorporated into the way organizations were working. With the advent of new methodologies, organizational teams were invigorated by hiring professionals from the best universities and incorporating new decision-making lines with different criteria and contemporary tools to manage resources.

With the opening of the frontiers for corporate growth, new methodologies for measuring people and their effectiveness were eagerly adopted by professional consultants wanting administrative tools for specific areas of business. Professional and systematic ways of learning new content emerged through training courses offering professional certifications for consultants. Organizational Development (OD), Balance Scorecard, Myers Brigg Type Indicators, Kaizen, Process Reengineering, Chains of Added-Value, SAP (which later gave way to *coaching*, and *mentoring*) and processes of leadership were some of the tools we used to transfer our learning to our clients. These tools were supposed to enhance reliability, quality, productivity and hence the profitability of organizational teams.

However, in many cases where these tools and skills were implemented, such improvements and changes faltered or failed. Many of the methodologies that came from abroad did not instil cultural changes and were not producing the expected effects. Integration between hardware, software and people-ware was not always achieved. Consultant's efforts were focused on trying to produce greater efficiency among teams who were confronted with rapidly accelerating advances in technology. But the processing of the unconscious, the organizational factors unique to state policies and politics, and the conditions and characteristics of the sociocultural environment were largely ignored.

Now, as a new client system with different sets of needs arises in Latin America, these needs are not being fulfilled with traditional-imported consultancy tools.

LEADERSHIP TODAY AND IN THE FUTURE

Leadership and culture research carried out by Hofstede (1983) and the Globe Study (House et al., 2004) find similarities between national cultures of Latin American countries. Specifically, the Globe study, which based the dimensions of culture used in their questionnaires on previous studies of Hofstede (1983), concluded that the leadership most valued in Latin America was being administratively competent, performance-focused, collaborative in group work and sacrificing a status-conscious ego for the common good. Attitudes were less favourable to the individualistic and autonomous leadership valued by many other cultures. In short, one of the most important findings of the study was the relative cultural homogeneity that exists among Latin American countries, both in the description of the current reality and what everyone wants. Argentina stood out as different in this respect: regarding the Argentine culture the study specifically mentions the simplification of the leader as hero, 'Messiah' idol, demigod, with followers having an uncritical acceptance of the leader, which inhibits their autonomy and actions.

CONCLUSION

The strengths of the lasting archetype of the gaucho leadership approach need to be balanced by a more integrated approach that enables Argentina to collectively build its society and economy. An entrepreneurial leadership led by strong-willed and independent thinkers can be a great strength, but only if this strength is harnessed to a collective identity, and a common good that builds a strong society and strong economy.

REFERENCES

Anguita, Edouardo and Caparrós, Martin (1997) *La Voluntad*. Buenos Aires: Norma.

Baschetti, Roberto (1996) *Documentos: 1973–1976*, Buenos Aires: De la Campana.

Botana, Natalio R. (1994) *El Orden Conservador: La Política Argentina entre 1880 y 1926*. Buenos Aires: Sudamericana.

Cortés Conde, Roberto and Gallo, Ezequiel (1972) *La República Conservadora*. Buenos Aires: Paidós.

Gambini, Hugo (1999) *Historia del Peronismo*. Buenos Aires: Planeta.

Godio, Julio (1991) *El Movimiento Obrero Argentino (1955–1990)*. Buenos Aires: Legasa.

Halperin Donghi, Tulio (1994) *La Larga Agonía de la Argentina Peronista*. Buenos Aires: Ariel.

Hofstede, Geert (1983) 'Dimensions of national cultures in fifty countries and three regions', in J. Deregowski, S. Dziurawiec and R.C. Annis (eds), *Expiscations in Cross-Cultural Psychology*. Lisse, The Netherlands: Swets and Zeitlinger.

House, Robert J., Hanges, Paul J., Javidan, Mansour, Dorfman, Peter W., and Gupta, Vipin (2004) *Culture, Leadership and Organizations: the Globe Study of 62 Societies*. London: Sage.

Mercado, Silvia (2015) *El Relato Peronista*. Buenos Aires: Planeta.

Petrella, Iván (2015) 'Que se metan todos: el desafío de cambiar la política argentina', E-BOOK, 2015, Random House Grupo Editor Argentina.

Romero, Luis Alberto (2004) *La Argentina en la Escuela*. Buenos Aires, Siglo XXI.

Sarlo, Beatriz (2007) *La Batalla de las Ideas (1943–1973)*. Buenos Aires: Emecé.

Salaverria Jose, M. (1934) *Vida de Martín Fierro: El Gaucho Ejemplar*. Madrid: Espasa Calpe.

3 ASSOCIATION OF SOUTHEAST ASIAN NATIONS (ASEAN)

In Pursuit of ASEAN Pride

Vaseehar Hassan Bin Abdul Razack: Chairman of Zilzar Tech Sdn Bhd; Senior Associate from the Kets de Vries Institute; former CEO and Director of the Dallah Al Baraka Group in Malaysia and Chairman of RHB Islamic Bank Berhad

Firoz Abdul Hamid: writer, strategist and adviser for government agencies and institutions, for private sector and think tanks

MEMORABLE QUOTES FROM ASEAN LEADERS

Perhaps now more than at any other moment in the history of the world, society, government and statesmanship need to be based upon the highest code of morality and ethics. And in political terms, what is the highest code of morality? It is the subordination of everything to the well-being of mankind. But today we are faced with a situation where the well-being of mankind is not always the primary consideration. Many who are in places of high power think, rather, of controlling the world. (Sukarno – Indonesia)

Here in Singapore, you didn't come across the white man so much. He was in a superior position. But there you are [in Britain] in a superior position meeting white men and white women in an inferior position, socially, I mean. They have to serve you and so on in the shops. And I saw no reason why they should be governing me; they're not superior. I decided when I got back; I was going to put an end to this. (Lee Kuan Yew – Singapore)

The Malays are spiritually inclined, tolerant and easy-going. The non-Malays, and especially the Chinese, are materialistic, aggressive and have an appetite for work. For equality to come about, it is necessary that these strikingly contrasting races adjust to each other. (Mahathir Mohamad – Malaysia)

PAST ROAD OF LEADERSHIP

The legendary Silk Road is a network of routes built some 2000 years ago over 5000 miles which started during the Han Dynasty in the second century BC. Linking the East to Eurasia, it started the exchange and circulation of commerce, ideas, culture and technology between major dynasties, between major ideologies. It brought Buddhism and Islam to the East. It even provided the route for global exploration to the likes of Marco Polo, Ibn Battuta, Vasco Da Gama, Christopher Columbus and many more.

Despite being backed by goliath dynasties, the Silk Road faded from its glory when land routes became obsolete as maritime routes emerged. It also dwindled out when China closed its doors to foreign influence amidst infighting within its dynasties which brought the collapse of the Mongols.

The Silk Road reflects the growth of today's ASEAN region. This chapter aims to uncover the influence of history, religion and culture in this region and stress the importance of a shared vision and leadership if ASEAN is to compete in the post-globalization era that we live in now.

THE MOULDING OF THE REGION

The Association of Southeast Asian Nations (ASEAN) was established in 1967 with an original membership of five nations – Indonesia, Malaysia, the Philippines, Singapore and Thailand. This later expanded to a membership of 10 countries which today includes Brunei, Cambodia, Laos, Myanmar and Vietnam as well. With a population reaching 650 million and growing, and a combined GDP of $2.5 trillion (ranked 7th in economic size in 2015), ASEAN has a wonderful story of optimism and hope to tell.

ASEAN is today deemed one of the two most successful economic and cultural global blocs (European Union the other), both aiming to promote economic success and peaceful coexistence.

The fabric of ASEAN is woven by its intellectual, cultural heritage and history from its past colonialists, such as the Portuguese, Dutch, British, French, Spanish, Japanese and Americans who colonized most of the 10 ASEAN countries at different times until the 1960s.

Over the last 50 years alone this region has seen memorable leaders. Some notables are Sukarno (first President of Indonesia), Tunku Abdul Rahman (first Prime Minister of Malaysia), Lee KuanYew (first Prime Minister of Singapore), Ho Chi Minh (founder of the Democratic Republic of Vietnam), Bhumibol Adulyadej (King of Thailand).

This list provides an insight into the diverse personalities, ideologies and leadership styles in the moulding of Southeast Asia. It shows a 'one-size-fits-all' approach does not work in this region.

THE ESSENCE OF ASEAN STABILITY

Bloc associations like the Organization of American States (OAS) and the South Asian Association for Regional Cooperation (SAARC) often struggle because the largest nations are too dominant in the organizations (the USA and India, for example).

To date, ASEAN's success is helped because its largest member, Indonesia, has not thrown its weight about. Kishore Mahbubani[1] wrote that Indonesia's role was critical as the largest member of ASEAN, as its population makes up to 40% of ASEAN's total population. Indonesia could have easily stifled the region's growth. Instead, President Suharto of Indonesia was remarkably wise and benign in his attitude towards ASEAN. Even though he was a strong ruler domestically, he took a laid-back approach towards ASEAN and allowed the smaller members to exercise leadership within the group. One reason why President Suharto did so was that he came to trust his fellow ASEAN leaders, and his own culture played a crucial role in his approach.

It would be safe to say that countries in ASEAN do not share the same model of leadership and governance (e.g. Laos, Vietnam, Brunei are not typical democracies). Their regimes are customized and tailor-made to their societies. Again, herein lie the uniqueness and intricacy of the ASEAN bloc.

[1]www.straitstimes.com/opinion/the-modern-miracle-that-is-asean (accessed 17 October 2017).

THE INFLUENCES ON FUTURE LEADERSHIP

As a bloc with a growing young population, rising middle class and partly Western-educated youth, ASEAN countries are seeking their own and unique identities. The foreign-educated population bring some characteristics from their education and social experience and they lean towards their own unique identities. These are well-spoken, eloquent, intelligent youth who want a world beyond the traditional Western model having witnessed the setbacks of Western democracies as well as its benefits. Further, countries individually and collectively no longer want to be associated with their former colonial powers and/or their founding fathers.

It can be said, leadership in the ASEAN region has been shaped by many endogenous and exogenous factors over the last 50 years alone:

- Colonialism and independence: the impact of outsider, imposed and authoritarian leadership and the impact of anti-colonial struggles and the leadership and followership associated with this. This can be seen in the continued struggle for individual and collective leadership identity search of ASEAN countries.
- Ethnic diversity with varying cultural attributes such as customs and traditions of clans and tribes have impacts on leadership. Where patriarchal leadership and kinship models prevail in some of the ASEAN societies, they have in many cases enabled continuity and stability, especially during turbulent times. Ethnic diversity produces a capacity for the societies to work across boundaries which is very important in 'adaptive leadership' (Razack, 2013).
- Diverse religions including Islam, Buddhism, Confucianism, Christianity and Hinduism also have diverse leadership impacts across the region.
- Monarchies and feudal traditions remain a very strong leadership and followership influence in some countries, and in some populations within countries albeit in different forms (this is not a homogeneous impact).
- Diverse political ideologies ranging from dictatorship, army-led governments to authoritarian democracies, people-led democracies, monarch-led democracies and communism. This is demonstrated, for instance, in the earlier listing in this chapter of past leaders.
- The recent rise of the middle-class impacts rising expectations in relation to consumerism, education and cultural changes linked to democratization.
- Digitalization and the growth of critical and social media place a spotlight on the work of governments and the integrity of leadership.
- The emergence of civil society is demanding openness and accountability in leaders.
- Globalization, and the movement of peoples and trade, has had an impact on government policies, international relations and social relations; some call for paternalistic leadership and protectionism, others for more open society and democratized leaders.
- Open market systems have transformed once-closed economies like Vietnam, Myanmar and Cambodia to join mainstream markets. This has caused huge rural migrations to cities and forced leaders to look outwards to improve global competitiveness.

WHAT IS ASEAN IDENTITY?

Finding the ASEAN pride

One of the key leadership issues that face ASEAN lies in its integration as a bloc. The new connectivity will involve physical, institutional and individual connectivity. The question is, will interconnectivity give rise to greater homogeneity or could it run the risk of encouraging protectionism and nationalism sentiments in the individual countries?

Arguably, shared vision and leadership is a key concern in ASEAN today. As we see the USA pivoting towards ASEAN, we have China turning towards Central and South Asia.[2] This pull between global superpowers will have a direct impact on ASEAN vis-à-vis its direction, priorities and agenda. The challenges for organizations and leaders in ASEAN are:

- Has ASEAN established its shared vision and identity?
- How will this vision affect organizational leadership and management in its public and private sectors?
- What kind(s) of culture is (are) needed for developing ASEAN identity and pride? and
- What kind of leadership do ASEAN organizations need to remain relevant beyond the twenty-first century?

Past leadership baggage

In the early nineteenth century, when countries around the world, including India, were rising against their monarchs, monarchs in Southeast Asia were treated obsequiously. This manifested the culture of *'special treatment' of leaders*, which continues to be practised to this day in some ASEAN countries. This culture has infiltrated into organizational management and business as well. An unspoken and open practice still exists in many ASEAN organizations, which has led to two specific perceptions of the region:

- to do business here you need to know the networks of power; and
- those in power must be corrupt

RELIGION IN ASEAN LEADERSHIP

Culture and religion are one of the biggest influences of post-colonial styles of leadership. Islam, Buddhism, Hinduism and Christianity coupled with the traditions of Confucianism and Taoism are embraced in most ASEAN countries. We will discuss just two examples:

---

[2]www.eastasiaforum.org/2017/02/20/east-asias-agreement-to-keep-the-world-economy-open (accessed 17 October 2017).

- *Islam* has the largest influence in ASEAN and Indonesia holds the largest number of Muslims in the world today. Thus, global geopolitics and the seeming vacuum in identity could potentially pivot the middle class towards a more conservative religious-based identity in the region, a way of being detached from a colonial past. This can have adverse repercussions if ASEAN does not establish its own identity coupled with the kind of leadership required to address the rising global concern on terrorism as well as Islamophobia.
- *Buddhism* emphasizes the individual unlike the collectivist values influenced by Confucianism and Islam. Buddhism has also played an important role in business cultures in ASEAN. One can observe this especially in Myanmar as it is often seen as one of the most individualistic societies in ASEAN. Arguably this has manifested in Myanmar's slow transition from its 'junta'[3] to its most recent democratic landscape.

BUSINESS LEADERSHIP IN ASEAN

Business styles are still based very much on ethnicity, religion and nationality in ASEAN. It has also been influenced by colonial powers, as discussed earlier.

The private sector in most of the ASEAN economies continues to be run by family businesses. Although this is slowly evolving into publicly owned entities, the change is debatably slow. Most of the big businesses in ASEAN are still owned by a handful of families. Doing business in those countries would mean doing business with a few entities and/or individuals. It is absolutely important to understand this structure as the leadership required in those countries and the partnership between public and private sectors is different from country to country in the region.

The large Muslim population in ASEAN as discussed earlier has also spurred Islam-based businesses. Malaysia, Indonesia and Thailand have led the Shariah[4]-based businesses such as Islamic finance and the Halal industry to thrive in the region.

Ethnicity of owners can determine the management and leadership styles of some companies. In Malaysia, for instance, a company owned by a Malaysian will operate differently than one owned by a Malaysian of Chinese or Indian origin. Trust is a sought-after commodity when transacting with family businesses. There is often a perception that family-owned businesses are difficult to access and their levels of governance and market transparency may not be up to the standards required in a capitalist market structure. Global governance structure is breaking down some of these ethnic gradations but they still exist.

The emergence of Sovereign Wealth Funds (SWFs) is yet another hallmark in ASEAN. SWFs were introduced after the 1998 financial crises as a means of revitalizing the

---

[3]A military or political group ruling a country after taking power by force.

[4]Islamic canonical law based on the teachings of the Koran and the traditions of the Prophet.

ASEAN economies. But many would argue that, as a result of the SWFs, there is no truly independent private sector leadership in ASEAN. The practice of SWFs is prevalent in Singapore, Malaysia, Indonesia and Brunei. Leadership in SWFs, which are mainly seen as market distorters, are mostly appointed by the governments (the main shareholder) and so the leadership allegiance in most instances is to the main shareholder. Given this, the rules by which SWFs are managed are not as per the private sector. There have been notable instances when SWFs are subjected to governments' official secrecy acts, a practice that is incompatible with the private sector, which hinges on transparency and governance. This presents leadership challenges in how businesses are run in some of these entities as they confound the public and the private sector.

PRECONCEIVED IDEAS OF LEADERSHIP OF THE EAST AND WEST

The chapter thus far has discussed the past and present that has and is moulding the leadership in ASEAN. Notwithstanding this, we would caution that there is a danger in pigeon-holing leadership styles by region and societies.

The late Edward Said of Columbia University, in his famous 1978 book *Orientalism*, argued that the East is a Western invention. It is an artificial device that has enabled the Westerners to worship as well as disparage the 'Orient', so to speak. In *Orientalism*, Said deliberates on why when we speak of a specific jurisdiction we have preconceived ideas of the culture and its people even though we may not have been there, and this he argues is the cause of many global troubles of the day. This argument from Said is poignant when analysing ASEAN leadership:

> Though the question of styles of western and eastern leadership needs to be confronted, the question of whether there is such a thing as a western or eastern leadership style need to also be challenged. (Said, 1978: 000)

There are too many stereotypes, e.g. hierarchy and allegiance as prerequisites for an ASEAN leadership versus governance and transparency as the Western model – but these notions break down in the face of recent collapses in Wall Street, for instance. The Chinese-style leadership which is prevalent in Southeast Asia can be said to be the Asian equivalent of what Europeans define as the 'Protestant work ethic' for instance, and seen on its own can be perceived as negative in a Western leadership model.

Further, though colonialism is discussed to an extent here, readers have to be cautioned that this is not a rebuff to Western-style leadership. Most countries in the region had their economic heydays when they were colonies. Many of the recent ASEAN problems such as, for example, the Asian financial crisis in 1998 (which was attributed to lack of governance to some extent) were resolved when 'Western' governance was infused.

Similarly, many businesses are family-based and hierarchical in places like South Korea and Japan where there is a completely different but successful corporate culture thus demystifying the myths of family-owned business. The working cultures in Japan and South Korea are being emulated by many institutions in the ASEAN region. Malaysia, for instance, ran the Look-East policy under the leadership of Mahathir Mohammad.

POSTMODERN ASEAN

The reality is that ASEAN faces the challenge of disparate nations with varying levels of growth. It houses one of the most competitive countries in the world (Singapore) and the newest democracy (Myanmar). It also has the largest Muslim population with its impact on regional stability, organizational leadership and business.

A new postmodern era of ASEAN leadership is morphing, but the question remains – what kind of leadership will place ASEAN in the limelight of global discourse? The question also remains if such a change is just enabling old prints in new covers or creating new postmodern leaders?

There is a danger ASEAN can dwindle like the Silk Road did if it is consumed by internal issues. But there is a real opportunity now for ASEAN to reinvent the heyday of the Silk Road. For this to happen, ASEAN needs new kinds of leaders able not only to have their voices heard globally, but have ASEAN organizations placed on the world map as the new force.[5]

CONCLUSION

ASEAN leadership cannot be defined in a simple way, however there are some key characteristics:

- Asian-inspired leadership approaches that do not fit Westernized individualistic trait models.
- 'Good' ASEAN leadership is defined by its capacity to bridge differences; this was so eloquently defined in Tommy Koh's writing in 'The way Asians settle disputes.[6]

---

[5]www.thestar.com.my/opinion/columnists/comment/2017/01/28/asean-todo-list-in-2017/ (accessed 24 November 2017).

[6]http://lkyspp.nus.edu.sg/ips/wp-content/uploads/sites/2/2013/04/pa_TK_ST_The-Asian-way-to-settle-disputes_1006151.pdf (accessed 24 November 2017).

- Relational leadership is important: whether family, public, private or political.
- Culture and religion are vital to understand ASEAN styles of leadership.

The leadership in ASEAN has been remarkable in its ability to work across national, cultural and ideological boundaries. The next phase of change will demand even greater levels of collaborative and focused leadership that can hold the bloc not only together but stronger in the face of nationalism and new economic realities that are emerging in the global world order today.[7]

REFERENCES

Razack, V.H.B.A. (2013) 'The Malay leadership mystique: Building a background to a psychoanalytic understanding of Malay leadership qualities in politics and business'. PhD Thesis, Vrije Universiteit Amsterdam, The Netherlands.

Said, Edward (1978) *Orientalism*. New York: Pantheon Books.

[7]www.thestar.com.my/opinion/columnists/comment/2017/01/14/asean-and-the-new-world-disorder (accessed 24 November 2017).

4
AUSTRALIA
Leadership Identity in the Making

Susan Long: Director of Research and Scholarship, NIODA, Australia; Visiting Professor INSEAD, Singapore; Associate Melbourne Business School; organizational consultant in private practice

Jane Chapman: Anglican priest of the Diocese of Sydney, Australia; former organizational and marketing consultant

In this chapter, we examine current and historical perspectives on leadership in Australia and present some hypotheses about its nature within the identity of the nation.[1] As Australians, we naturally demonstrate some of the characteristics of the culture, which include individualism and an open and critical evaluation of our leaders, alongside pride in the achievements of the nation.

A FLAVOUR FROM HISTORY

Australia is a country with a long history of Indigenous occupation and a more recent European settlement of just over 200 years.

Two points are important. First, although the colonial leaders knew of the Indigenous inhabitants, they referred to the land as 'Terra Nullius' – land belonging to no one. The mindset of colonialism denied previous occupants their rights of ownership and even their existence despite the many contacts made with them. Murder and disease brought by the Europeans devastated the Indigenous population. A denial narrative was frequently taught in schools up until the late twentieth century. Only in 1992 was the doctrine of Terra Nullius legally overturned. Despite this and land and voting rights, our Indigenous population is unrecognized in the constitution and still disadvantaged across all indices of well-being: health, education and employment. In this context, we can say that a perverse leadership was established in relation to the Indigenous population where turning a blind eye was central along with other indicators of perverse leadership (Long, 2008). This attitude permeated government policy through the 'White Australia Policy' of the 1930s–50s and the policy of taking Indigenous children with European heritage away from their families right through to the 1970s.

Second, European settlement began as a series of penal colonies that cast their shadow on future generations. Times were tough for the convicts, most of whom were from poverty-stricken backgrounds. Yet it was from their ranks that the early settlements grew. The ideas of 'Mateship' and the 'Aussie battler' were immortalized by our early poets and writers such as Banjo Patterson and Henry Lawson who wrote of the isolated settlers, the cattle drovers and their struggles on the land. Nowadays there is a pride among those who can trace their heritage back to the convicts, especially those on the First Fleet. The persisting strong egalitarian, democratic and anti-authority ethos is expressed in the use of first names rather than titles at all levels of organizational life, the preference for casual clothing in the workplace, and positive attitudes to publicly shared spaces, including the protection of coastal parks and beaches against private ownership. Ned

[1]Thanks are given to Michael Long – formerly Associate Professor in Economics of Education Monash University for his help with details from the trade union movement and VET-based education.

Kelly, a highwayman with Irish heritage, is a historical national hero. Yet, as with so much of history, there are also suggestions that the convict origins led to a petty bourgeois and authoritarian culture expressed in a persistent conservatism in government.

From this early history, has grown a paradoxical flavour in the Australian culture of social equality alongside a conservative sense of ownership and entitlement. Two other factors are evident. First, it is a somewhat male-oriented culture – seen in the lower numbers of women in parliament, senior corporate positions and on boards. There are still great gender inequalities in pay and superannuation benefits (ASFA, 2015; Workplace Gender Equality Agency, 2016) perhaps due to undervaluing women's contributions to leadership (Piterman, 2015). Second, the phenomenon known as 'the tall poppy syndrome', which occurs where anybody who rises above their peers is liable to be 'cut down', usually through envy, is evident in many areas of endeavour. Despite this, there is a strong work ethos.

A FLAVOUR FROM AUSTRALIAN MYTHS OF LEADERSHIP

The stories and myths surrounding the country have a deeply unconscious influence (Levi-Strauss, 1966) on how Australian leaders take up their roles. Myths can be 'country romances' (Boccara, 2014) or traumatic events that form a part of group identity often re-enacted unconsciously (Volkan, 2004).

One Australian romance is the ANZAC story. This derives from a battle during World War I that was a disaster for Australian and New Zealand troops. Its story, now celebrated in a national holiday, is one of heroism and valour. Built upon the earlier cultural ideals of egalitarianism and mateship that grew up during early European settlement, it displays characteristics supporting collective endeavours.

Such country romances may strongly influence country government and policy in areas such as economics, social service and international affairs and may also influence organizational policies in terms of strategy. This may be so much so that reasonable decisions are overridden. For example, the somewhat mythical pride in Australian sports leadership means that many successful sporting figures are employed to give advice to business leaders. The appropriateness of this practice across disciplines is rarely questioned.

The myths and realities of egalitarianism, hopefulness and prosperity have drawn a wide range of people to Australia and, in general, economic growth has been positive despite the depression of the 1930s and the minor recessions since then. Australia rode out the 2009 world financial crisis with minimal losses. Population growth came through the gold rush periods in the mid-nineteenth century and the immigration movements of the twentieth century. Australia is seen as the land of opportunity. There have been waves of immigrants from different parts of the world; each making its mark: the post-World War II

Italian immigrants, for example, grew and dominated market garden vegetable production; Vietnamese and Turkish female migrants made up the largest percentage of factory workers in the 1970s and 80s. In the twenty-first century, migrants are taken more into service industries and as agricultural labourers. The Australian government has a policy of targeted immigration to encourage skilled people as well as a policy to accept a limited number of refugees. Each wave of immigrants feels grateful for the chances they have. But as the population grows so does the sentiment of strong border control. It is as if each wave of migrants and refugees seeks to maintain their own hold on the prosperity offered by Australia, fearing that this might be lost to the influx of new groups. Political leadership can often reflect these fears, producing a defensive populist approach to politics.

Sanders (2008) notes a dearth of Indigenous representation in mainstream Australian political and administrative leadership and points to the debate among Indigenous community leaders as to whether it is strategically best for Indigenous leaders to work from either 'inside' or 'outside' mainstream institutions to gain better recognition. This debate speaks to the split that lies within the community around Indigenous/mainstream cultures. Nonetheless, Indigenous Australians have held prominent positions in artistic, sporting and community endeavours. Cathy Freeman, Indigenous athlete and Olympic gold medallist, for instance, founded an institute to aid Indigenous children to succeed at school.[2] Indigenous leader Noel Pearson, lawyer, academic and land rights activist, has, to a large extent, charted a path independent of any particular political party, hence furthering the cause of Indigenous communities. However, despite land rights successes in the late twentieth century, there is still much to be done to give the Indigenous community access to the benefits enjoyed by the wider community.

A FLAVOUR FROM CURRENT PERCEPTIONS OF LEADERS

Australians perceive and form opinions about their leaders from many sources. Political and government leadership is primarily understood through the media, as is major industrial and corporate leadership. Sporting and celebrity leadership is understood also through the media, but more of the populace is able to have direct experience in these fields through public events. Perceptions are also built from everyday leadership in the workplace, in the community and from the Internet.

There is a strong competitive ethos around political and corporate leadership. Recent years have seen leadership changes in the major political parties during their exercise of government, resulting in changes of prime minister outside of elections. This appears on

[2] www.cathyfreemanfoundation.org.au

the surface to be a result of the parties' response to public opinion and the fear of losing the next election. The media, including the new social media, has a large influence. Corporate leadership too may be short-lived and vulnerable to short-term market fluctuations and increasing or declining profits. Today's political and business leaders work with the feeling of having to 'watch your back' and having to work quickly as your tenure may be short-lived.

Trade union leaders provide many leaders of the Australian Labour Party, but over time more union leaders have come from their professional secretariat (e.g. lawyers such as Bob Hawke, Prime Minister, 1983–91) rather than rising through the ranks (e.g. the former locomotive driver Ben Chifley, Prime Minister 1945–49). Although the proportion of workers who are members of trade unions has more than halved since the 1960s and is now only about a fifth of the workforce, the union movement continues to exert considerable political and social influence, yet is contested and leadership in this sector appears vulnerable.

Schools play an important role in shaping leadership as does professional post-secondary education and training. Increasing numbers of Australian parents are choosing private education over the state system, mostly due to the funding decisions of current governments and increasing standards of living. This trend allows sector-separate diverse belief systems (e.g. different religions having their own school systems), with little opportunity for cross-fertilization of different leadership examples within a child's formative years. The state system, however, has the possibility of diverse models of leadership (Sherington and Campbell, 2013). Schooling is critical because both conscious and unconscious beliefs and attitudes are developed when children first are exposed to and try out leadership behaviours.

What of leadership in the workplace? University business schools provide major industry and administrative training with senior leadership education. These schools develop curricula according to current leadership research, and which is strongly influenced by US leadership examples such as the Harvard Business School. However, counter to such influences, many business schools now pride themselves on having industry leaders as adjunct staff members who bring their own Australian examples of leadership style and influence. Unfortunately, much of the research on leadership that influences the MBA and other management programmes focuses on the qualities of leaders' personalities alone, in itself reflecting Australia's individualistic culture.

Twenty years ago, the Industry Task Force on Leadership and Management Skills released a major report entitled *Enterprising Nation: Renewing Australia's Managers to Meet the Challenges of the AISA–Pacific Century* (Karpin, 1995). One area that Task Force chairman David Karpin noted as requiring improvement was what he termed 'soft skills', that is, the need for leaders to develop improved skills in people management, communication and working with diversity, including providing opportunities for women. Indeed, the best Australian leaders are those who are able to combine deep industry knowledge with generalist management capability. An example is the 'Telstrar Business Woman of the Year' Uniting Care Queensland chief executive Ann Cross, whose leadership consolidated 100 different separate organizations scattered around this vast state. Ms Cross was originally a front-line social worker whose career grew into management responsibilities.

The context for leadership has developed in many of the directions anticipated by the report: a global economy and more trade with Asia means a greater need for leaders to develop skills in dealing with diversity and cross-cultural communication. Many Australian industry leaders find themselves working in foreign-owned multinational corporations. This sits alongside a decade of the erosion of Australian manufacturing industries due partly to the rise in the Australian dollar and the impact of cheaper imports (although this is changing more recently with deliberate lowering of the Australian dollar in order to invite foreign investment). Leadership is primarily now in service and knowledge industries despite the mining boom of the early twenty-first century. Medical research, university education and sport are examples of Australian world leadership. Fred Hollows, the specialist eye doctor who treated outback Indigenous populations and saved the sight of thousands and then did the same in Africa, is but one medical leader. The names of Greg Norman (golf), Donald Bradman and Dennis Lillee (cricket), Lionel Rose (boxing) and Margaret Court (tennis) are but a few among world sports leaders. Plus, there are many prominent Australian women leaders who have fought for social justice: Edith Cowan and Elizabeth Kenny being early examples.

The current leadership in these fields has had to adapt to environmental challenges and technology advances. For example, the Internet and video conferencing have had a great influence, especially given the tyranny of distance across the continent. While the flying doctor service, begun by the Reverend Dr John Flynn in 1928, is still an important service, medical specialists are now able to respond promptly to local practitioners at a distance through online streaming of procedural instructions. But also, due to the Internet, medical practitioners and researchers no longer have the close-held monopoly on research findings that they once had, thus prompting the development of different clinical practices in dealing with informed or semi-informed patients (Dowton, 2004). University educators have now to deliver courses online due to national and international competition in this sector. This is especially important for those students in remote areas.

Australian organizations are increasingly aware that developing personal capacity is not enough. From our own consulting work and that of colleagues, we are aware that for senior leadership teams two areas are of predominant interest: first, a concern with developing the capacity for strategic thinking across all levels of leadership, and second, a concern with the capacity to lead high-performing teams. These concerns are reflected in a recent survey done by Swinburne University in Melbourne (2015). That leaders may have high competence in their own specialized fields is more or less a given; that they are able to understand and identify with the organization context as a whole; that is, to have a systemic perspective rather than a localized view, is less apparent. But it is these capacities that are most needed and are currently in organizational development plans.

DRAWING THE STRANDS TOGETHER

We now offer some hypotheses that link leadership to national identity

1. *A derivative identity.* Why have many Australian leaders found it hard to think strategically about the whole country and its future and have tended to get stuck in operational reactivity within their own industries? We think this may be linked to an unconscious identity that is still not felt to be uniquely Australian and authority for identity links back to the 'old countries' of the migrants. Unlike the American colonies, Australia never had a war of independence and has always had an ambivalent relationship with the British monarchy. Moreover, we went through a period colloquially regarded as 'the cultural cringe' where everything we did in the arts, sciences and in organizational leadership and business seemed derivative of the UK and later the USA. With Australian innovations in industry, medicine and the arts, this identity is shifting.

   Linked to this, is the question of Australia's war participation. It is the history of our nation that we engage in wars following the USA in particular: Vietnam and Iraq being examples. It is as if there is an underlying defensiveness to prove we exist as a Western country and not be forgotten by the West despite our geographical location. This is despite our increasing trade with Asia and the importance of being seen as part of the Asia/Pacific region.
2. *A leaky identity.* Psychoanalytic theory and practice proposes that one cannot creatively use what has been stolen; unconsciously guilt is aroused and interferes with productive learning (Meltzer in Tyminski, 2014). Australians are still coming to terms with their history of having stolen the country, saying 'sorry' to the Indigenous population only a few years ago. Enacting this apology through legislative changes for the Indigenous population is only in its beginnings and until real equality occurs the social unconscious is filled with guilt, anger and divisiveness. So, the hypothesis is that unconsciously we are unable fully to take up a creative national identity due to this theft. Following this, we argue that unconsciously our identity borders are leaky and this is translated into policy around seemingly leaky national borders – hence inhumane government policies towards the 'boat people' (refugees seeking to come to Australia via unseaworthy boats).
3. *Constructing our identity.* More positively, the Australian identity is still in continuous making with much to be proud of as well as dismayed by. Fractured, previously derivative and at times leaky, the question of Australian identity and how Australians take up leadership includes having the potential to be flexible and not dragged down by centuries of tradition. There is a sense of 'giving it a go' when it comes to new ventures and the creation of small businesses. The egalitarian and maverick quality of the culture breeds leaders likely to take risks, many of which prove to be constructive and highly innovative.

If increased strategic thinking and high-performing teams are the result of good leadership, then some Australian leaders are attempting to cultivate work cultures where members think systemically and are united in their diversity.

REFERENCES

ASFA (The Association of Superannuation Funds Australia) partnered with State Street Global Advisors, 'The future of retirement income', March 2015.

Boccara, Bruno (2014) *Socioanalytic Dialogue: Incorporating Psychosocial Dynamics into Public Policies*. New York: Lexington Books.

Dowton, S.B. (2004) 'Leadership in medicine: where are the leaders?', *Medical Journal of Australia*, 181 (11): 652–54.

Karpin, D. (1995) 'Enterprising nation: renewing Australia's managers to meet the challenges of the AISA–Pacific century'. Karpin Report. www.voced.edu.au/content/ngv%3A21108 (accessed October 2015).

Lévi-Strauss, Claude (1966) *The Raw and the Cooked: Introduction to a Science of Mythology: 1* (translated from the French). London: Penguin.

Long, Susan D. (2008) *The Perverse Organisation and its Deadly Sins*. London: Karnac.

Piterman, H. (2015) 'All that glitters is not gold – the allure of the business case for gender equality – an Australian perspective', *Socioanalysis*, 17: 64–83.

Sanders, W. (2008) 'Outsiders or Insiders? Strategic choices for Australian Indigenous leadership', in Paul t'Hart and John Uhr (eds), Public Leadership: Perspectives and Practices [electronic resource]. http://press.anu.edu.au/anzsog/public_leadership/mobile_devices/ch12.html (accessed December 2015).

Sherington, Geoffrey and Campbell, Craig (2013) *The Comprehensive Public High School*. New York: Palgrave Macmillan.

Tyminski, Robert (2014) *The Psychology of Theft and Loss: Stolen and Fleeced*. London: Routledge.

Volkan, V.D. (2004) 'Chosen trauma, the political ideology of entitlement and violence'. Paper presented in Berlin 10 June 2004. www.vamikvolkan.com/Volkan%27s-Papers%3A-2000-present.php (weblink no longer available).

Wilson, S. and Fien, J. (2015) Swinburne University Leadership Survey: Index of Leadership for the Greater Good (2015) www.swinburne.edu.au/news/latest-news/2015/04/swinburne-leadership-survey-launched.php (accessed 9 November 2017).

Workplace Gender Equality Agency (2016) Gender pay gap statistics, March 2016. www.wgea.gov.au/sites/default/files/Gender_Pay_Gap_Factsheet.pdf (accessed 9 November 2017).

5
BRAZIL
Tensions, Contradictions and Development

Maria José Tonelli: Professor in Organizational Behaviour at FGV-EAESP – São Paulo School of Business Administration, Brazil

INTRODUCTION

Despite the populist images promoted by carnival, Brazil remains very conservative and adopts a patriarchal style of leadership up to this day. Personal relations are still extremely important and paternalism overrides meritocracy in many Brazilian organizations (Motta and Caldas, 1997). Yet, old styles or premodern forms of organizations coexist with new and innovative models of organizations.

These characteristics permeate the Brazilian organizational cultures which, combined with the low level of education, weaken Brazilian productivity. Inequalities permeate gender questions, and despite having a higher level of education nowadays women still suffer with lower salaries than men for the same position.

This chapter aims to describe the sociocultural reference for leadership development. To this end, we will start with a brief description of the Brazilian context and then highlight the connections between culture, politics and leadership behaviour. At the end, we will discuss the importance of ethics for Brazilian leaders.

BRAZILIAN CONTEXT

Brazil is the biggest country in South America in size, wealth and population. With approximately 200 million inhabitants concentrated in urban areas (only 10% of the total population lives in the rural area today), the Brazilian trade balance is mainly composed of raw products (71%), followed by semi-manufactured products (8.5%) and manufactured products (7.9%). The country has a diverse range of organizations: global multinationals, Brazilian multinationals, family businesses, small businesses, public organizations and NGOs. It also has the highest labour taxation rates: while the global average is 25%, Brazilian employers pay 57.5% over an employee's wages in labour taxes. Such a rate in a country with poor education and healthcare systems, informal work and fragile contracts contributes to the instability of living conditions.

Latin America still ranks among the most unequal region in the world and Brazil, its largest economy, faces the same problem. This country is threatened by the persistence of poverty, informal employment, youth unemployment and poor education. As the only country in South America to be colonized by Portugal, Brazil has little social and cultural connections with the other countries in the region. Despite similarities between Spanish and Portuguese, language is still a barrier between the countries in the region. To a certain extent, Brazilians live and feel quite isolated from their neighbours (Fishlow, 2011).

A typical image of Brazil would show people living in an ambiance made of very good relationships, friendships and happiness. The carnival presented on TV promotes this unique atmosphere spiced with sex. Many stereotypes persist: samba, beautiful women, soccer and beautiful landscapes. Are they true? Such images really are stereotyped! Brazil is full of paradoxes in different spheres. *Machismo* (male chauvinism) pervades the culture. Although women represent more than 50% of the workforce they continue to struggle to find leadership positions. Black people suffer from more or less subtle discrimination. Brazilians are mainly religious therefore the image of free sex is questioned by conservative behaviour from the majority of the population.

Nonetheless, Brazil is a secular country. Different religions coexist in a syncretic and pragmatic way. Brazilian society is violent, especially in areas with high poverty and dominated by drug dealers. But the country is also ludic, loving celebrations, barbecues and any kind of social events, with personal contact being extremely appreciated (Skidmore, 1998; Sorj, 2001; Fishlow, 2011; Fausto, 2012). Brazilians are also very connected, with over 250 million smartphones spread among different social classes. Discussion of Brazilian leadership requires consideration of these diverse narratives that coexist within the country as well as their consequences for organizational life.

During the first half of the twentieth century the economy was dominated by agriculture. The industrialization process flourished in the latter half of the century driven by the presence of multinationals. Many important Brazilian companies were founded in this period (Bresser Pereira, 1962, 1966, 1974). The post-colonization process after World War II promoted the USA as the aspired model for the country (Wood et al., 2011; Alcadipani and Bertero, 2012; Alcadipani and Caldas, 2012). However, the dictatorship period from the 1960s to the 1980s delayed the experience of a true democracy. Even until now, the notion of democracy is controversial and does not fully permeate the civic society.

The globalization process, the development during the 1990s and the first decade of twenty-first century allowed for better conditions at the base of the social pyramid regarding consumerism. But education has not improved. For decades, Brazil has suffered with a lack of talent and many open job positions have not been filled. Alongside successful companies, inequalities and social differences mark the country and some isolated focus of slavery persists. Corruption in public and private companies coexists with solid examples of entrepreneurs who have constructed and developed successful businesses. Brazil is a very mixed picture!

Considered as an emergent nation in the last decades, heralded as one of the fast-rising BRIC economies (Brazil, Russia, India, China), success turned to anger and despair as Brazil in 2016 faced the effects of a recession and a profound political crisis. Throughout its history, Brazil has been developing from crisis to crisis, but in spite of many problems, one aspect must be celebrated: all people in Brazil identify themselves as Brazilian. Even though there are many regions with different accents, the country has only one language, which emphasizes the sense of belonging. Hope is still a characteristic of many and this feeling is associated with religiosity. Predominantly Catholic but also with practising African and local spirituality such as Candomble in the mix, and with a growing evangelical and Pentecostal movement, Brazil has a living religious tradition that inspires many. Brazilians believe in the future.

After this brief overview of the country, the next section explores some aspects of the leadership models in Brazil. Gender aspects will also be discussed.

THE MAIN INFLUENCES ON LEADERSHIP

Brazilian organizational behaviour can be characterized by five general frames (adapted from Chu and Wood, 2008): (a) *personalism*, the individual has privileges contrasting with not so high values of the public sphere, meritocracy and community; (b) *ambiguity*; (c) *high distance of power*, with the social relations influenced by slavery and colonial heritage; (d) *plasticity and permeability*: Brazilians are open to novelty and have a strong fascination with foreigners; (e) *formalism* with the existence of many laws but laws are (or are not) applied depending on the circumstances (Motta and Caldas, 1997; Caldas and Wood, 2007).

The Brazilian business environment is marked by flexibility and plasticity that coexist with power inequalities and hierarchy. Such conditions, connected with other cultural aspects, inhibit exchanges between upper and lower classes. Chu and Wood (2008) showed that two other components could be seen within the contemporary culture of Brazilian organizations. First, the existence of authoritarian leaders side by side with the obedience at the bottom as symmetrical parts. Workers never complain or contest the order; in general, they respect the authority of the leader because of fear and aversion to conflict. In this last decade, with development of the educational level of the population and new technologies that intensify communication, the cities are facing mass demonstrations and popular movements on the streets. Second, leaders have to deal with a complex and unstable environment, which leads to a short-term vision. Managers in Brazil tend to inefficiently cope with time.

There is great need for meritocracy and it is desired by many. Research with young managers of 113 companies in Brazil showed that besides flexibility and compensation, meritocracy and respect are the most desired working conditions (Tonelli et al., 2014).

Behaviours are embedded in the organizational culture: (a) companies are very hierarchical and have primitive forms of work organization; (b) management style is marked by authoritarian and centralized decisions; and (c) there is a fascination with models and fashions from abroad in an attempt to develop new and creative forms of management. Implementation of imported management techniques is typically used without reflection and adaptation to the local context (Wood and Caldas, 1998; Wood and Paes de Paula, 2008; Wood et al., 2011).

These conditions, associated with low levels of education, could explain the very low index of productivity of the Brazilians workers: five Brazilian workers are required to achieve the same productivity of one North American worker. The role of education inside the companies is thus essential for developing new leadership skills. Many companies prepare their key executives by promoting in-house programmes or offering them opportunity to study abroad. Yet, being a leader in Brazil means having to deal with all aspects that permeate the Brazilian context and the local organizational cultures.

Brazilian leaders are known to be cordial, which entails a friendly and superficial behaviour with subordinates. They are also reputed to exhibit a paradoxical behaviour, namely democratic and authoritarian (Islam, 2011). At the same time, they are inclined to avoid conflicts while being uneasy with divergences (Chu and Wood, 2008) and more flexible than, say, Chinese leaders, according to Nelson (2014). With such a behaviour, Brazilian leaders tend to emphasize results, performance and goals, planning, agility and environment sustainability.

Another strong influence of management in Brazil is the Americanization process that spread over much of the world post 1940s (Alcadipani and Caldas, 2012). The post-war American way of management started with the idea of separating 'brains' and 'hands', implying task divisions and hierarchy. Such an influence reinforced the historic Portuguese influence that already emphasized hierarchy. As a result, Brazilian leaders' behaviour is made of a mix of European and American models which produces contradictions such as flexibility with formalism, and democratic with authoritarian features.

WHO ARE THE LEADERS?

Brazil had some great political leaders, such as Getulio Vargas, Juscelino Kubitischek, Fernando Henrique Cardoso, former presidents of the country. As noted by Fausto (2016), Getulio Vargas and Fernando Henrique Cardoso shared the same vision despite their distinct political perspectives. They pushed the nation beyond their private interests. Lula da Silva, a great leader who came from the shop floor to become president, promoted social inclusion of the so-called 'new middle class'. He is now under investigation due to possible corruption during his term of government.

Who are the Brazilian business leaders? Irineu Evangelista de Souza, Baron of Maua, around 1850, was a farmer, a politician, an industrialist and a banker who lost most of his fortune. Bertero and Iwai (2005) argue that Baron of Maua was a victim of the institutional context but also a defender of its environment. In an agricultural country, he dedicated himself to industry development by promoting the construction of the first railway in Brazil. Despite all the controversial aspects of his business, he is still considered as the first Brazilian entrepreneur.

Since then, industry has developed with strong links between business and the political arena, with the predominance of the banking sector after the 90s. According to Bresser Pereira and Diniz (2009), Brazil is characterized by a contradiction between business leaders who support a nationalist government but also look for liberal and international perspectives that connect with the financial mode of contemporary capitalism.

Contradiction is not the privilege of these leaders but expresses some typical behaviours that permeate Brazilian culture.

Since the 1960s the business field has been growing with huge companies such as Companhia Siderúrgica Nacional (CSN), Gerdau, Itaú-Unibanco, AMBEV, Natura, Azul, Renner, Maganizes Luiza, Oderbrecht, Klabin, Suzano, Grendene, Votoranti. Executives such as Carlos Brito, Roberto Egydio Setubal, Carlos Ghosn, Laercio Cosentino, Antonio Luis Seabra, David Neeleman, among others, are widely regarded as being among the best leaders in Brazil. Understandably, these leaders have inspired many young people, such as Abilio Diniz, Luiza Trajano, Jorge Paulo Lehman, Marcel Telles, Carlos Sicupira, Fabio Barbosa, Jorge Gerdau, Samuel Kein, Roberto Civita, Antonio Luiz Seabra, Pedro Passos, Claudio Luiz Gottemberg (Época Negócios, 2015; Infomoney, 2015).

FEMALE LEADERSHIP

The development of women as executives or business leaders in Brazil followed the same global movement. From the 1970s, a growing number of women contributed to the Brazilian economy.

Progressively, they gained responsibilities in Brazilian or multinational companies (Bruschini and Puppin, 2004). Yet, despite having more years of education than men today, Brazilian women have to deal with a *machismo* embedded in the culture:

- First, Brazilian men are not used to dealing with domestic tasks so women have a double day of work. Although middle-class women can be helped by domestic employees, they are still responsible for the perfect functioning of the house.
- Second, there is glass ceiling since men control the access of women to better positions and are responsible for structuring organizations.
- Third, women are still paid less than men for similar tasks.

As a result, female middle managers are reluctant to pay the price of their career progress, namely getting more responsibilities at work for less money than men and still being in charge of their home.

Interestingly today, the majority of entrepreneurs starting a new business are women (GEM, 2014). Despite that, they do not succeed as well as men and they run only 30% of the mature business in the country. On top of that, black women suffer gender and racist prejudices. There is only one black woman as a CEO in Brazil.

This challenging context did not prevent the emergence of a large number of national and international groups, promoting women empowerment. For instance, the so-called 'Mulheres do Brasil', under the leadership of Luiza Trajano, owner and CEO of Magazine Luiza, a big retail business in Brazil, actively promotes the development of women as business leaders in Brazil.

LEADERSHIP TODAY AND IN THE FUTURE

On a general basis, Brazilians are resilient, hard workers and love to communicate. Many companies are sustainable while young people fight for more respect and equality. Recent feminists' groups have promoted all over Brazil respectable discussions about women's conditions at work. These movements went viral on the Internet, denouncing unacceptable behaviours and praising gender equality for a better country in the future. The recent corruption scandals also contribute to change Brazilian behaviour. Today, conflicts are being more and more discussed and mass demonstrations are becoming more frequent.

It is worth mentioning that as executives become frequently confronted with crises in increasingly complex organizations, they become more resilient, creative, team-builders and also appreciated in international working environments.

We hope Brazil will benefit from the current crisis and that ethics will become a central part in the education and development of future business leaders. More than ever, Brazilians political and business leaders will be valued by their ethical behaviour and their ability to promote a more equal environment at work.

REFERENCES

Alcadipani, R. and Bertero, C.O. (2012) 'Guerra fria e ensino do management no Brasil: caso da FGV-EAESP', *Revista de Administração de Empresas*. São Paulo, Fundação Getulio Vargas, 52 (3).

Alcadipani, R. and Caldas, M.P. (2012) 'Americanizing Brazilian management', *Critical Perspectives on International Business*, 8 (1): 37–55.

Bertero, C.A. and Iwai, T. (2005) 'Uma visita ao Barão', *RAC – Revista de Administração Contemporânea*, Curitiba, 9 (2).

Bresser Pereira, L.C. (1962) 'Desenvolvimento econômico e o empresário', *Revista de Administração de Empresas'*, São Paulo, Fundação Getulio Vargas, 2 (4).

Bresser Pereira, L.C. (1966) 'O administrador profissional e as perspectivas da sociedade Brasileira', *Revista de Administração de Empresas'*, São Paulo, Fundação Getulio Vargas, 6 (20).

Bresser Pereira, Luiz C. (1974) *Empresários e Administradores no Brasil*. São Paulo: Ed. Brasiliense.

Bresser Pereira, L.C. and Diniz, E. (2009) 'Empresariado industrial, democracia e poder político. Novos estudos CEBRAP', no. 84, São Paulo.

Bruschini, C. and Puppin, A.B. (2004) 'Trabalho de mulheres executivas no Brasil no final do século XX', *Cadernos de Pesquisa*, 34 (121): 105–38.

Caldas, M. and Wood, T. Jr (2007) *Comportamento Organizacional: Uma Perspectiva Brasileira*, 2nd edn. São Paulo: Editora Atlas.

Chu, R. and Wood, T. Jr (2008) 'Cultura organizacional brasileira pós-globalização: global ou local?', *RAP – Revista Brasileira de Administração Pública*, Rio de Janeiro, 42 (5): 969–91.

Época Negócios (2015) Os 10 líderes brasileiros mais admirados pelos jovens. http://epocanegocios.globo.com/Inspiracao/Carreira/noticia/2015/09/os-10-lideres-brasileiros-mais-admirados-pelos-jovens.html (accessed 3 September 2015).

Fausto, Boris A. (2012) *Concise History of Brazil*. New York: Cambridge University Press.

Fausto, B. (2016) 'GV e FHC em seus diários: o confronto intimo de dois chefes de Estado', *Folha de Sao Paulo, Ilustríssima*, 13 March.

Fishlow, Albert (2011) *O Novo Brasil: As Conquistas Políticas, Econômicas, Sociais e Nas Relações Internacionais*. São Paulo: St Paul Editora.

GEM (2014) *Global Entrepreneurship Monitor*. Curitiba, IBQP/FGV–EAESP.

Infomoney (2015) www.infomoney.com.br/carreira/gestao-e-lideranca/noticia/4344262/conheca-cem-melhores-ceos-mundo-quatro-brasileiros-estao-lista (accessed 14 October 2015).

Islam, G. (2011) 'Can the subaltern eat? Anthropophagic culture as a Brazilian lens on post-colonial theory', *Organization*, 19 (2): 1–22.

Motta, Fernando P. and Caldas, Miguel P. (1997) *Cultura Organizacional e Cultura Brasileira*. São Paulo: Editora Atlas.

Nelson, R.E. (2014) 'Leadership, personal values, and cultural context in Brazil, China and the USA', *BAR- Brazilian Administrative Review*, Rio de Janeiro, 11 (1): 47–63.

Skidmore, Thomas (1998) *Uma História do Brasil*. São Paulo: Paz e Terra.

Sorj, Bernardo (2001) *A Nova Sociedade Brasileira* (Jorge Zahar, ed.). Rio de Janeiro.

Tonelli, M.J. et al. (2014) 'O futuro do trabalho: impactos e desafios para as organizações'. PWC, FGV–EAESP, São Paulo.

Wood, T. Jr and Caldas, M.P. (1998) 'Antropofagia organizacional', *RAE – Revista de Administração de Empresas*, São Paulo, 38 (4): 6–17.

Wood, T. Jr and Paes de Paula, A.P. (2008) 'Pop-management literature: popular business press and management culture in Brazil', *Canadian Journal of Administrative Sciences*, 25(3): 185–200.

Wood, T. Jr, Tonelli, M.J. and Cooke, B. (2011) 'Colonização e neocolonialização da gestão de recursos humanos no Brasil (1950–2010)', *Revista de Administração de Empresas*, Fundação Getulio Vargas, São Paulo, 51 (3): 232–43.

6 CHINA

Paternalism and Paradox of Leadership at the Dawn of a New Era

Jeff de Kleijn: Sinologist and General Manager Asia–Pacific at HP

Nai-keung Lau: Member of the Basic Law Committee of the NPC Standing Committee, China

Jian Liang: Associate Professor at the Antai College of Economics and Management at the Shanghai Jiaotong University, China

Chao Chen: Professor of Organization Management and Global Business at Rutgers University, USA

INTRODUCTION

Research in Chinese leadership has been gathering some momentum in recent years, driven by the rise of China's influence in global economy and politics. However, overall the topic still holds important misconceptions in the international world. An aspect that complicates the understanding of Chinese leadership is that in China it has been dealing with paradoxes as one of its defining features. These seemingly perpetuating paradoxes can make Chinese leadership hard to comprehend from more linear and unambiguous cultures.

Despite the great progress made, the emerging understanding of Chinese leadership in the West is often still stereotypical and perceived through a lens of Western leadership practice. Consequently, a feature of Chinese leadership like paternalism is too often interpreted not only as a single dominate aspect but linked to an assumption of strong top-down authoritarianism, high power distance (Hofstede, 1997 [1991]), and uniformity over diversity and creativity. While the objective of this chapter is not to argue against common assumptions about Chinese leadership, the authors of this chapter are aiming to refine the picture of the practice of leadership in China.

CULTURAL CONTEXT

It will be impossible to discuss any form of human behaviour in a sensible and understandable way without first painting the cultural setting of the behaviour. A risk one takes when placing the cultural setting, however, is that the reader might assume the culture as a fixed phenomenon and use it to make hasty deductions about expected behaviour of individuals. Culture is in fact dynamic and may be carried less by stable internal value orientations than by the external social situations and structures that define the possibilities for action in a given cultural setting (Morris et al., 2001; Kitayama, 2002). Still, when one contrasts Chinese culture with Western culture, many remarkable differences do appear.

One fundamental difference is that Chinese tend to think holistically, in contrast to the analytical style of thought favoured by Westerners (Nisbett et al., 2001). One of the most highly developed skills in contemporary Western civilization is dissection: the split-up of problems into their smallest possible components and finding a solution applying the principle of *ceteris paribus* – all other things being equal (Prigogine and Stengers, 1984). Cultures with an Aristotelian heritage tend more towards practical logic and mechanical rules. Chinese culture, on the other hand, is much more holistic, intuitive and contextual. In general, the Chinese believe that it is not effective to directly treat specific problems without resolving the issues in the system that caused the problem. This ability to think more intuitively and contextually also enables Chinese leaders to be more comfortable and effective in managing paradoxes. The management process is not to control but to reflect like a mirror, to flow like the water, and to blossom like nature (McElhatton and Jackson, 2012). Traditional Chinese philosophies, Taoism and Buddhism in particular, make people view management tasks or situations as a holistic process with particular characteristics. Effective Chinese leaders thus conduct their organizing role by 'following the nature' and understand their tasks as the 'combination of conditions' (Alves et al., 2005).

Similar principles apply to social relations in China. The hierarchy of Confucian paternalism is extensively described. This hierarchical paternalism is a prerequisite of maintaining social harmony, where each actor should behave strictly in accordance with the hierarchical position that specifies the individual to a prescribed role (Yang, 1993). Confucian paternalism has a strong emphasis on familism and the values of respect for authority, particularism, reciprocity, interpersonal harmony and leadership by virtuous example. Therefore, individual agency is strongly constrained by family roles, organizational hierarchy and social norms (Morris et al., 2001). We should note, however, that ancient Chinese philosophers did not treat maintaining social harmony as a static process. For example, in the Taoist conception, social harmony is the result of *wu-wei* (无为), or 'yielding' (McElhatton and Jackson, 2012). The social hierarchy is mitigated by clear rules of compassion, equality in opportunity and freedom of action. The senior role within this hierarchy comes with many obligations of care for juniors, self-sacrifice and self-development. Historically hierarchical and social mobility has been high in China. Chinese farmers shed the shackles of slavery during the Warring States period (572–221 BCE). Ever since they have been agents enjoying much higher levels of freedom than their peers in cultures with Graeco-Roman roots. People in China could move up through the social stratifications based on academic achievement and were not forced to remain in the social group in which they were born. Many famous leaders in Chinese history, even including emperors, were born in simple farmer families. This tradition has continued until the present day when Chinese leaders continue to be praised for their humble backgrounds. The rules of organizational hierarchy and social rules developed in China within this highly dynamic social environment.

KEY PRINCIPLES OF CHINESE LEADERSHIP PRACTICE

Chinese leadership philosophy holds three defining principles: concern for the overall welfare, paternalistic style and managing with paradoxes.

Traditionally, the Chinese have 'the ability ... to hold different propositions simultaneously without distress' (Cotterell, 2002: 30). The mindset derived from the Yin of Confucian paternalism and the Yang of Taoist holistic thinking does not see opposites but rather different aspects of the same system (Li, 2012). Multiple themes of Chinese leadership philosophies have been identified, including: individualism, relationalism and collectivism; humanism (benevolence); social hierarchy and equality; and dialecticism and holism (Yang et al., 2008). Chinese leadership as such is a dynamic paradox that makes it hard to place Chinese leaders neatly in any one dominant category. They are consciously balancing among many competing opposites, refusing to permanently settle on one side, preferring to leave themselves opportunities to fall back on a broad base of mental and cultural resources. For example, the Chinese executive continues to navigate between pragmatism and spirituality, socialism and capitalism, universalism and particularism (the rule of man and law) etc. Because of holistic thinking and paternalism, Chinese culture tends to view leaders as the role models for developing social order and the main source for maintaining social harmony and group effectiveness (Redding, 1990; Farh and Cheng, 2000). This was brought to the extreme by the regard for emperors and later for autocratic leaders like Mao Ze Dong (毛泽东)and Chiang Kai Shek (蒋介石).

Whereas the West focuses on the individual, China places more emphasis on the collective. When contrasting human needs of Westerners and Chinese, the former tend to consider their utmost need for self-actualization of the individual, whereas the latter consider it to be self-actualization in the service of society (Yang, 1993). Related to this, Chinese organizations are more likely to share results and benefits in the collective.

To develop Chinese leaders with an altruistic, benefit-sharing mindset, Confucianism strongly advances the cultivation of conscience and character through education and reflection on one's actions, as well as a lifetime commitment to character-building. Five virtues are emphasized for self-cultivation: *ren* (仁 – humanity-benevolence), *yi* (义 – righteousness), *li* (礼 – propriety), *zhi* (知 – wisdom) and *xin* (信 – trustworthiness). Among them, *ren* – humanity is the source of all virtues and the highest morality. Confucianism recognizes that people connect with each other and live in social-relational networks. To achieve or sustain social harmony within a collective, Confucianism proposes a set of defined roles and mutual obligations to guide how people treat each other: Let the ruler be a ruler; the subject, a subject; the father, a father; the son, a son (Yang, 1993). A consequence of Chinese collective thinking is conservatism in initial change relative to more individualistic cultures. Members of collective cultures have less willingness to be a first mover than members of more individualistic cultures. When change does gain reference, general adoption frequently gains much faster momentum in collective cultures.

Confucianism emphasizes the importance of a leader to provide guidance and care for the welfare of the follower as a whole person. According to Farh et al. (2008), a good leader in China is expected to provide individualized care within a work domain, such as allowing opportunities to correct mistakes, avoiding the public embarrassment of subordinates, providing coaching and mentoring, and showing concern for subordinates' career development. Meanwhile, a leader must also demonstrate his/her individualized care within a non-work domain, such as treating subordinates as family members, assisting subordinates during their personal crises, and showing overall concern beyond professional relationships. Due to an expectation of paternalistic benevolence from their leader, Chinese employees believe that an ideal leader should have not only a high level of personal morality and managerial skills, but also needs to be multi-talented, such as have extraordinary knowledge, broad interests, to be imaginative and willing to take risk etc. (Ling et al., 2000).

The superior in a company is expected to lead morally by example, maintain authority and control, provide guidance, protection and care to the subordinate. The subordinate, in return, is obligated to be loyal and deferential to the superior. Farh and Cheng (2000) use a three-dimensional model in which Chinese paternalistic leadership is defined as a type of leadership that combines strong and clear authority with concern, consideration and elements of moral leadership. At the heart of the model are three dimensions of paternalistic leadership: authoritarian leadership, moral leadership and benevolent leadership.

Authoritarian leadership is defined as leadership behaviours that rely primarily on legitimate authority and professional expertise to influence subordinates, such as making final calls on key decisions, expecting employees to comply with and follow through on directives, holding employees accountable for work rules and high-performance standards (Chen and Farh, 2010: 614). Moral leadership is defined as leader behaviours that demonstrate superior moral character and integrity in leading by example and not acting selfishly. Finally, benevolent leadership is defined as leadership behaviour that demonstrates individualized, holistic concern for subordinates' personal and familial well-being.

Competence has always been a key criterion of Chinese organization and management in personnel selection, appraisal and reward. But an important distinction that must be made is that Chinese paternalistic leadership also holds other competing criteria of differentiation as equally or even more important as competence or performance, be those criteria kinship, personal loyalty, or political correctness (Hui and Graen, 1997). Thus, the competence criterion in practice often becomes displaced by or secondary to 'guanxi' (关系) or relationship considerations.

EMPOWERMENT AND AUTHORITARIANISM IN CHINESE LEADERSHIP

In a study of Chinese empowering leadership, Chen, Wang and Zhang found that power-sharing and delegation had a positive impact on employee job satisfaction, task performance and employee engagement, and that such effects were mediated through psychological empowerment (Zhang et al., 2008). The authors also found that control behaviour of the supervisors, defined as setting performance goals and monitoring work processes, enhanced the positive effect of greater power-sharing with subordinates.

In another study (Chen and Tjosvold, 2006), it was found that cooperative goals had a positive effect on leader–member relationship (guanxi – 关系) and leader–member exchange quality, which in turn affected perceived participative leadership. Chinese employees and their managers seem to expect cooperative goals as necessary for relationship-building and relationship quality, and guanxi (关系)-building outside work as essential means of establishing the trust necessary for constructive controversy.

There is evidence that subordinates' responses to authoritarianism are contingent on the resource dependency of subordinates (Farh et al., 2006). When subordinates depend heavily on their leaders for resources, authoritarian and benevolent leadership tends to have stronger effects on subordinates. Interestingly, Farh et al. (2006) reported a 'reverse' moderating effect for moral leadership. That is, the leader's morality had a stronger positive effect on the subordinates' identification, compliance and commitment when subordinates' dependence was low than when it was high. In other words, leaders' morality had a more potent effect when subordinates did not depend on their leaders for resources. Given that transformational leadership is based on charismatic leadership, which according to Weber (1968) derives authority from the superior quality of the person, whereas Confucian governance rests on the superior character and conduct of the sagely king, it is no coincidence that there is much overlap between transformational leadership and Confucian paternalistic leadership.

One striking difference, however, is in the latter's emphasis on the leader's continuous self-cultivation and high moral integrity, an exhortation largely missing in transformational leadership (Chen and Lee, 2008). Transformational and charismatic leadership needed for successfully empowered organizations elaborates certain aspects of Confucian leadership philosophy and paternalistic leadership. For example, the notion of visionary leadership, which is deeply rooted in Confucian value-based leadership (Fernandez, 2004; Peng et al., 2008) and to some extent in paternalistic leadership (e.g. the didactic behaviour of the leader).

Although traditional Chinese leadership philosophy holds much to encourage highly empowered organizations, its paternalism equally holds the ability for highly directive styles of leadership. One other angle to evaluate Chinese leadership are the two highly valued ingredients of *wen* (文) and *wu* (武). *Wen* (文) refers to the culture and literary sophistication of the leader, but the equally important *wu* (武) element refers to a military type of heroism. A Chinese leader is expected to be fully versed in both aspects, and able to alternate between the two modes. Few nations struggled more to enter the modern era than China. While the West entered the modern era during the eighteenth century, and Japan successfully followed after the Meiji restoration, China experienced 200 years of decline and unmatched human suffering after the passing of the Qianlong (乾隆) emperor in 1799. This period was concluded with the final sociopolitical disasters of the Mao (毛) period. Those long years of civil war, famine, invasion and humiliation by Western nations and Japan have left deep scars in the collective memory and subconscious of the Chinese nation. The remnants of this period are mostly expressed through the trust levels in Chinese society, which are often still too low to allow for a highly empowered style of leadership.

The historic tension between the power of the state and the power of the families provides an important additional context causing elements within the state to incline towards a rigid control-type leadership to maintain the harmony and unity of the state. But simultaneously the sentiment of vindication after humiliations by the West and Japan in the late nineteenth and early twentieth century is still providing much of the energy to progress with the aim to combine the best of Chinese tradition and the most useful aspects of Western thought, like analytical thinking and a higher degree of individual initiative, to regain the position as a powerful global leader. This shared national vision pulls the nation together and drives the resolve to overcome any obstacles preventing China from reaching its ultimate aim of national rehabilitation.

REFERENCES

Alves, J.C., Manz, C.C. and Butterfield, D. A. (2005) 'Developing leadership theory in Asia: the role of Chinese philosophy', *International Journal of Leadership Studies*, 1: 3–27.

Chen, C.C. and Farh, J.L. (2010) *Developments in Understanding Chinese Leadership: Paternalism and Its Elaborations, Moderations, and Alternatives*. Oxford: Oxford University Press.

Chen, C.C. and Lee, Y.T. (2008) 'The diversity and dynamism of Chinese philosophies on leadership', in Chao-chuan Chen and Yueh-ting Lee (eds), *Leadership and Management in China: Philosophies, Theories, and Practices*. New York: Cambridge University Press. pp. 1–27.

Chen, Y.F. and Tjosvold, D. (2006) 'Participative leadership by American and Chinese 'managers in China: the role of relationships', *Journal of Management Studies*, 43: 1727–52.

Cotterell, Arthur (2002) *East Asia: From Chinese Predominance to the Rise of the Pacific Rim*. London: Pimlico.

Farh, J.L. and Cheng, B.S. (2000) 'A cultural analysis of paternalistic leadership in Chinese organizations', in J.T. Li, Anne S. Tsui and Elisabeth Weldon (eds), *Management and Organizations in the Chinese Context*. London: Macmillan. pp. 94–127.

Farh, J.L., Cheng, B.S., Chou, L.F. and Chu, X.P. (2006) 'Authority and benevolence: employees' responses to paternalistic leadership in China', in Anne S. Tsui, Yanjie Bian and Leonard Cheng (eds), *China's Domestic Private Firms: Multidisciplinary Perspectives on Management and Performance*. New York: Sharpe. pp. 230–60.

Farh, J.L., Liang, J., Chou, L.F. and Cheng, B.S. (2008) 'Paternalistic leadership in Chinese organizations: research progress and future research directions', in Chao-chuan Chen and Yueh-ting Lee (eds), *Leadership and Management in China: Philosophies, Theories, and Practices*. New York: Cambridge University Press. pp. 171–205.

Fernandez, J.A. (2004) 'The gentleman's code of Confucius: leadership by values', *Organizational Dynamics*, 33: 21–31.

Hofstede, Geert H. (1997 [1991]) *Cultures and Organizations: Software of the Mind*, 2nd edn. New York: McGraw-Hill. p. 27. (Originally published in 1991 as *Cultures and Organizations: Software of the Mind: Intercultural Cooperation and Its Importance for Survival*.)

Hui, C. and Graen, G. (1997) 'Guanxi and professional leadership in contemporary Sino-American joint ventures in Mainland China', *Leadership Quarterly*, 8: 451–65.

Kitayama, S. (2002) 'Culture and basic psychological processes: toward a system view of culture', *Psychology Bulletin* 128: 189–96.

Li, P.P. (2012) 'Toward an integrative framework of indigenous research: the geocentric implications of yin–yang balance', *Asia Pacific Journal of Management*, 29: 849–72.

Ling, W., Chia, R.C. and Fang, L. (2000) 'Chinese implicit leadership theory', *Journal of Social Psychology*, 140: 729–39.

McElhatton, E. and Jackson, B. (2012) 'Paradox in harmony: formulating a Chinese model of leadership', *Leadership*, 8: 441–61.

Morris, M.W., Menon, T. and Ames, D. (2001) 'Culturally conferred conceptions of agency: a key to the social perceptions of persons, groups, and other actors', *Personality and Social Psychology Review*, 5 (2): 169–82.

Nisbett, R.E., Peng, K., Choi, I. and Norenzayan, A. (2001) 'Culture and systems of thought: holistic versus analytic cognition', *Psychological Review*, 108: 291–310.

Peng, Y.Q, Chen, C.C. and Yang, X.H. (2008) 'Bridging Confucianism and legalism: Xunzi's philosophy of sage-kingship', in Chao-chuan Chen and Yueh-ting Lee (eds), *Leadership and Management in China: Philosophies, Theories, and Practices*. New York: Cambridge University Press. pp. 51–79.

Prigogine, I. and Stengers, I. (1984) *Order of Our Chaos*. New York: University of Michigan/ Bantam Books.

Redding, Gordon S. (1990) *The Spirit of Chinese Capitalism*. New York: Walter de Gruyter.

Weber, Max (1968) *On Charisma and Institution Building* (selected papers, edited and with an introduction by S.N. Eisenstadt). Chicago: The University of Chicago Press.

Yang, K.S. (1993) 'Chinese social orientation: an integrative analysis', in L.Y. Cheng, F.M.C. Cheung and C.N. Chen (eds), *Psychotherapy for the Chinese: Selected Papers from the First International Conference*. Hong Kong: Chinese University of Hong Kong. pp. 19–56.

Yang, X.H., Peng, V.Q. and Lee, Y.T. (2008) 'The Confucian and Mencian philosophy of benevolent leadership', in Chao-chuan Chen and Yueh-ting Lee (eds), *Leadership and Management in China: Philosophies, Theories, and Practices*. New York: Cambridge University Press. pp. 31–50.

Zhang, Y. Chen, C.C. and Wang, H. (2008) 'How does individualized consideration foster OCB? A comparison of three psychological mechanisms'. Paper presented at the Academy of Management, Anaheim, CA, July.

7
DEMOCRATIC REPUBLIC OF CONGO (DRC)

Ambiguities and Challenges of Leadership

Déo M. Nyamusenge: General Director of International Space Consulting (Abidjan, Ivory Coast) and African Leadership Alliance (Kinshasa, DRC)

INTRODUCTION: FRAMING DRC LEADERSHIP IN A HISTORICAL AND SOCIOPOLITICAL CONTEXT

Approaching the study of leadership in DRC, we start with a brief portrait of the country. Located between the Atlantic Ocean, the Cabinda enclave and Congo-Brazzaville; Uganda, Rwanda, Burundi and Tanzania; Central Africa Republic and South Sudan; and Zambia and Angola, DRC is a big African country, extremely rich in natural resources which provokes neighbours' aggressions. It has 97 million inhabitants (INS-RDC, 2015) distributed among 300 tribes, of whom 80% are Christians (Index Mundi, 2015). There are 477 political parties (Le Soft International, 2015). None is socially integrated to the extent of ANC in South Africa.

People have lived on Congolese territory for at least 200,000 years (Clist, 2005) and have been fighting for dignity, peace and security for as long as we can trace their history.

Before 1885, the territory was composed of independent kingdoms and empires (Mambi, 2010), which had their own currencies and practised 'collective democracy' (Paraire, 1998) in the villages. From the fourteenth century, the impact of the slave trade decimated social, economic and political structures, contributing to the introduction of capitalistic industries which impacted negatively on population size and composition. Between 1510 and 1860, there were about 50 men for 100 women, and the shared identity declined from one of 'nationalism' to 'tribalism' (Paraire, 1998). This regression may have been a defence strategy to draw on intra-tribal cohesion; however, colonialism thrived in this context.

The Berlin 'world' Conference (1885) shared Africa among the Western powers. The Belgian king, Leopold II, acquired DRC, named 'Independent State of Congo'. He later gave it to Belgium as a colony. Through incomparable violence, mistreatment and corruption, the Belgians tried to overcome local resistances. Eventually, they established partnerships whereby kings became interfaces between their people and the colonial power, which now invested massively in the country. Meanwhile the two world wars occurred, in which many Congolese served as soldiers for the Belgian army; and in the midst of which independence was claimed.

Independence (on 30 June 1960) opened a succession of alternately peaceful and troubled periods, marked by confrontation between those for and against 'a single Congolese state with total independence in a united country'. Considering escalation of the chaos (secessions of Katanga and South Kasaï, assassination of the Prime Minister, Lumumba, civil war), the United Nations provided peacemaking forces until Mobutu's second coup d'état on 24 November 1965. This initiated a period of dictatorship, peace with rebellions, economic recovery strengthening the national currency, yet embedded in corruption and embezzlement, which eventually caused deep economic collapse and the sharp fall of the national currency.

The Mobutu regime fell (17 May 1997), defeated by popular resistances and the war of liberation conducted by Laurent D. Kabila, who was assassinated on 16 January 2001, in a multi-rebellions context. His son, Joseph K. Kabila, organized a constitutional referendum in 2006. His regime has been marked by peace with localized rebellions, economic growth, but also corruption and embezzlement as a reproduction of the past. There is now huge tension around his succession.

With this war–peace pattern and the complexity of its history of political leadership and authority, DRC is among the poorest countries in the world, despite its richness in resources. This contrast increases the interest of this chapter.

THE ESSENCE OF LEADERSHIP IN DRC

Perceptions of leaderships in DRC are ambiguous and ambivalent, hanging between autonomous and 'dependence' views of ruling, which can be broken into five clusters, as follow.

Authoritarian leadership balanced with collective practices

Sometimes, leadership is seen in fearful 'top-down' ways. I heard of a director in a company in Kinshasa who reprimanded his former classmate, a middle manager, because he had greeted him by his name instead of his title as required by the enterprise's chart. Here, leadership appears individualistic and 'clannish'; based on kinship and in-group models for controlling resources. These serve the leader's self-interest and sometimes also his/her community's.

Such authoritarianism reflects the Niheer Dasandi's (2014) 'predatory state' characterized by almost similar roles between politicians and bureaucrats, low autonomy of bureaucrats, and 'the use of the state apparatus by ruling elite to extract personal wealth, such as in Zaïre (DRC) under Mobutu Sese Seko'. However, the overlap in 'belonging' implies that authoritarian leadership observed in institutions and organizations may be balanced elsewhere by 'collective leadership', which is a process where members of a given group assume collective responsibility and reciprocal influences for the common goals. Thus, a person from an institution may shift from authoritarian to participative behaviour in his/her other belonging spaces. This situation invites us to question the Congolese sense of responsibility: why some people, honest in their churches or tribal communities, simultaneously appear dishonest in public spheres?

Messianic–heroic leadership

During our training-workshops in leadership development, we often ask attendants to characterize the leaders they admire and look to and those they reject. They admire leaders who assemble people around a common big and exciting project; behave as role models, strengthen the people's dignity, fight for liberty, equity and security; and who bring people to socioeconomic well-being. Thus, some Congolese believe in 'altruistic–messianic' leadership, which they may say is symbolized by Patrice E. Lumumba, Laurent D. Kabila, Jesus Christ, Nelson Mandela, Mahatma Gandhi, Mao Ze Dong and Robert Mugabe, although Mugabe is also often classified on the opposite side due to Zimbabwe's socioeconomic deterioration. Otherwise, leaders are distrusted and rejected.

Leadership as an elder-masculine affair

Some other Congolese perceive leadership as a male and patriarchal quality, allocating the first roles to elders and men. 'Women can never build a village,' says one proverb. We also hear '*Mokolo se mokolo*', which means 'An elder is still an elder' in Lingala language. However, many poor Congolese families push young people of both sexes to undertake economic activities at an early age, and hence bear the role of family support. As a result, a class of young male and female leaders has emerged all over the country and we now see female managers in many organizations, though seldom as senior managers.

Racial-based leadership contradicting Congolese authenticity-based claims

There is a real 'white' perception of leadership-power. The 'white' people are frequently perceived as rich and powerful or very close to the source of formal power. They access and utilize power more easily, e.g. getting bank loans or public contracts; and live in the most comfortable areas. Among them, European people and, especially the Belgians, are called 'maternal uncle' (*noko*) in Kinshasa. This wording is ambiguous. In matriarchal areas of DRC, maternal uncles have solid relationships with nephews because they are their inheritors. But uncles are also feared; accused of causing mysterious deaths of nephews. So, Belgians are appreciated for having opened the country to modern progress but they are also criticized for their mistreatment.

However, an opposite trend exists following 'authenticity'-based leadership promoted by Lumumba, Mobutu and Laurent Kabila. This 'approach' is understood as an individual and collective expression of Congolese assertiveness using Congolese cultures and values.

Leadership as natural or divine gift

In local traditional areas, leadership effectiveness relies on the belief that each ruling family holds its power from God. Then, replacement of any ruler is made within the same family following the specific local regulations and customs. Kings are admired or not depending on their appropriate behaviours. 'Bad' leaders are rarely rejected, except in some kingdoms like Buyeke (former Katanga), where the succeeding king is always chosen by the court among princes according to their personal merits.

Many political and organizational leaders may use biblical verses (e.g. Roman 13:2; 1 Peter 2:13–14) asserting that rulers are established by God, and inviting everyone to respect them. Not surprisingly, political, social and religious leaders tend to use these traditions and beliefs to illegally perpetuate their mandates.

The next section will now analyse other factors influencing leadership.

WHAT INFLUENCES LEADERSHIP PERCEPTIONS IN DRC?

Colonization and trapped independence

The oppressive (Putzel et al., 2008) and degrading governance during colonization, described as 'soft apartheid' (Braeckman, 2010), faced real resistances. Then, colonial power concomitantly opted for partnerships with the local traditional leaders. They developed a governance model called 'apparently hybridized power' by Mambi (2010), which reinforced an elitist system of acculturation. Belgians created Congolese classes from which those who learned to copy the 'whites' for apparent emancipation were named 'evolved' people. The worthy were even given 'certificates of evolved' within registration numbers. Later many political leaders came from the 'evolved' class. Belgians had given to themselves the 'status of power-givers'.

Thus, Congolese perceived leadership in the national sphere as 'others' property', racially oriented, authoritarian, elitist, paternalistic and extorting. However, in their resistance, people were practising a mélange of messianic, paternalistic and shared leadership. They expected that independence would formalize these practices as legitimate indigenous approaches. Effectively, they hoped a locally authentic leadership, as previously described, could meet this expectation. Unfortunately, it has never lasted, for two reasons.

First, this approach has never been developed as a managerial concept. Second, the independence movement was hi-jacked. One of the expressions of this is the declaration made in July 1960 by General Janssens, a Belgian who was still Commander in Chief in Kinshasa. For him, 'after independence' equalled 'before independence'

(Ndaywel è Nziem, 1998), a comment that provoked a generalized military mutiny. Thence up to today DRC has regularly alternated between periods of peace and war, forcing tumultuous changes of governments. I refer to this as 'war-pattern', opposing overtly 'defenders of national interests' and 'protectors of foreign godfathers' interests, with the involvement of 'international communities' such as a few Western governments, business corporations, and the UN system, all pursuing different objectives: peacekeeping/maker, emergency aid, mediator, investor, managerial concepts provider, but also instigator, and stakeholder in some unethical practices.

Professor Banza Malale (2011) has justified the right of Western powers to nurture such a pattern due to business contracts signed during the colonization and that Congolese would be wrong if they failed to respect these contracts. I do not totally share his conclusions as they tend to legitimate the *fait accompli* of the colonization without considering its ethical and moral dimension. Unfortunately, the fact is there.

Therefore, many Congolese are now convinced that the *noko*'s quality of power-givers perpetuates the racial and authoritarian-paternalistic perceptions that leadership is 'others' property'. As Tony Busselen (2015) puts it: '[the] Congolese political world, even some politicians from the ruling majority, consider declarations about their country from Washington, Paris and Brussels like God's word ...: there is a lack of confidence in the Congolese population's capacities and a resignation in pursuing the nation's real interests'. Beside the above considerations, unethical enrichment is an additional factor.

Corruption and embezzlement: tribal-based leadership

The war-pattern has exacerbated the trend towards tribal-based leadership. Among other cases, evaluation of a bilateral medical project in 2014 revealed that people were reporting to their protectors' relatives, more than to their hierarchical supervisors. However, behind the support to one's tribe, political or other coalitions are often motivations of personal interest, especially through corruption and embezzlement.

In fact, the CEPAS's international conference on corruption (2008) showed that, through Congolese managers and international financial institutions' practices, corruption and embezzlement are deeply generalized, and provoke socioeconomic inequalities between public authorities and the population at large. Therefore, perceptions of leadership as associated with extortion, economically segregating, individualistic, authoritarian and framed in a paternalistic-based power persist and tend to be deeply internalized. Such internalization might partially explain the slowness of the Congolese in claiming sociopolitical changes. Otherwise Mobutu's dictatorship could never have lasted three decades.

Furthermore, the machismo of the war-pattern reinforces the association of masculinity with power-oriented leadership. Nonetheless, this perception and the elder-view are also cultural products and not easily isolated as specific to war-pattern.

Globalization and media/ICT

The Berlin Conference unilaterally declared DRC as an 'international common space for commerce ...' secured by the USA (Malale, 2011). But, while the international community considers such an arrangement as acquired rights, Congolese see it like an attempt at extortion. This conflictual interpretation about the ownership of the country reinforces the ambiguous and ambivalent perceptions and practices of leadership.

International media, press and more recently social media prompted by Information and Communication Technologies or ICT (e.g. mobile phone, emails, social networks) contribute to reinforce such ambiguities through subtle or overt propaganda of a Western ethnocentric view of leadership. However, Congolese political opposition and civilian society members are keen on these means as strategic supports for democracy. Indeed, the decentralized use of ICT could inductively transform every Congolese into a 'public opinion' influencer, as happened in Kinshasa (January 2015) when a mass protest supported by ICT forced the government to stop modifying the constitution. New media may play a very important part in reshaping Congolese leadership perceptions and practices, particularly as the young increasingly use ICT to gain information, to socialize and to do their business.

MISSING LINKS

There are a few missing factors that could help people to perceive leadership more optimistically.

First, a shared vision of the country's future and related consensual plans – the last was the 10-year 1950–59 plan. According to Lukusa Mendo, who had been the General Secretary of Planning and with whom I facilitated a strategic workshop in Kinshasa in 2013, all Mobutu's plans were elaborated just for external marketing.

Second, an integrating and original concept for national development: As I have put it (Nyamusenge, 2012), it is necessary to develop African concepts of management inspired by local culture, especially Ubuntu philosophy which stresses individuals' responsibility towards the community, and vice versa; through the spirit of unconditional collective contribution, solidarity, dignity and stewardship.

Third, constructive dialogue and cooperation between national authorities, traditional local powers and religious authorities, all considered as complementary entities in the process of elaborating and implementing a shared vision. This is crucial because it is established that 'in African countries allegiance of people to their king or that of believers to their religious guide is more strong and fixed than the submission of a citizen to the authority from official power' (N'Dah, 2003).

Fourth, appropriate information on national development opportunities and challenges should be readily available. For instance, colonial treaties and arrangements should be widely distributed and deeply analysed and discussed.

LEADERSHIP TODAY AND IN THE FUTURE

Considering the complexity of the DRC's situation and the ambiguities previously pointed out, it is difficult to determine the direction in which leadership should evolve. However, there are fundamental unanswered questions that require particular attention in the future. They cover three main themes:

1. Building a solid and lasting national basis of 'ownership' so that development is seen as producing and distributing wealth to every citizen sustainably and responsibly: How to create a critical mass of aware leaders and followers about the common interest and required sacrifice? How to develop an appropriate 'model of development and human well-being'; and operational 'authentic' leadership concepts? How to promote ethical practices and behaviours in the public and private governance-leadership?
2. Modernizing without harming traditional local leadership; developing true partnerships between them and the national and provincial governments for an authentic and effective development: How to optimize partnership between national government and traditional local powers? How to better use the churches' assets and availability in the national and local development plans and actions? What role should civil society play in such a perspective?
3. Transforming the colonial and postcolonial experience into a chance for lasting peace and development. How to negotiate a real and transparent win–win partnership with the 'international community'?

These themes invite us to think of leadership not in terms of individual strong leaders, even if they are necessary, but in terms of a strong consensus about the common destination and a strong coalition about the way we want to get there. Such a view implies creating new leadership concepts and approaches, from existing leadership concepts. 'Indigenous' action-research about leadership and people's well-being might be a critical means for generating such creations and adaptations.

REFERENCES

Braeckman, C. (2010) 'L'apartheid "soft" des Belges au Congo', *Bruxelles: Journal Le Soir*, 28 April 2010, p. 17.

Busselen, T. (2015) 'Les USA ont un agenda caché en République démocratique du Congo', Interview conducted by Olivier Atemsing Ndenkop, in *Le Journal de l'Afrique*, no. 7, Investig'Action, February 2015- CIA Website, 17 February.

CEPAS (2008) Conférence Internationale : Institutions Financières Internationales et les Pratiques de la Corruption en République Démocratique du Congo. Kinshasa.

Clist, B. (2005) *Découvertes archéologiques en République Démocratique du Congo*. Saint Maur-des-Fossés: Editions Sepia.

Dasandi, N. (2014) 'The politics–bureaucracy interface: impact on development reform', *The Developmental Leadership Program (DLP) – State of the Art 2*. Birmingham, UK: University of Birmingham: International Development Department, School of Government and Society, College of Social Sciences.

Index Mundi (2015) Congo, Democratic Republic of Congo Profile 2014. www.indexmundi.com. Source: CIA World Factbook, updated 30 June.

INS-RD (2015) Congo. *Annuaire Statistique 2014*. Kinshasa-Gombe.

Le Soft International (2015) Liste intégrale des partis politiques congolais. www.lesoftonline.net, No. 1310/ 11th edn. 17 March 2015.

Malale, B. (2011) *Les Aspects juridiques dans les enjeux des crises congolaises, des origines à nos jours*. Doctoral thesis, University of Lubumbashi, DR Congo.

Mambi, T.B.H. (2010) *Pouvoir traditionnel et pouvoir d'etat en République Démocratique du Congo: esquisse d'une théorie d'hybridation des pouvoirs politiques*. Kinshasa: MEDIASPAUL.

N'Dah, A.P. (2003) *Moderniser l'etat africain*. Abidjan : Les éditions du CERAP.

Ndaywel è Nziem, I. (1998) *Histoire générale du Congo – de l'héritage ancien à la République Démocratique du Congo*. Paris/Brussels: De Boeck & Larcier s.a.

Nyamusenge, M.D. (2012) 'How to develop leadership in a hospital in Ghana?' Dissertation towards the degree of Master of Research by advanced study in Leadership Studies. University of Exeter, Business School, UK.

Paraire, P. (1998) 'Economie servile et capitalisme: un bilan quantifiable', in *Le Livre noir du capitalisme*. Montreuil: Le Temps des Cerises.

Putzel, James, et al. (2008) 'Vecteurs de changement au sein de la République Démocratique du Congo: ascension et déclin de l'etat et enjeux liés à la reconstruction'. Working paper no. 26. London: Crisis States Research Centre, DESTIN, LSE.

8
ETHIOPIA
The Faces of Leadership in Ethiopia

Fentahun Mengistu: Lecturer at Wollo University, Ethiopia, and PhD Student in Education Policy and Leadership at Bahir Dar University, Ethiopia

Vachel Miller: Associate Professor and Higher Education Programme Director at Reich College of Education, Appalachian State University, USA

Girma Shimelis: Lecturer and Researcher at Jigjiga University, Ethiopia, and PhD Student in Education Policy and Leadership at Bahir Dar University, Ethiopia

ETHIOPIA IN A NUTSHELL

Different. That's the most succinct way we can describe the context for leadership in Ethiopia. Located in the Horn of Africa, Ethiopia stands apart from both its northern and southern neighbours. In Ethiopia, Orthodox Christianity coexists with Islam and multiple indigenous cultural/linguistic groups in a stable state. However, state-driven industrial growth is rapidly creating new forms of inequity in a country in which most people rely on subsistence agricultural shaped by traditional ways of life.

Unlike other countries in East Africa, Ethiopia did not undergo sustained colonization by European powers. Apart from brief periods of Italian occupation (1895–6; 1935–41), Ethiopia has long maintained its autonomy. Because Ethiopians never served a colonial master, they maintain a sense of cultural pride that was systematically crushed elsewhere in Africa. Since the reign of Emperor Haile Sellasie, Ethiopia has embraced a role of political leadership for the African continent.

There is a relatively thin research base on leadership in Ethiopia. A recent review of 60 years of leadership research in Africa noted that there are few studies of leadership in Ethiopia, despite the country's unique circumstances (Fourie et al., 2015). Given the dearth of published leadership research, our writing in this chapter is based on our extended conversations about leadership theory, as well as informal observations of leadership practice in educational and community settings. Where possible, we link our own observations with findings from available research, with the expectation that our insights will be subject to further dialogue and enquiry.

LEADERSHIP IN POLITICAL AND CULTURAL CONTEXT

Despite long-standing national autonomy and cultural pride, Ethiopians have enjoyed little political freedom. Leadership practice in Ethiopia has been shaped by an autocratic political culture, running from a long line of imperial rulers to the contemporary one-party state. In the most recent national election in 2015, the ruling party won 100% of the seats in Parliament, leaving little doubt about the party's control over governmental institutions and political spaces (Arriola and Lyons, 2016). In late 2016, anti-government protests resulted in hundreds of deaths and a declaration by the Ethiopian government of a 'state of emergency' with broad police powers to ensure security (Al Jazeera, 2016).

Political culture in Ethiopia is intensively hierarchical (Vaughan and Tronvall, 2003), with decision-making authority located at the top and obedient implementation expected at all organizational strata. Political considerations are often involved in the selection of institutional leaders. Because positional leaders typically gain their legitimacy through political selection, they are sometimes viewed with suspicion by staff members. In this context, it may be difficult for leaders to gain others' trust and commitment to organizational change initiatives. Positional leadership is observed to be politicized, with the common assumption that career advancement can only come through affiliation with and allegiance to the dominant party.

Because of the status/power inequities attached to positional leadership, staff members tend to feel distant from their leaders. An Amharic proverb says that 'too much appreciation leads to bad behaviour', reflecting a pessimistic tenor in superior–subordinate relations. Superiors typically engage in 'fault finding', looking for mistakes that will diminish the accomplishments of subordinates. Similarly, Ethiopian leaders have been conditioned by the nation's historical experience of radical regime change. In organizations, newly appointed leaders tend to ignore or suppress the achievements of their predecessors in order to elevate themselves. This practice limits organizational capacity for sustaining adaptation and growth.

In terms of gender hierarchies, women leaders are almost non-existent in decision-making roles in Ethiopian institutions. Hora (2014) observed several barriers to women's positional leadership, including limited educational opportunity, patriarchal cultural attitudes, burdensome domestic responsibilities and the lack of role models. Women's access to leadership posts is largely determined by powerful male gatekeepers, as patriarchic culture still dominates organizational life. Overall, the conditions and expectations of leadership in Ethiopia are shaped by larger systems of social power and gender inequality.

MYTHIC FACES OF HEROIC LEADERSHIP

Ethiopians love imperial heroes. On the streets of Ethiopia, shopkeepers sell T-shirts with images of heroic leaders from Ethiopia's past. These mythic male leaders include Emperor Tewodros, Emperor Menelik II and Emperor Haile Selassie. In the mid-1800s, Emperor Tewodros defeated feuding regional warlords and brought Ethiopia together as a unified kingdom. Later, in the late 1800s, Emperor Menelik II mobilized a national army to confront and defeat invading Italian forces in the Battle of Adwa. Menelik's victory assured Ethiopian independence in the modern era. Following Menelik, Emperor Haile Selassie elevated Ethiopia onto the global stage and made the Ethiopian capital, Addis Ababa, the headquarters of the African Union. Haile Selassie also introduced Western education and bureaucracy (Haregot, 2013), promoting the nation's development under professional public management. On the streets of contemporary Ethiopia, each of these leaders represents a culturally idealized narrative of strong nation-building leadership. Their continued visibility in popular culture indicates a deep reverence for national heroes in the collective Ethiopian psyche.

There are no T-shirts in Ethiopia celebrating leaders of the Marxist revolution that overthrew Haile Selassie in 1974. For 17 years, from 1974 to 1991, the Derg regime limited individual rights and attempted radical redistribution of wealth. The Derg regime also instituted an effective mass literacy campaign, increasing opportunities for basic education while restricting higher education and individual mobility. This period of modern Ethiopian history produced even more highly centralized authority, replacing the autocratic power of the Emperor with the monolithic power of a one-party, one-ideology state.

A FOLLOWER'S TASK: LEARNING 'NEGATIVE KNOWLEDGE'

For centuries, leaders in Ethiopia have held onto power by maintaining relations of distance and dependence among subordinates. In Kapuscinski's (1983) reconstructed interviews with former officials of Haile Selassie's imperial court, one official recounts how the Emperor would suppress the leadership capacity of subordinates:

> Whoever wanted to climb the steps of the Palace had first of all to master the negative knowledge: what was forbidden to him and his subalterns, what was not to be said or written, what should not be done, what should not be overlooked or neglected. Only from such negative knowledge could positive knowledge be born – but that positive knowledge always remained obscure and worrisome, because no matter how well they knew what *not* [italics original] to do, the Emperor's favourites ventured only with extreme caution and uncertainty into the area of propositions and postulates. There they would immediately look to His Distinguished Majesty, waiting to hear what he would say. And since His Majesty had the habit of being silent, waiting, and postponing things, they, too, were silent, waited, and postponed things. (1983 [1978]: 49)

This notion of 'negative knowledge' remains salient in contemporary organizational life in Ethiopia. Often, staff members maintain a passive stance, cautious about making independent decisions for fear that mistakes or missteps will be sharply criticized. Safety is found in mastering the 'negative knowledge' of what not to do, and when taking action, only implementing explicit directives from above. As noted in a 2003 study of political culture in Ethiopia, folk tradition affirms the wisdom of obeying authority in this aphorism: 'As long as one says nothing and makes no remarks, neither can one be punished for one's actions' (cited in Vaughan and Tronvall, 2003: 34–35).

Leadership positions are widely viewed as gateways to prestige, power and material gain. Another local proverb admonishes leaders to exploit their positions: 'If a person does not accrue benefits as a leader, he will regret it when he steps down.' This proverb illustrates the popular belief that individuals should look out for themselves rather than being public servants first. Viewing leadership as a source of prestige and material reward also encourages staff to be loyal and obedient to superiors, in order to position themselves for future benefit.

Mid-level managers typically take directives from the top without questioning, thus passing the burden of implementation to lower-level officials and line workers. Ethiopians refer to this practice as *tikus denich* ('hot potato'). Once a 'hot potato' is received from the top, no one can hold it for long, and it is passed rapidly down to the next level of organization, and down again, until the burden falls into the hands of the lower-level workers. This practice affords mid-level management little autonomy or leadership capacity to initiate productive action. The focus of leadership power at the top of organizational hierarchies often results in weak capacity to sustain system improvement as positional leaders change over time.

Inside the leader's office

In Ethiopian universities, it is common to see a sign that says 'Use next door' on the closed office doors of upper administrators. This sign directs clients to pass through an outer office guarded by an executive secretary who has the power to withhold access to the inner office of her boss. If admitted inside the leader's office, a client will sit at a long conference table placed perpendicular to the administrator's desk, in a T-shape. This spatial configuration centres the administrator at the 'head' of any meeting and makes the conference table an extension of the administrator's own desk. It reinforces vertical relations of power and the patriarchal authority of the positional leader.

TWO FACES OF LEADERSHIP

Rigid, hierarchical traditions often rub up against liberal discourses of leadership flowing into Ethiopian academic discourse from the West. In this respect, we have observed what might be called 'leadership schizophrenia' in Ethiopia. With the phrase 'leadership schizophrenia' we are attempting to describe the ways in which leaders simultaneously espouse progressive leadership ideals while actually practising leadership in a traditional authoritarian style that erodes trust and constrains organizational learning capacity.

We have observed large gaps between leaders' self-perception and followers' experiences of both servant-oriented forms of leadership (Spears, 2010) and adaptive forms of leadership (Heifitz et al., 2009). Similarly, a recent study of ethical leadership in three Ethiopian universities (Amsale et al., 2016), found statistically significant differences between leaders' self-perceptions and staff perceptions of their leaders' ethical behaviour. As the researchers summarized, 'Academic leaders reported 'we are doing well', while the teachers indicated the opposite' (Amsale et al., 2016: 375). This mismatch between leaders' self-perception and followers' experience of leadership has created a two-faced discourse of leadership, as we discuss further below.

COLONIZED BY THEORY

In Ethiopian universities, the learning objectives for undergraduate leadership courses are shaped and approved by the Ministry of Education. The standard leadership curriculum includes a spectrum of traditional leadership theory found in American textbooks. In Ethiopia, however, the map of leadership theory has a hard border, with little discussion of theory beyond the highly leader-centric notions of transformational leadership. Feminist leadership theory is largely ignored, as are other forms of leadership theory focused on social justice and/or environmental concerns.

Awra Amba: An indigenous leadership alternative

A counter-hegemonic model of leadership can be found within Ethiopia. In the Amhara region of northern Ethiopia, there is a small intentional community known as Awra Amba. This community is grounded in a non-religious philosophy of human equality and self-sufficiency. In this community, leadership work has been decentralized. Women and men in the community participate in various committees tasked with organizing education, hospitality, community health, etc. The community has built its own childcare centre as well as an elder care centre to provide for the needs of its members. Nevertheless, the Awra Amba community is viewed with some suspicion by neighbours, particularly due to its non-religious stance and its requirement that men and women share equally in all forms of work, regardless of traditional gender roles (Halpern, 2007; Duncan, 2013).

Generally, there seems to be little formal development of indigenous Ethiopian leadership models, concepts, or theories grounded in local community traditions. Rather, scholars and students typically employ Western theoretical frameworks in their research practice, with only superficial adaptation to the Ethiopian political-economic context. A Masters' student in educational leadership, for example, might conduct a study on the leadership styles of school directors, using imported categories and instrumentation downloaded from foreign universities. Those survey instruments may have little direct relevance in a context of chronic poverty and limited organizational capacity for change.

At another level, we wonder: could the dominance of Western leadership theory, especially in the 'Messiah' paradigm (Western, 2013) of transformative leadership, contribute to leadership schizophrenia? Ethiopian leaders may feel a normative pressure to espouse the higher ideals of such theory – or may feel an authentic desire for distributing power – while being embedded within a very different set of cultural/operational expectations that drive a wedge between espoused theory and daily practice.

In the southern African context, there has been much affirmation of the concept of *Ubuntu* as an indigenous African-approach leadership focused on caring, harmony and connection (Ncube, 2010). We anticipate that this notion could be productively adapted to fit the particular nuances of the Ethiopian cultural context. For the purpose of this chapter, what is remarkable is that even an African leadership framework like *Ubuntu* is relatively unknown in Ethiopia, perhaps because the knowledge flows that inform leadership thinking have been shaped by Ethiopian scholars studying abroad (whether in North America or Europe), as well as foreign scholars teaching in Ethiopia. Prestige in knowledge production is found largely by engaging in discursive communities outside the country, rather than in localized discussions/adaptations of theory.

LEADERSHIP TODAY AND IN THE FUTURE

In Ethiopia, heroic male leadership holds mythical power, as embodied in the narratives of past emperors such as Tewedros, Menelik II, and Haile Selassie. Even as Internet access expands and smartphones become commonplace, Ethiopia remains a relatively insular society, with great pride in cultural traditions woven with thick strands of patriarchal, authoritarian power. Decision-making in Ethiopia remains highly centralized and power remains carefully guarded. Our observations tell us that distrust, suspicion and passivity remain prevalent in organizational culture, amid an espoused discourse of progressive, transformational leadership.

In recent years, the government has introduced several organizational change efforts designed to promote greater organizational effectiveness and efficiency. Such initiatives are typically based on isomorphic adoption of imported practices (Woldegiyorgis, 2014) rather than locally-produced solutions. We suggest that future leaders need to open critical space for stakeholders to design and debate their own organizational change initiatives, in order to facilitate greater local ownership of change. Leadership that does not welcome public dialogue about social/organizational change will likely drive dissent underground. In daily life, much of the critical dialogue in Ethiopia happens in social media – a medium carefully monitored and controlled by the current government due to its potential use as a vehicle for mobilizing organized resistance.

All too often, leadership research in Ethiopia attempts to measure and categorize leadership practice according to imported theoretical constructs. We advocate for a surge of culturally- and institutionally-grounded leadership research and dialogue in Ethiopia. Such an approach would develop more complex, nuanced interpretations of leadership practices on the ground, listening to the aspirations and frustrations of people across organizational spaces.

Overall, the challenge of fresh leadership thinking in Ethiopia will be breaking with the historical pattern of one authoritarian form of power replacing another. Liberating leadership thinking will require space (often found in social media) for the proliferation of difference – welcoming multiplicity in discourse, identity, and practice – rather than demanding a new 'right way' of doing leadership that comes down from the top. There are many possible faces of leadership in Ethiopia; moving forward, they should be more clearly recognized and valued.

REFERENCES

Al Jazeera (2016) 'Ethiopia declares state of emergency over protests', 9 October. www.aljazeera.com/news/2016/10/ethiopia-declares-state-emergency-protests-161009110506730.html (accessed 9 November 2017).

Amsale, F., Bekele, M. and Tafessa, M. (2016) 'The ethical behaviours of educational leaders in Ethiopian public universities: the case of the western cluster universities', *European Scientific Journal*, 12 (13): 359–79.

Arriola, L.R. and Lyons, T. (2016) 'The 100% election', *Journal of Democracy*, 27 (1): 76–88.

Duncan, D. (2013) 'This Ethiopian village has gained wealth, but has bred hostility'. PRI, 12 December. www.pri.org/stories/2013-12-12/ethiopian-village-has-gained-wealth-has-bred-hostility (accessed 9 November 2017).

Fourie, W., van der Merwe, S.C. and van der Merwe, B. (2015) 'Sixty years of research on leadership in Africa: a review of the literature', *Leadership*, Online first, 29 April. DOI: 10.1177/1742715015580665.

Halpern, O. (2007) 'In Ethiopia, one man's model for a just society', *The Christian Science Monitor*, 21 August. www.csmonitor.com/2007/0821/p01s02-woaf.html (accessed 9 November 2017).

Haregot, Seyoum A. (2013) *The Bureaucratic Empire: Serving Emperor Haile Selassie*. Trenton, NJ: The Red Sea Press.

Heifetz, Ronald A., Grashow, Alexander and Linsky, Marty (2009) *The Practice of Adaptive Leadership: Tools and Tactics for Changing Your Organization and the World*. Boston, MA: Harvard Business Press.

Hora, E. (2014) 'Factors that affect women participation in leadership and decision-making positions', *Asian Journal of Humanity, Art and Literature*, 1 (2): 97–117.

Kapuscinski, R. (1983 [1978]) *The Emperor: Downfall of an Autocrat* (trans. W.R. Brand and K. Mroczkowska-Brand). San Diego, CA: Harcourt Brace Jovanovich.

Ncube, L.B. (2010) 'Ubuntu: a transformative leadership philosophy', *Journal of Leadership Studies*, 4 (3): 77–82.

Spears, L.C. (2010) 'Character and servant leadership: ten characteristics of effective, caring leaders, *The Journal of Virtues & Leadership*, 1 (1): 25–30.

Vaughan, S. and Tronvall, K. (2003) 'The culture of power in contemporary Ethiopian political life'. Sida Studies #10. http://ehrp.org/wp-content/uploads/2014/05/VaughnandTronvoll-The-Culture-of-Power-in-Contemporary-Ethiopian-Political-Life.pdf (accessed 24 November 2017).

Western, Simon (2013) *Leadership: A Critical Text*, 2nd edn. London: Sage.

Woldegiyorgis, A. (2014) 'Adapting to global trends: why and how is the Ethiopian higher education changing?', *The Online Journal of New Horizons in Education*, 3 (4): 23–9.

9
FRANCE
Exploring the French Paradoxes and Promises of Leadership

Valérie Petit: Professor of Management,
Director of Open Leadership Innovation Center,
EDHEC Business School

INTRODUCTION

'To me, a leader is Napoleon on the Pont d'Arcole!',[1] the CEO of a major French group told me in the early 2000s (Petit, 2013). Fifteen years later, I invariably hear references to Napoleon when I ask French people about leadership. I am always surprised by the persistence of this reference even though it is an accurate reflection of French representation of leadership and leaders. This Napoleonic syndrome is indicative of the terribly romantic and also paradoxical vision of leadership held by the French. In this chapter, I built on recent research and the case-study of Jean-Marie Messier, former CEO of Vivendi Universal and an emblematic corporate French leader, to introduce the reader to the French implicit leadership theories and the paradoxical conditions of leadership in France. I use this example to provide new insights and future analysis into French leadership.

LEADERS AND LEADERSHIP: EXPLORING THE FRENCH PANTHÉON[2]

How do French people collectively represent leaders? Few academic studies have explored the implicit theories of leadership (Schyns and Meindl, 2005) in France. The Globe Study (House et al., 2004) shows that the French have a preference for leaders who are both charismatic and autonomous. They favour a heroic and solitary vision of the leader figure and have little time for forms of leadership in which the key figure is undecided or delegates to followers.

Studies conducted in the French context (Petit, 2012, 2013; Garcia, 2013) reveal that the French place charisma at the top of the list of leadership traits. They describe the charismatic leader as a particularly eloquent visionary with an aura and a magnetic presence, someone who is charming and seductive. They see charisma as an innate and almost magical quality, and cite Charles de Gaulle and Napoleon, as well as Gandhi and

---

[1]The battle of the Pont d'Arcole took place in 1796 during Italy's first military campaign. It was fought between the 19,000 Frenchmen of the Italian army, under the orders of Napoleon Bonaparte, and 24,000 Austrian troops. Napoleon won the battle, having crossed the bridge alone, where he planted the flag unaccompanied by his troops after his generals had failed. It is a symbol of the individual heroic act.

[2]The Panthéon is a monument located in the Latin Quarter in Paris. It is used to honour major figures from French history and houses the remains of Voltaire, Rousseau, Hugo, Zola, Jaurès, Malraux and Alexandre Dumas, among others.

Xavier Niel,[3] as iconic figures (Petit, 2012). In this respect, the French broadly reflect the universal preference for charismatic leaders (Den Hartog et al., 1999), yet they stand out in two ways. First, they include seductive qualities in their portrait of the ideal leader. Although such qualities are not striking characteristics of the historic and military figures mentioned above, they feature strongly in the more qualitative studies I have conducted in which senior French managers have told me about their expectations and experiences of leadership (Petit, 2009, 2012), highlighting the French fondness for the ambivalent and roguish qualities of the trickster (Radin, 1987 [1956]). This points to the second distinction: The French also resist references to morality, which they do not put at the heart of leadership (Ciulla, 1995). The moral integrity of a leader, identified by House et al. (2004) as a cultural invariant, is not seen as a priority in France. This is a reflection of one of France's peculiar features: the strict separation between the private and professional spheres. For the French, morality, like religion, belongs to the private sphere and can be separated from the exercise of leadership in the professional sphere.

Beyond this vision of the charismatic leader as someone who is charming, amoral and individualistic, the French strictly associate leadership with the male gender: leaders are men with so-called masculine traits (Eagly et al., 1992). They also consider leadership to be inextricably linked to hierarchical position. For many of them, people in high political or economic positions are de facto leaders, and to some extent one's position continues to determine leadership. This is particularly true in the case of senior French civil servants (Petit et al., 2017), where status and position carry their own charisma which is reflected onto the individual, as pointed out by Max Weber in his analysis of the personal and institutional foundations of charisma (Weber, 1968).

THE GENESIS OF LEADERSHIP: NAVIGATING THE FRENCH PARADOXES

Focusing on the figures of leadership is not enough to understand it, as it is profoundly situational and contingent (Liden and Antonakis, 2009; Garcia, 2013). To understand leadership in France, one must look beyond individual figures and consider the collective and objective conditions of leadership (social, economic and political): the archetypal story of Jean-Marie Messier provides the perfect opportunity for such analysis and can help us better understand and highlight the paradoxes of leadership in France.

---

[3]Xavier Niel is a French entrepreneur and businessman. He is CEO of Iliad group, which owns the telecommunications operator Free. He is also joint owner of *Le Monde*, France's leading daily newspaper. He is sometimes referred to as France's Steve Jobs.

Jean-Marie Messier's story: the rise and fall of a French leader

In 2001, the cover of *Fortune* magazine ran with the title *'He's not just France's famous businessman; he is the country's first rock star CEO'* in reference to Jean-Marie Messier. The former CEO of Vivendi Universal group (1996–2002) was also described as the most powerful leader in France, a man who had bought the world with his policy of frenetic and wilful acquisitions, caricaturized as the Napoleon of the business world (Orange and Johnson, 2003; Khurana, 2010; Petit, 2013).

Jean-Marie Messier was born in Grenoble in 1956 into a Catholic family from France's 'petite bourgeoisie' He obtained his baccalaureate two years early, and having completed preparatory studies in science, went on to study at two of the country's most renowned schools: École Polytechnique, which provides French companies with engineers and senior executives, and the Ecole Nationale d'Administration, which trains the elite of political leaders but also prominent French civil servants and French companies' CEOs.[4] He began his career as the cabinet director for the Finance Ministry, where he oversaw the privatization of a major TV channel (TF1) and several industrial companies (e.g. Matra) that had previously been nationalized. In 1988, he joined the investment bank Lazard, where he became the 'dealmaker' for major French corporate figures, and notably oversaw the first successful hostile takeover by a French company in the USA (Schneider). In 1994, he joined the Compagnie Générale des Eaux, later renamed Vivendi Universal (VU), and became CEO two years later. He transformed the water services company into a global media giant, merging with Seagram and Universal Studios.[5] Despite foreseeing the convergence between media and telecommunications, he proved unable to ensure the profitability of VU[6] and had to leave his post under combined pressure from company shareholders, the French management community, the media and the financial markets, which had previously elevated this charismatic leader to dizzying heights and now cast the first stone against a 'hubristic' boss. His forced resignation played out like a national melodrama in a flurry of excitement rarely observed in the French business world.

---

[4]Among others: the current and also former Presidents (François Hollande, Jacques Chirac, Valery Giscard d'Estaing), and CEO of French leading companies (Guillaume Pepy, CEO of the French Railways, Frédéric Oudea, CEO of Societe Generale Bank, Philippe Wahl, CEO of the French Post or Clara Gaymard, CEO of General Electric France, Henri de Castres, CEO of Axa Insurances).

[5]Messier was convinced that the control of contents-production was key in achieving the convergence strategy and the vertical integration of the group (from content acquisition to content distribution). At that time, Vivendi Group already controlled the distribution but needed to secure content production: the merger with Seagram served this goal and was a second chapter of his strategy.

[6]In 2002, VU group announced a loss of 23 billion euros (the largest loss in the French history of capitalism ... just behind its competitor, Orange (21 billion).

Messier and the French stereotype of a leader

Jean-Marie Messier perfectly embodies the French stereotype of a leader. He is first and foremost the man who, like Napoleon, alone conquered the media industry and, through a series of ground-breaking deals, managed to impose his vision and turn a French company into a heavyweight on the global economic stage. Messier has all the attributes of charisma as envisioned by the French: he is a leader driven by a modern vision that looks beyond the company; in 1996, he stood as the French neo-prophet of the new economy, called for media convergence and ensured the Internet would revolutionize culture and the wider world; he has proven seductive through his charm, down-to-earth demeanour and his ability to listen, particularly as the darling of the media. Between 1998 and 2001, Messier was the perfect embodiment of the charismatic and heroic leader of which the French are so fond of. However, his leadership was not only linked to his personality and the fact that it was looked favourably upon by the collective imagination – far from it. It was above all based on his ability, at one point, to represent and resolve the paradoxes of the French fabric and practice of leadership.

Messier and the paradoxes of leadership in France

The notion of a paradox (Smith and Lewis, 2011), which implies 'contradictory yet interrelated elements', is also relevant in understanding French Leadership (Petit et al., 2015). The paradox scholars point out that the most productive but also the most difficult way to manage paradoxes is to succeed in what they call a both/and strategy, i.e. one of hybridization. This is clearly the kind of strategy implemented by Jean-Marie Messier.

Egalitarianism versus elitism

The first paradox of French society is in the way it produces its future leaders. The French educational system is the product of a paradoxical injunction: on the one hand, it aspires to equality for all so that each young pupil can obtain the baccalaureate regardless of his or her social origins or financial means, and on the other this mass egalitarian system is transformed into a machine to produce an over-selected and over-networked elite that will be capable of interchangeably governing state or business organizations. Under the French ideal, it is personal merit that reconciles these two antagonistic realities. In reality, there are two paths for future leaders: that of excellence in the country's Grandes Ecoles,[7] and that of university education. Most major companies are governed by graduates from

[7]Grandes Ecoles meaning 'state elite schools', such as Ecole Polytechnique, Ecole Nationale d'Administration or Ecole Nationale supérieure des Arts et Métiers.

the former. Jean-Marie Messier is a good illustration of how to resolve this paradox and propagates the myth of French meritocracy: he showed that the system could enable a middle-class child from the provinces to reach the upper echelons of the political and economic sphere by recognizing his personal merit and providing him with the highest level of training. His case also serves as a reminder that it is indeed the state that produces the nation's future leaders, through its public Grandes Ecoles.

State capitalism versus financial capitalism

The second paradox of French society lies in the antagonism between two capitalist models: that governed by the state and that governed by the financial markets. France has long oscillated without making a clear choice between these two visions of capitalism, which extend beyond political rivalries but make the economic context particularly complex and often uncertain for business leaders. Jean-Marie Messier was able to assert his leadership because over a certain period he successfully represented the resolution of this paradox, combining both capitalist practices. Like many French leaders, he developed his leadership by to-ing and fro-ing between the public and private sectors and playing on the permeability between the two.

With responsibility for the privatization of state companies, Messier learned how to get the country's political leaders and captains of industry to collaborate and took on board the rules of French-style capitalism, in which the state and industry are inextricably linked. His time at Lazard investment bank later taught him how to convince the markets and master the rules of a more Anglo-Saxon brand of capitalism. At the head of Vivendi, he drew on both of these strengths and managed to sell his business project both to the financial markets and the French state in a sector that was heavily regulated (water and telecommunications). And while conquering the markets, he continued to nurture his relations with senior French executives with a very French form of complicity based on his place within the French elite, having attended the same schools and acquired experience in both the public and private spheres.[8]

Revolution vs tradition

The third paradox of French society is the tension that exists between two mindsets – revolutionary and attached to traditions. This complicates the task of transformational

[8]Such as the current French President and former Minister of Economy, Emmanuel Macron: graduated from ENA, former banker at Rothschild & Cie.

and reformative leaders – indeed, makes it a tragic endeavour. The history of France has of course been marked by a succession of sometimes brutal revolutionary acts and the restoration of the old order. The major figures of French leadership such as Napoleon or De Gaulle were above all revolutionaries, who challenged the incumbent order but in turn came to embody a tradition that was itself challenged, fell out of favour and were forced into exile. This is a process very well depicted by Weber (1968) in his analysis of charisma, which he describes as the revolutionary force par excellence that emerges to put down the established order (Petit, 2012) but which over time sees its revolutionary lustre eroded and is ultimately condemned to disappear as quickly as it first emerged.

This depiction of the charismatic and revolutionary hero is, for me, the most productive basis from which to understand the destiny of French leaders, and in particular that of Messier, who was a product of French tradition and took on the role of a revolutionary. Messier's first revolution was a strategic one: he was the charismatic leader who transformed a French company into a global giant based only on his incredible vision and ambition. However, this revolution was to clash with the traditional orders represented by the French media and political sphere: when during a press conference in New York following the acquisition of USA Networks he announced that the French cultural exception could not survive the globalization of media and culture, he was no longer the figure who resolved one of the paradoxes of French society but instead someone who was attacking its most prized asset – its culture. The French media never forgave him. When he considered selling off part of Vivendi Universal to a foreign group, he was depicted as 'pawning off' a jewel of French industry and betraying French economic patriotism. France's political leaders never forgave him either.

Messier's second revolution was a leadership revolution: he was the boss who sought to change the way leadership was exercised in France. He broke some of the taboos of French management: that of financial matters by revealing his salary, that of political neutrality by supporting the 35-hour working week introduced by a left-wing government, and that of secrecy by sharing the details of his daily working life with the press. His management peers in France were unwilling to forgive him for seeking to change the traditional leadership culture and later adopted a united position to secure his resignation in 2002.

In both of these revolutionary roles, Messier played against and was ultimately defeated by French leadership traditions, despite perfectly embodying these traditions in the early part of his career. He also lost control of himself, succumbing to the hubris of power. His story highlights how the ability to combine revolution and tradition is central to the mould of French leadership. It also introduces us to the tragedy and the paradoxes of the French vision and practice of leadership.

THE FUTURE OF LEADERSHIP: BUILDING A FRENCH THEORY OF LEADERSHIP

As a French leadership scholar, when I look to the past, I regret the fact that French intellectuals have not always engaged with the field of leadership studies. This lack of interest and the absence of leadership research is due to relatively similar preconceptions to those found in the wider population: leadership, a theme forged in American culture and thought, is not considered appropriate to understand the French context, it is too managerial and bereft of the critical dimension so dear to the social sciences in France. This reluctance does not favour pluralism and diversity in the making of leadership knowledge. Therefore, who can enrich the debate about the contingency of leadership, the diversity of leaders or the emergence and destiny of a global form of leadership? And who ultimately will show that France is also a rich source of lessons to learn when it comes to leadership?

Now, as I look to the future, I hope that here in France we will manage to produce a *French Theory* of leadership in years to come and contribute to the global intellectual life as French philosophers and sociologist did (Cusset, 2008). If I had to outline two paths for future research on leadership in France, they would be as follows:

First, a French theory of leadership could no doubt contribute a critical perspective of leadership through the deconstruction of the French romance of leadership (Meindl et al., 1985) and, going beyond the critics, study French leadership in the postmodern, post-Napoleonic era. Leadership in the France of today is being reinvented, whether by leaders – like Xavier Niel – who circumvented the traditional system responsible for producing the country's elite, or in alternative or hybrid organizations (Bayle et al., 2016), who have given rise to a form of leadership that is democratic and shared at the scale of the company. Understanding this transition and transformation is both of theoretical and practical interest.

Second, a French theory could explore and build on the study of the paradoxes of leadership: the story of Jean-Marie Messier tells us that in France you have to be able to navigate paradoxes to demonstrate leadership. For my part, I see this less as a French exception than as a lesson in leadership handed down to us by the country's leaders. At a time of complexity and uncertainty, they encourage us to reflect on leadership as the capacity to resolve paradoxes in order to continue to act in a positive way for companies and society in general. A critical and contradictory approach that is bound to resonate with the French mindset! So, calling on all *French academics: one more effort if you want to be leadership scholars*![9]

---

[9]A reference to the title of a text by the Marquis de Sade: '*Frenchmen, one more effort if you want to be Republicans!*'

REFERENCES

Bayle, J., Petit, V. and Stervinou, S. (2016) 'Leadership in hybrid organizations: the case of French cooperatives', ICA annual conference.

Ciulla, J.B. (1995) 'Leadership ethics: mapping the territory', *The Business Ethics Quarterly*, 5 (1): 5–24.

Cusset, François (2008) *French Theory: How Foucault, Derrida, Deleuze, and Co. Transformed the Intellectual Life of the United States*. Minneapolis, MN: University of Minnesota Press.

Den Hartog, D.N., House, R.J., Hanges, P.J., Ruiz-Quintanilla, S.A. and Dorfmann, P.W. (1999) 'Culture specific and cross-culturally generalizable implicit leadership theories: are attributes of charismatic/transformational leadership universally endorsed?', *Leadership Quarterly*, 10: 219–56.

Eagly, A.H., Makhijani, M.G. and Klonsky, B.G. (1992) 'Gender and the evaluation of leaders: a meta-analysis', *Psychological Bulletin*, 111: 3–22.

Garcia, Éric-Jean (2013) *Le Génie du leadership: Mythes et Défis de l'Action Managériale*. Paris: Dunod.

House, Robert J., Hanges, Paul J., Javidan, Mansour, Dorfman, Peter W. and Gupta, Vipin (2004) *Culture, Leadership and Organizations: the Globe Study of 62 Societies*. London: Sage.

Khurana, R. (2010), 'Messier's reign at Vivendi Universal', *Harvard Business School Teaching Note*, pp. 407–9.

Liden, R.C. and Antonakis, J. (2009) 'Considering context in psychological leadership research', *Human Relations*, 62 (11): 1587–605.

Meindl, J.R., Ehrlich, S.B. and Dukerich, J.M. (1985) 'The romance of leadership', *Administrative Science Quarterly*, 30: 521–51.

Orange, Martine and Johnson, Joe (2003) *The Man Who Tried to Buy the World: Jean-Marie Messier and Vivendi Universal*. London: Portfolio.

Petit, V. (2009) 'Les habits neuf du pouvoir: regards critiques sur le leadership', in *Les Etudes Critiques en Management: Une Perspective Française*, edited by Damon Golsorkhi, Isabelle Huault and Bernard Leca. Laval: Presses Universitaires de Laval.

Petit, V. (2012) 'Les théories implicites du leadership des dirigeants français', *Revue Internationale de Psychosociologie*, pp. 247–66.

Petit, Valérie (2013) *Leadership, l'art et la science de la direction d'entreprise*. Montreuil: Pearson France.

Petit, V. and Delanghe, M. (2015) *La Revolution du leadership/The French Revolution of Leadership?* EDHEC Publication. Available at https://fr.slideshare.net/lesechos2/la-revolution-du-leadership-rapport-rpondants (accessed 13 November 2017).

Petit, V., Delangue, M. and Jemel-Fornetty, H. (2017) 'Promesses et paradoxes du leadership public: une étude sur les cadres-dirigeants de la sphere publique', EDHEC Publications.

Available at http://edhecopenleadership.com/promesses-et-paradoxes-du-leadership-public/ (accessed 13 November 2017).

Petit, V., Pradies, C. and Uhlaner, L. (2015) *Paradox-Based Leadership: Top Executives' Leadership in the Paradoxical Age*. EGOS annual conference, Athens.

Radin, Paul (1987 [1956]) *The Trickster: A Study in American Indian Mythology*. New York: Schocken Books.

Schyns, Birgit and Meindl, James R. (2005) *Implicit Leadership Theories: Essays and Implications*. Greenwich: Information Age Publishing.

Smith, W.K. and Lewis, M.W. (2011) 'Toward a theory of paradox: a dynamic equilibrium model of organizing', *Academy of Management Review*, 36 (2): 381–403.

Weber, Max (1968), *On Charisma and Institution Building* (selected papers, edited and with an introduction by S.N. Eisenstadt). Chicago: The University of Chicago Press.

10
GERMANY

German Leadership: A Dialectical Approach

Claudia Nagel: Managing Partner, Nagel & Company GmbH, Germany, and Visiting Professor at Hull University Business School, UK

THE ESSENCE OF LEADERSHIP

In Germany, the topic of leadership is a difficult one because it is historically burdened. In German companies, leadership is most often talked about by using terms such as 'senior leaders' and 'leadership principles'. It is becoming more and more common that English-language terminology is used, but not for reasons of increasing internationalization or globalization. Due to Germany's history, the shame felt about what transpired, during World War II the still existing dismay and the deep moral rejection of what occurred continue to lead to – consciously and unconsciously – the avoidance of using the term 'Führer', which means leader. At the same time, in terms of the economy, Germany is a pioneer and leader of the European Community and, in turn, also globally. In addition, the German Chancellor Angela Merkel is viewed as one of the leading global politicians. Yet within Europe, for Germans it is still considered presumptuous to discuss the country's role as a leader. This perfectly illustrates how Germans deal with the term 'leadership'. Ambivalence pervades through all segments; the German leadership culture is a complex network that consists of a wide variety of polarities. Some of these terminological poles are located at the forefront, while the other side is only unconsciously or partially integrated. This broad area of tension makes it so difficult to speak about German leadership; however, it does allow us to draw a characteristic picture.

The ideas of leadership in Germany are defined by historical aspects, by military thought, by German engineering and craftsmanship, as well as by German high-class workmanship, all of which are reflected by the 'Made in Germany' quality seal. They are closely tied to the religious-based ideas of life and work that are found in the Protestant-based ethics of Weber as well as in the Catholic Social Doctrine and the resulting Rhine Capitalism.

From an external perspective, the character of the corporate landscape is especially defined by the DAX 30 companies, in which male networks and male-dominated management boards determine the view of leadership while, at the same time, the typical German handling of the fear of failing is often equated with 'German angst'. In this first superficial overview, the other side of the coin, which is subsequently described in further detail, must be integrated, since it also plays an important role when it comes to understanding German leadership.

THE MAIN INFLUENCES ON LEADERSHIP

The dialectical interplay of the different characteristics and influences is diverse, making it difficult to generate a stereotypical idea of typical German leadership, as is depicted in the following.

Let us begin with the history and the military imprint of the idea of leadership in Germany. In Germany, historically the military and leadership have been closely intertwined. Even today, strategic thinkers are viewed as the most important leaders in companies as well as in the consulting industry, just as strategy continues to belong to the core tasks of the management team. However, the image that was drawn up by one of the greatest strategic military thinkers, von Clausewitz, did not prevail over time. Von Clausewitz (1780–1831) extolled the individual genius of the strategic general in other words, the role of leader was largely defined by his extraordinary character and as a harmonious combination of intellectual and emotional expertise paired with experience. In contrast, von Moltke (1800–1891) demanded from the Prussian general staff that they consider and investigate all potential scenarios and required at the same time that they be able to react to reality in a flexible and situational manner. For him, the art of war consisted of practical decisions as a reaction to the uncertain, unforeseeable situation in the reality of war, made on the basis of qualities of mind and character in the pursuit of a selected strategy and goal.

The major military successes in the second half of the nineteenth century led to further appreciation of military role models and strengthened the application of military principles in the economy (Staehle and Conrad, 1991). As a result, the German economy was driven by Prussian precision, accuracy, rigour, neutrality and dedication to principles in the political administration.

Closely linked to this concept of leadership influenced by military is the archetype of the hero as described by the (Swiss-born) Jacob Burckhardt in 1868: 'Then the great men are necessary for our lives so that the world historical movement are periodically and suddenly set free from dead wood and deliberate chatter' (as quoted by Neuberger, 2001: 114). This archetypical hero figure suits the military-based idea of leadership; the hero takes his own road, stays untouched, defeats his enemies and leads the company through difficult times. This narcissistic idea of grandeur is just as widely prevalent in the German upper echelon as the unconscious desire of many employees for the projection of stability, security and to be saved.

Even the father as an archetypical background of German leadership is part of this militaristic-inspired image of leadership, which can be seen in the nineteenth century in the early assumption of responsibility for the upbringing of orphaned young men by the military. Both archetypes – the one of the father and the one of the hero – enable the defence of individual and collective fears, which are triggered by an uncertain and unclear future.

On the other, unconscious side of this pair of opposites is the resistance movement – such as, for example, the Scholl siblings and their small but effective resistance group named 'The White Rose' during the reign of National Socialism and also the democratic movement of the workers, such as in the Weimar Republic.

On the basis of Christian and humanitarian ideas, the members of the White Rose, in particular the siblings Hans and Sophie Scholl, used numerous leaflets to actively criticize the National Socialist regime and its inhuman practices in 1942–3. Five students and one professor were the core of this alliance. Because they freed others from blame and saved them from punishment, they represented – in the face of death – a different image of German leadership. Their sister Inge wrote that they 'didn't do anything inhuman. They defended something simple: they stood up for something simple – for human rights and the freedom of every individual to enjoy a self-determined life of freedom. They did not sacrifice themselves for an extraordinary cause; they did not follow any utopian vision; what they wanted was that people like you and I could live in a humane world.' (Scholl, 1986 [1955], p.12).

Even in today's German leadership culture there are some examples for an economic resistance movement – although this comparison must be made with the utmost care – as can be seen, for example, in the growing foundation of start-ups and social businesses. They represent a different way of leadership and economic attitude.

Additionally, an important development for the German leadership culture was the social democratic movement, for which Friedrich Ebert stood as the first German Reich president of the Weimar Republic in 1919 and which established civil rights, that is, the same rights for men and women as well as for employees and employers.

The development of labour unions, which – as a result of the introduction of the power of co-determination – have a position of power in companies that is rarely understood outside of Germany, has created a type of counter-movement to the military organization and bureaucracy. The importance given to labour unions' role can be seen as a critically positive reaction against the principle of alienation derived from the increasing industrial rationalization described by Karl Marx.

The social responsibility of the 'ruling class' towards the 'factory work' that was called for and necessary in order to alleviate social conflict, also led to a particular understanding of leadership in family businesses. On the one hand, large multinational corporations such as the DAX 30 companies shape the image of German companies abroad. The (leadership) systems of German companies are still largely defined by hierarchical and bureaucratic structures. They are still shaped by a network of a male elite whose affiliation continues to be determined by its members' upbringing and where they attended university.

This is opposed by a large number of family-owned companies that are understood to be the backbone of the German economy. These companies operate very successfully in their respective niche markets as 'hidden champions'. In this segment, a change in leadership culture has already taken place, since many of these companies are already being run differently. Countless examples of participative and cooperative leadership structures can be noted and a large percentage of those family-run companies are already led by women.

Generally speaking, these companies are known for highly assuming regional and social responsibility. Leadership is seen as a discipline of service to society and to the local region. The basis of company management is a long-term, asset-retaining attitude, which is less interested in quarterly earnings reports and corporate growth rates, but instead emphasizes stability and sustainability. At the same time, family-run companies try to be highly innovative and flexible. Their leadership culture is often defined by personal recognition and appreciation. In these and around these family businesses the world looks very different. While German large corporates are generally located in densely populated, metropolitan regions, the employees and managers of family businesses are often based in rural Germany. Internationally aligned manager personalities are less often found here. Instead, the managers are typically down-to-earth and less oriented towards material values. However, this attitude often limits a modernization as well as a transfer of the business to the next generation.

Religious aspects also influence the understanding of leadership in Germany. At this religious level, we find Weber's Protestant Ethic opposed and connected with the Catholic Social Doctrine – depicted in the first social encyclical 'Rerum Novarum' by Pope Leo XIII. Both of these created the ethical framework for the leadership culture in Germany. While the content of the Catholic Social Doctrine was used as the basis for the economic, social and regulatory framework of the social market economy – in other words had an influence on the social structure – the ideas of Weber's Protestant Ethic are more closely tied to the level of the individual, especially that of the entrepreneur.

The Catholic Social Doctrine is based on the convictions that the world was not 'simply predetermined for humans, but shall be determined and shaped by them'. This resulted from the belief 'that, because the goal of human life is the salvation of the soul, all activities for improvement of the material situation can only be means, but never an end unto itself.' (Weber, 1982: 42). The fundamental principles of the Catholic Social Doctrine include the triad of personality, solidarity and subsidiarity that created the basis of a societal – and later economic – structure, and which justify the claim to private ownership through natural law. On the basis of these thoughts, the idea of social market economy was born, via the so-called Rhine Capitalism as a precursor. The founding fathers of the social market economy in Germany were Erhard, Adenauer and Frings. They integrated the Protestant and Catholic ideas and introduced the concept of co-determination. In order to understand German leadership, it is therefore helpful to bring to mind the core of the social market economy in its original meaning. The essence is the 'principles of the individual freedom and competition, the existence of a strong, constitutionally legitimized state as the guardian of the economic and social order, recognition through the principle of subsidiarity and solidarity-based equal (life) opportunities' with human dignity being an unalienable prerequisite (Körner, 2008: 238).

The insights of Max Weber regarding the Protestant Ethic are based on the result of his own analysis. He discerned that capital investment and entrepreneurship are essentially Protestant by nature in Germany, whereby he saw this denominational character as a consequence, rather than a reason (Weber, 2015 [1905]). As a side note, Prussia can also not be understood without understanding the Protestant Ethic.

The guiding maxims of his Protestant Ethic for successful entrepreneurs are: proficiency, systematic ascetic way of life, deliberate modesty as well as joy in the obligatory fulfilment in the secular occupation as the highest content of moral self-exertion. The special role that the occupation has as a calling and place of inner-worldly fulfilment, is described by the idea that the occupation is a God-given task for the expression of brotherly love and a service to the useful design of his [*sic*] surroundings with the goal of serving the glory of God (for the Calvinists) and a self-reassurance of a personal state of grace through tireless professional work. One was either vessel (Luther) or tool (Calvin) of divine power. Success in work was seen as a sign of blessing and for being a chosen one of God; wasting time was seen as a sin and work as prescribed by God as an end of life itself. Wealth was there to be retained for the glory of God and to be proliferated through tireless work. This attitude is still widespread among German entrepreneurs and managers.

There is a further polarity embedded behind this religiously based pair of terms, which was religiously motivated at least for quite some time. The traditional role model of the genders, which is strongly based on the long successful male society and old boys' network, is now opposed by a new female pragmatic leadership style that is embodied by Chancellor Angela Merkel. In the eighteenth century, women played absolutely no role in the utterly male martial state of Prussia (under the two kings, the 'Soldier King' Frederick Wilhelm I [1713–40] and Frederick the Great [1740–86]) and even in the nineteenth century women had no civil rights. This extremely misogynistic behaviour by men, who viewed females as second-class citizens, was in every respect normal. Even Wilhelm II and Bismarck scorned women as soon as they wanted to interfere (Craig, 1982; Krockow, 2000).

After World War I, admittedly women were given the right to vote (1919) and tasted the first phase of freedom. However, under National Socialist rule, women were not intentioned to work (if a woman withdrew from her profession she was given a large number of benefits and public praise). Instead, a woman should care for her family and her nation – as a child-rearing machine who ensured that new war heroes were born. Even though the work in the munitions plants during World War II and the subsequent reconstruction of war-ravaged Germany was mainly performed by women, the role distribution was largely reinstituted after the war. When German soldiers returned to Germany in the decade following 1945 many of these women again took a step back in order to allow their husbands not only to perform meaningful work in the new economic development but also to help them overcome the psychological effects of their war experiences. Although these events occurred 70 years ago, today traditional ideas regarding gender roles remain imprinted in the minds of men and women; this makes it still more difficult for women to access management positions. However, through the party-based quota system, the political system has already undergone a significant change – the result of which is now clearly evidenced through the female Chancellor and numerous female prime ministers and federal ministers.

More critical evaluation is required for the pair of opposites whose one side is viewed as typically German: particularly in English-speaking regions, Germans are often saddled with the term 'German angst', a fear of failing combined with a type of hesitation and a general inferiority complex (Balzer, 2015: 43). At the same time, one could attest to a

German display of a great deal of courage, represented, for example, by the reconstruction of the country after the war and the introduction of the social market economy (Gemper, 2008). However, these types of national stereotypes must be generally viewed carefully, since they go hand in hand with a moral assessment.

The fundamental tension that characterizes the German approach to leadership is best shown in the most unusual and most important pair of opposites – the art of engineering, desiring perfection and rational thinking and, on the flip side, the philosophical mode of thinking of German Idealism (Kant, Fichte, Hegel, Schopenhauer, Schelling, among others) paired with the art of German Romanticism (e.g. Novalis, ETA Hoffmann, Goethe, Eichendorff, Wagner and also Karl May).

Especially German engineers, inventors, tinkerers and perfectionists have fostered the reputation of German reliability, durability, precision and pioneering technical and technological innovations, driven as well by the desire for planning security and control. And since for decades the best specialist was promoted to the position of manager, we find these characteristics and traits in the ideas of leadership. Volkswagen, which has been in the press for its diesel engine emissions scandal, is a good, although negative example of a one-sided, authoritarian–autocratic-led system.

On the other side, traces of Idealism and German Romanticism can be found in the German soul, which also has a strong influence on the idea of leadership. Perhaps the connection is best seen in the example that there are covertly a greater number of managers than expected playing a musical instrument at a high level (the manager as the conductor of an orchestra represents a newer way of thinking, but belongs in this category) as well as a greater number of managers interested in the topics of philosophy, literature, theatre and opera, even if this is rarely talked about. This hidden desire to achieve something greater, more beautiful, deeper and higher at the same time, which is essential to German Romanticism and German Idealism, is probably the more unconscious part of this leadership-influencing pair of opposite notions. Also, Karl May influenced generations of men in their leadership ideas. Albeit the generation of the reconstruction years has been described as being cured of the Romantic (Schelsky, 1957, cited after Safranski, 2007), today's narcissistic search for fame and fortune in the dazzling world of the Internet could be reinterpreted as this romantic desire for a higher purpose.

In conclusion, these described polar-opposite terms define German leadership and can be depicted as shown in Figure 10.1.

LEADERSHIP TODAY AND IN THE FUTURE

Ideas of leadership in Germany are shaped by the historically influenced polarities outlined above. However, over the course of the decade-long economic growth, the attitude towards leadership has become increasingly interchangeable due to the level of complexity

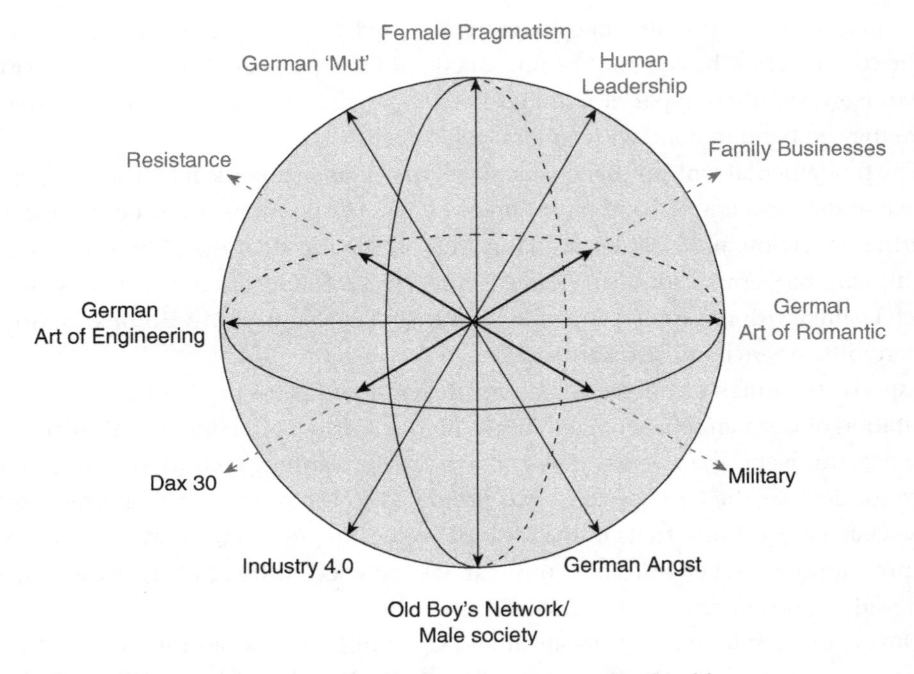

Figure 10.1 The system of complex polarities of German leadership

just described. The superficially perceived one-sidedness and the 'typical German' are slowly disappearing. On the one hand, there is a desire for a flexible and agile start-up culture – whether these companies are Internet-based in Berlin, or whether they are more scientific, life-science-oriented firms in Munich. On the other hand, one large German corporation is fighting for its survival. Volkswagen particularly represents the male-autocratic-hierarchical-engineering-driven, zero-faults-made-in-Germany culture, and it must now witness the end of this era, because it (still) has not properly integrated the other side. With this fear-driven leadership system, other leading German corporations will also face these issues. It is not only Generation Y that will not tolerate the leadership mechanisms that are in place, also customers and suppliers are calling for a change in the leadership culture.

In addition, the digitization and the respective technological change also require a rethinking of processes, products and business models. This digitization of the entire value chain – intensely contemplated by the German automotive industry and mechanical engineering companies – in other words, the technological approach behind the current trend of automatic controls and data exchange in manufacturing technologies (i.e., Industry 4.0) – is therefore making an entirely new understanding of leadership necessary. The challenges for the managers will be how they will design leadership in a digital, networked man/machine world. This new leadership culture will have to ensure that a framework is created in order to solve complex problems through actively thinking together. And, conversely, it will have to create a sense-making and appreciative environment in which human encounter is still possible and necessary beyond the machine-to-human-to-machine interaction. Therefore empathy – which is one of the biggest differences between humans and machines – will likely become one of the 'new leadership competencies'. It will be required for lateral leadership far removed from hierarchies and training, as cross-cultural diversity management competence will gain in significance. This new world of leadership – not only for Germany – will be challenging, but without an altered concept of leadership, the companies cannot and will not be successful in the long term. The possibilities of freedom that are offered by the digital intelligence must be understood and used. For Germany, this could mean the opportunity for establishing an economy that intelligently combines the digital with the analogue world and that does not defer to the disempowerment of the analogue world. Germany could become a trailblazer in the development of new democratic-participative-integrated-lateral understanding of leadership already laid out in history.

REFERENCES

Balzer, S. (2015) 'Scheitern auf Deutsch', *Frankfurter Allgemeine Zeitung*, 25 October, Issue 43, p. 43.

Craig, Gordon (1982) *Über die Deutschen*. Munich: Beck.

Gemper, Bodo (2008) 'Rheinische Wegbereiter der Sozialen Marktwirtschaft: Charakter zeigen im Aufbruch' [Rhenish forerunners of the social market economy: displaying character in times of [social)]wakening]', in *Ordnungspolitische Diskurse*, No. 2008-02.

Krockow, C. von (2000) *Über die Deutschen*. Munich: List.

Körner, H. (2008) 'Soziale Marktwirtschaft in der pluralistischen Gesellschaft', *Wirtschaftsdienst*, April, 88 (4): 237–41.

Neuberger, Oswald (2001) *Führen und Führen Lassen*. 6. Aufl. Stuttgart: Lucius & Lucius.

Safranski, Rüdiger (2007) *Romantik: Eine Deutsche Affäre*. Munich: Hanser.

Schelsky, Helmut (1957) *Die Skeptische Generation*. Düsseldorf: Diederichs.

Scholl, I. (1986 [1955]) *Die Weisse Rose*. Frankfurt: Fischer.

Staehle, Wolfgand. and Conrad, Peter (1991) *Management: Eine Verhaltenswissenschaftliche Perspektive*. Munich: Vahlen.

Weber, B (1982) 'Technischer Fortschritt und Katholische Soziallehre', *JCSW*, 23: 82.

Weber, M. (2015 [1905]) *Die protestantische Ethik und der Geist des Kapitalismus*. Complete edition. Hamburg: Nikol.

11
INDIA
Cultural Ethos and Leadership Styles: Indian Perspectives

Asha Bhandarker: Asha Bhandarker, Distinguished Professor of Org Beh, IMI-Delhi, India

Pritam Singh: Pritam Singh, CEO of the Lead Centre, Gurgaon, India

This chapter explores leadership in India, a country characterized by its complex cultural ethos, apparent contradictions and multitude of problems including sharp inequalities. More specifically, we will focus on the relationship between a few prominent features of the Indian sociocultural history and leadership in organizations.[1] The content of this chapter reflects our experiences as researchers, consultants, trainers and, in some cases, as board members of Indian organizations with nearly a hundred CEOs and thousands of managers at senior and top management levels.

A SOCIOHISTORICAL PERSPECTIVE

India is a symbol of diversity, aptly referred to as a cultural mosaic due to its incredible mix of ethnic groups, languages and cultures. It is the birthplace of four officially recognized religions, a nation with followers of eight different faiths, a land where 22 official languages and 1,652 mother tongues flourish, a country where colour of skin varies from region to region and caste compounds the complexity. This mosaic has evolved over thousands of years through waves of migration, age-old wars and conquests. As a result, India's national identity has long been talked about as 'unity in diversity'.

In regard to unity, the myth of the ideal leader has percolated from ancient times till today through two of India's beloved and sacred books, namely *Ramayana* and the *Mahabharata* (Gopalkrishnan and Kaur, 2010). The concept of Guru – the remover of darkness, who leads one towards enlightenment – is also embedded in Indian religion and philosophy. Faith in Gurus can be seen even today in the manner in which religious cults flourish in India and the complete faith and suspension of judgement which Gurus evoke among their acolytes.

The importance of religion in India is another commonality. Preponderantly, Indians have been religious and an important aspect of this religiosity is faith in Punarjanma, the ongoing cycle of birth and rebirth, before the soul achieves liberation (Moksha). This cycle of birth and rebirth results in strong faith in the fact that one's past deeds, good or bad, influence one's present life and in turn one's deeds in the present life influence one's future life. So, Punarjanma leads to the related belief in destiny, and depending on the individual characteristics, gets interpreted either to affirm the person or to provide an alibi when faced with failure.

From a family perspective, Indian society typically operates on the joint family system where early socialization experiences are characterized by experiences of a '*Kartha*' or head of the family who is typically protective, nurturing and creates a sense of safety and security (Singh and Bhandarker, 1987). The positive Kartha experience leads to trust in

---

[1]See Den Hartog et al. (1999) and Dickson et al. (2012) for an analysis.

authority figures. The negative experience with an over-controlling Kartha leads to indecision, looking upwards for guidance and direction, preference to play safe and enormous delays in decision-making.

According to Gannon (1994), this family system explains why Indians are known to be highly emotional, to strongly value relationships and invest considerable energy in them. For instance, there is a preponderance of the joint family and strong ties with '*Kutumb*' meaning the extended family (Beteille, 1964; Sethi, 1989). Nuclear families continue to hold the mindset of the joint family helping and taking care of each other. In return, there is tremendous loyalty to family, especially to its senior members.

At the same time, although Indian society has been a shining example of diversity, regrettably it is as caste-ridden as ever. Historically, Varna Vyavastha was the system which categorized people on the basis of their competencies and interests in the professional realm. The Brahmins, Kshatriya and Vaishyas used to be respectively known for knowledge, bravery and wealth. It was later distorted and propagated as a caste system based on birth, by a nexus of vested interests, namely the ruling communities who had wealth, power and knowledge. The caste system then became a categorization of those born to rule and those born to serve and has afflicted Indian society for millennia. Even during the period soon after independence, politicians, bureaucrats, businessmen and professionals were preponderantly from the forward classes.

Today, the electoral mathematics of candidates' selection centres around three Cs, i.e. communities, clans and caste. As a result, the caste mindset continues to influence people's perceptions, attitudes and their decisions – in all spheres, with members of the forward castes being respected more by their ascribed status than by their personal achievements. For instance, many private organizations are still dominated by particular communities, not only at the operational levels but also at the board levels, rendering them into country clubs.

However, the situation might not be forever immutable. For instance, India launched in the 1950s the world's oldest affirmative action programme in the form of initiatives to protect the interests of the Dalits ('broken people', formerly known as 'untouchables'). As a result, over the years there has been a change in the composition of the ruling class, wherein more members from the so-called backward classes have joined the ruling elite. This shift has been aided not only by positive discrimination but also by the forces of democracy where voting rights have powerfully thrown up leaders from communities other than the forward castes.

The economic deregulation of 1992 and the subsequent thriving of economic activity has been another major game-changer for India. The last two decades have seen the rise of the great Indian middle class, fuelling relative economic prosperity among millions, built on the foundations of education, sheer hard work, a booming internal economy and great strides made in the service economy using the power of the Internet. Knowledge is a strong value among certain castes and regions, and has seen people from these groups rising to unprecedented levels based on their knowledge capacity.

LEADERSHIP IN INDIAN ORGANIZATIONS

The particular sociohistorical context highlighted above continues to influence organizational structures, leadership and leader acceptance. From a general standpoint, in both public and private organizations leadership is likely to be directive and somewhat toxic. For instance, it has been found that Indian executives demonstrate highly power-oriented (Trompenaars and Turner, 1993) and controlling behaviour with a feudalistic mindset. Such a mindset is evident in the pomp and show that many heads of organizations seem to favour.

In fact, people holding top management positions are inclined to expect special treatment like the erstwhile ruling elite – the kings and other high-ranking officers. We have actually seen those who were humble when they occupied lower or middle-level positions in the hierarchy changing their behaviour overnight when getting a top position such as president, director or chairman of their organization. This is true for the private sector and to a greater extent for the public sector, where bureaucracy is institutionalized, probably a legacy of British India's government departments. Although such a situation is not pervasive in every Indian organizations, it is still worth highlighting as one of the peculiarities of demonstrating 'status' and superiority.

Evidence of religious and spiritual orientation was found in a recent study (Spencer et al., 2005) which concluded that Indian CEOs have reported greater spiritual and or religious sources of inner strength as compared to their global peers. From our experiences, the belief in destiny based on the faith in Punarjanma mentioned earlier influences individuals' philosophy, values, beliefs and attitudes reflected in workplace behaviour. On the positive side, we have observed that those leaders who believe in destiny (karma) attribute their success to destiny rather than attributing it to self. This protects the person from hubris, generates humility and open-mindedness. This belief also provides a psychological placebo to those who are unable to cope with the terrible tragedies that might occur in life. However, continued negative interpretation of karma, blaming past life for one's non-performance rather than taking responsibility for one's actions in the present life, is one of the real dangers of a continued use of this approach. The latter interpretation is seen quite often in the face of delays or non-performance leading to procrastination, laziness, low focus and perseverance to convert failure into success. Those who have imbibed the true essence of karma have been found to be transformational, catalytic, making ceaseless efforts to bring about change.

As mentioned earlier, owing to socialization, joint and extended family system, Indians are used to warmth, proximity and personal relationships (Sinha, 1979). As a result, the success of leaders also depends on the manner in which they handle this need. While focus on both task and people is considered important in the leadership literature, it has been found that 'good' leaders in India build relationships first and then focus on task. Well-known and acknowledged Indian leaders practise humility, respect and value people, build personal connection and robust teams. While all of them are well travelled, most of them are India-educated. It is not surprising therefore that their leadership styles are in sync with broad expectations of Indians.

From the employees' perspective, we found that the majority of them exhibit compliant behaviour with directive bosses owing to the Kartha archetype in their subconscious mind. When leaders play the positive Kartha role at the workplace (i.e., nurturing, protective and mentoring the team) they are able to mobilize people and influence them as well as channel their energy for organizational goal achievement. In other words, developing such familial relationships is likely to elicit high commitment and involvement. However, when leaders play the negative Kartha role, they become not only directive but also critical and punitive. Such leaders are disliked (Singh et al., 2015) and employees retaliate by withdrawing and becoming non-cooperative.

In the last 30 years, we have observed companies introducing various schemes to improve workers' involvement, such as TQM (Total Quality Management) and TPM (Total Productive Maintenance). The results have not been as successful as in Japan and in some other countries because of the hierarchical mindset. Many leaders and organizations have, however, transcended the hierarchical-caste mindset and successfully implemented broader involvement and participation across their organizations. As a matter of fact, a recent study of Indian CEOs (Cappelli et al., 2015) found that Indian executives are inclined to use transformational styles and believe that the success of their firms is closely linked to handling the people factor positively. It is worthwhile to mention names of companies like Tatas, ABG, Bharat Forge, Biocon, BHEL, Hero Motors, Maruti Suzuki, Siemens among others where the above-cited mindsets have helped in the successful implementation of participation schemes.

The principle of relying on workers' creativity and self-organizing capabilities has been epitomized and promoted by Vineet Nayar, the former CEO of HCL Technologies Ltd(HCLT), a $5.5 billion global information technology services company based in India. In a world-bestselling book entitled *Employees First, Customers Second: Turning Conventional Management Upside Down* Vineet Nayar promotes the idea of unleashing the power of the many and loosens the stranglehold of the few for the sake of quality and performance.

Many Indian leaders are found to be suffering from tribalistic, clannish, regionalistic and linguistic preferences and biases. Such preference leads to 'we–they' classification of employees. Those who are in the 'we' or 'in-group' are powerful whereas the rest live with power deprivation. Those out of power vigorously seek to capture power through clique formation, sycophancy and jockeying. Such behaviour gets further accentuated by the hierarchical family structure where individuals experience powerlessness for many years into adulthood, especially when the Kartha is over-controlling, a common Indian failing. During our 30 years of work across a wide variety of Indian organizations we have seen widespread prevalence of this phenomenon. Over the years, it has come down considerably, owing to the emergence of the Millennials and the rise of the knowledge society.

CHANGING SCENARIO AND NEW CHALLENGES

Since independence, democracy has unleashed various forces at the individual and group levels and rendered India into a noisy democracy where there is an upsurge in the quest for regional, linguistic, religious as well as caste identities. There is a high degree of entitlement orientation and people are focused on their rights and rewards. These factors pose serious challenges for those in positions of authority to influence and mobilize people. Identity-related issues affect decisions and actions not only at a national political level, but also at governmental levels and even at corporate levels, especially those owned by the government.

Young Indians have embraced technology with great passion and their exposure is more global. Educated Millennials coming of age in this period have experienced greater prosperity and creature comforts provided by their hard-working middle-class parents who have seen unprecedented improvement in their quality of life. Family sizes have shrunk with a steep increase in the percentage of nuclear families in the educated class. As a result, today's youth are completely different in their orientation to leadership and work organizations. According to a recent study (Singh et al., 2012), Millennial Indians look for leaders who are mentors and coaches, who give them greater independence and autonomy. Hierarchy, seniority, currying favour, flaunting status, compliance, which are some of the outcomes of hierarchical mindset, are disliked by them. India is poised to become the country with the youngest population in the world by 2021. Gen X will have no choice but to become less hierarchical and directive and more flexible and participative in their approach if they have to attract and retain young talent.

CONCLUSION

There are many factors that impact leadership in India: broad historical and socioreligious and cultural influences, Westernized and global leadership expectations and also new technologies that embolden a new generation and connect them with a wider world. The emerging multigenerational employees of organizations will have to mutually adapt and accommodate in order to work together and build successful organizations.

REFERENCES

Beteille, A. (1964) 'Family and social change in India and other South Asian countries', *The Economic and Political Weekly*, Annual Number, February, pp. 237–44.

Cappelli, P., Singh, H., Singh, J. and Useem, M. (2015) 'Indian business leadership: broad mission and creative value', *The Leadership Quarterly*,26 (1): 7–12

Den Hartog, D.N., House, R.J., Hanges, P.J. and Zhou, J. (1999) 'Culture specific and cross-culturally generalizable implicit leadership theories: are attributes of charismatic/transformational leadership universally endorsed?', *The Leadership Quarterly*, 10 (2): 219–56.

Dickson, N.W., Castano, N., Magomaeva A. and Den Hartog, D.N. (2012) 'Conceptualizing leadership across cultures', *Journal of World Business*, 47 (4): 483–92.

Gannon, Martin J. (1994) *Understanding Global Cultures: Metaphorical Journeys through 17 Countries*. London: Sage.

Gopalkrishnan, S. and Kaur, R. (2010) 'Cultural mythology and global leadership in India', in Eric H. Kessler and Diana J. Wong-MingJi (eds), *Cultural Mythology and Global Leadership*. Cheltenham: Edward Elgar.

Sethi, B.B. (1989) 'Family as a potent therapeutic force', *Indian Journal of Psychiatry*, 3: 22–30.

Singh, P. and Bhandarker, A. (1988) 'Cultural ethos in organizational milieu', *Indian Management*, October, AIMA.

Singh, Pritam, Bhandarker, Asha and Rai, Singdha (2012) *Millennials and the Workplace: Challenges for Architecting the Organizations of Tomorrow.* New Delhi: Sage.

Singh, Pritam, Bhandarker, Asha and Rai, Singdha (2015) *The Leadership Odyssey: From Darkness to Light*. New Delhi: Sage.

Sinha, J.B.P. (1979) 'The nurturant-task leader: a model of effective executive', *ASCI Journal of Management*, 8: 109–19.

Spencer, S.M., Rajah, T., Mohan, S. and Lahiri, G. (2008) 'The Indian CEOs: competencies for success', *Vision: The Journal of Business Perspectives*, 12 (1).

Trompenaars, Fons and Turner, Charles H. (1993) *Riding the Waves of Culture: Understanding Cultural Diversity of Business*. London: Economists Books.

12
JAPAN

You're the Leader? The Long-Term Relational Approach to Japanese Leadership

Yasuhiro Hattori: Associate Professor of Organizational Behaviour at Yokohama National University, Japan

Daniel Arturo Heller: Professor of Strategy at Yokohama National University, Japan

THE ESSENCE OF LEADERSHIP

In Japan, there is a striking lack of academic research on leadership. Unlike the many English-language journals, there are no Japanese journals devoted to the subject of leadership. When we surveyed all of the articles published over the past 10 years in four of the leading Japanese-language management journals, the results were even lower than our already low expectations. There were only 22 out of 639 articles (3.4%) that had leadership in their title or as a keyword.[1]

Yet, despite this apparent dearth of academic research, Japanese management scholars and business practitioners are likely to be quick to acknowledge leadership as an important subject. Like the rest of the world, Japan has a booming leadership development industry, Japanese business schools typically offer leadership courses, many business books on leadership are published every year, and one can easily find seminars and training programmes in Japan with a leadership theme.

So, we find a paradox. There is an enduring interest in leadership in Japan, but a very real lack of scholarly research on the subject. The source of this paradox lies right at the heart of the present volume, namely that management literature has tended to look at the subject of leadership from a highly Western-orientated industrial/organizational perspective. Leadership as it is generally practised in Japan simply does not fit well into the 'individual behaviours and traits' box that dominates academic discussion of leadership.

Japan has approached the issues embodied in leadership differently than in the West. While the word leadership may not have been used, the Japanese have long been concerned with questions such as: How is a thriving work community created? How can a group of people be managed efficiently and effectively? How should the person who is legally or morally responsible for an organization relate to others?

Japanese people understand leadership as social relationships, not traits/behaviours. The leader–follower relationship and the way the leader and follower interact within a specific social context are the touchstones of leadership in Japan. Such an understanding clearly fits with the obvious fact that a leader can only be one if there are other people.

---

[1]The four journals we surveyed were: *soshiki kagaku* (Organizational Science), *nihon keiei gakkaishi* (The Journal of Business Management), *sangyo shinri – soshiki shinri gaku kenkyu* (Industrial and Organizational Psychology Research) and *keiei koudou kagaku* (Japanese Journal of Administrative Science). The highest number of articles with leadership in the title or keywords was 11 out of 276 in Organizational Science, and the highest percentage was 6.7% (6 out of 90) in Research on Industrial and Organizational Psychology.

THE MAIN INFLUENCES ON LEADERSHIP

The Japanese philosopher Tetsuro Watsuji posited that a human being should not be regarded solely as an individual, but as a relational existence between people (Watsuji, 1966 [1935]). In this view, called *aida-gara*, it is critical to recognize that a human being is necessarily a member of many different social groupings. We must nurture and maintain our relationships with other people and with society at large in order to retain our humanity.

The connectedness of people that is inherent in the healthy human condition comes through in written Japanese. The Japanese language, like Chinese, does not usually make a clear distinction between singular or plural. One says 'human being' exactly the same way one says 'human beings'. The two *kanji*[2] used to write human being(s) are 'person/people' and 'between'. We can understand the Japanese language as socializing its speakers to view an individual as connected with other people. The cooperative culture needed for the rice farming that flourished in feudal Japan is said to be a deeply rooted source of this view of the interconnected self.

Hamaguchi (1977) articulated an explicit theory of Japanese selfhood based on the notion of a 'contextualized-person (or people)' who is governed by ritual interactions in social groups. Hamaguchi's model establishes a contrast between the Euro-American egocentric model of self as an individual versus the Japanese model of self which is a social-self (*kanjin*). In this contextualized worldview, who a person is and the actions he or she takes is based on the person's relationship with others. Following both Watsuji and Hamaguchi, one must adjust appropriately whenever the people with whom one interacts changes.

Discussion of leadership in Japan, both by practitioners and academics, generally is in line with the approach of Watsuji and Hamaguchi. The choice of who to make a leader is profoundly influenced by the perception that who we are is determined by the context in which we are embedded. In such a worldview, rather than look to an individual's general characteristics and behavioural traits, it is more rational to evaluate a person's suitability for leadership based on the way in which the person has behaved and expressed him- or herself over a long period of time among a variety of different types of people. Selecting a leader in this way places severe constraints on those who seek to lead in a very independent manner or who use strong-arm tactics (Nakane, 1970).

---

[2]*Kanji* are Chinese characters that were imported into Japan over 1500 years ago to allow spoken Japanese to be written down.

The I-do-not-want-to-be-a-leader syndrome

In recent years, there has been a growing trend in the English-language academic literature to describe career paths as becoming more diverse, with people seeking leadership opportunities in ways other than simply rising to head an organization (Charan et al., 2001). Japan has experienced a similar trend, but it has been amplified by a longstanding but now growing parallel tendency, especially among younger Japanese, to avoid positions where one needs to exercise leadership (Kanai, 2005).

There are at least three drivers of the intensification of this leadership-avoidance tendency. For one, cross-firm employability has been increasing since the collapse of the Japanese economic bubble in the early 1990s. With greater opportunity to move between companies, people are more willing and able to change to another employer if a job asks for more leadership than one wants to give.

Second, many more people in Japan, both young and old, are presently expressing a desire to live a more balanced and meaningful life. There is a growing rejection of the extremely high levels of commitment to one's company that some Japanese business people have exhibited, even to the point of being caricatured for it. Japanese born in the 1980s or later commonly say that doing something beneficial for society is more important than achieving a position of power in a company. For many Japanese, the power that comes together with leadership is simply viewed as unattractive and unwelcome.

Third, more and more Japanese businesspersons are pursuing increased specialization in a primary field of work, such as obtaining some kind of a third-party certification, perhaps in bookkeeping or foreign language ability, and/or attending seminars and workshops relevant to their field. A leadership position pushes one away from the day-to-day work and thus decreases the value of specialization. Becoming a leader reduces both the incentive and time one is able to devote to pursuing increased specialization.

On top of these three specific drivers of the leadership-avoidance syndrome is the widespread perception that leaders in Japanese companies will have to expend a lot of time and effort on intractable management tasks. Greater stress can certainly be expected but rewards will be limited. In short, Japanese business people do not have a positive image of the managing that a leader has to do (Kanai, 2005).

Dispersed-leadership system

As a response to ever-more complex markets and technology, there have been growing demands on leaders to be able to deal with an ever-wider array of issues. Against this backdrop, in the English-language literature on leadership there have been calls for shared leadership roles and distributing leadership responsibilities among multiple individuals.

Japan has long championed this kind of thinking, although for a different reason than what is being described today.

The present push for shared leadership is typically understood to be a response to the inability of a single person to adequately fulfil all of the responsibilities and exercise all of the authority that is required of a leader in an environment of high and rising external complexity. Multiple leaders are used in order to maintain the ability of an organization to achieve a good fit with a dynamic and unpredictable environment. In Japan, dividing up the power of a leader, in other words shared leadership, has been done not so much as a response to growing complexity, but rather as a means to force a greater variety of opinions to come to the surface in decision-making regardless of the environmental context.

In Japan, organizations have tended to avoid letting a lot of power and authority be concentrated in a single individual. As such, it has been typical for a decision to be made in the negotiated space between multiple individuals who share responsibility for a decision. *Nemawashi* is a Japanese business term that refers to working carefully behind the scenes to obtain buy-in from key voices in an organization before a decision is made.

Leadership without a silver tongue – the silent leader

Since the 1980s, there has been much discussion in the English-language literature on transformational and visionary leadership, where a powerful leader uses his or her words to inspire people to follow. We have seen that Japan is already quite different in tending to avoid concentrating power in one person. In addition, it is relatively rare for people in a Japanese organization to seek a leader who is particularly skilled with using words for persuasion.

In recognition that words can also frequently be a source of misunderstanding, a Japanese leader is asked to show his or her attitude without using any words. It is partly about speaking through actions, but more importantly a leader or future leader is evaluated by how consistent his or her efforts have been over an extended period of time. It is true that words are at times important and effective tools of persuasion in Japan, too. However, a silver tongue is generally not enough to win over others. The silent leader is often viewed as the best leader.

Hirshman's exit–voice–loyalty

The single most defining characteristic of a Japanese organization is the high value that is placed on long-term relationships. This value is embodied in the traditional core pillar of Japanese management: lifetime employment. The idea that a company should look after an employee until retirement is under strain but still it remains in place in many large organizations in Japan. We can view long-term ties between people and between a company and its employees, ties that often span decades, as the operating software of Japanese organizations. Hiring, performance evaluation, promotion and job assignments are the application software that run on top of this operating system.

In the typical Western organization, contracts are the operating system. People are constantly aware that there exists a formal agreement between an employee and his or her employer. The need to keep the contract provides an ongoing incentive for both parties to contribute to realizing individual and organizational objectives. In Japan, there are no such clear guidelines by which the behaviour of the employer and the employees is controlled. This ambiguity is embodied in the fact that few newly hired college graduates in Japan will be given anything more than a rudimentary job description. In fact, explicit detailed job descriptions seldom even exist.

In Japanese organizations, both leaders and followers can rarely choose the exit option in Hirshman's (1970) exit–voice–loyalty model. For better or worse, the two sides are more or less stuck with each other. Where such long-term relationships are the norm, it makes sense to choose a relatively weak form of leadership that will be less likely to strain ties. It also helps explain why many Japanese actively avoid taking leadership positions: there is not much to be gained personally (or financially) from becoming a leader.

When a task requires that a leader must be chosen, ideally the choice will be made based on careful consideration of how individuals have expressed themselves over a long period of time in a variety of situations. Frequently, leadership positions will be rotated periodically among the available members of the organization. It is considered equitable to select a leader in this manner, and dispersed leadership means that even people who are not particularly suited to the job can still do it. When a leader is chosen in these ways, he or she[3] will seldom become bossy or seek to hold onto power. If something new is needed, the leader will try to introduce it without totally disrupting what was there before. Indeed, achieving an optimal marriage between the new and the old may be considered the essence of Japanese management.

LEADERSHIP TODAY AND IN THE FUTURE

Meyer (2014) has brought Hall's (1976) classic work on communication patterns and culture back to the attention of the business world. We can interpret Japanese leadership and

---

[3]Even though leadership positions in Japan are overwhelmingly male dominated, we intentionally wrote 'he or she' instead of just 'he' to bring to the surface the pressing need to change attitudes and corporate systems (i.e. greater childcare support) in Japanese organizations to allow more women to take leadership positions.

its lack of a silver tongue as being a good fit with the high-context culture that is Japan. In a high-context culture people are expected to have sufficient background knowledge and use it to read between the lines.

In a culture like Japan, it is okay to assume that people will already share a lot of common knowledge and understanding, even before a conversation is held. Since the shared context embeds deep meaning in each word, fewer words are needed. In a low-context culture, it is quite risky to assume that people already know something before anything is said. The most important aspect of communication in a low-context culture is to impart clarity.

Of course, even in a high-context culture there are times when the lack of a clear message will lead to misunderstanding. Someone to whom a task is delegated may underestimate the span of his or her responsibility. Or, a leader will not be able to get his or her intention communicated to someone with whom there is insufficient shared context. As long as relationships have stayed within the relatively closed sphere in which Japan has tended to operate throughout its history, these issues have not surfaced as major problems.

At present, however, new challenges of globalization are putting strains on Japan's ability to keep such problems under control. Many young Japanese are reluctant to go abroad: in the 2010s, the number of Japanese students studying overseas has declined by more than 25% compared with the peak that occurred around the year 2000. This trend coupled with a rapidly ageing society means there are fewer Japanese people who are able to support the growing international operations of Japanese companies and who also share a common context.

At the same time, non-Japanese leaders such as Carlos Ghosn at Nissan, are also increasingly called upon to lead Japanese organizations. If the common language changes to English, basic communication patterns will be severely disrupted. Subtle words spoken in Japanese will be replaced with blunt expressions in English. New forms of Japanese-style leadership that work outside of the Japanese language are desperately needed.

Thus, there is a pressing need for Japanese leadership practices to be adjusted so that they will function in different and often low-context cultures. Not only do methods of communication need to be changed, but the basic assumption of long-term relationships is also challenged. It is typically quite hard to find employees overseas who have ever seen a company that is genuinely interested in building a long-term relationship with them. A change in the operating software from long-term relationships to contract-based relationships requires a major re-write of a company's management practices.

We find that the paradox described at the beginning of this chapter is hardly academic. The enduring interest in Japanese leadership must be met with robust scholarly research that reveals how Japanese leadership can function outside of a traditional Japanese context. One hopes the success shown in the global achievements of other forms of Japanese management, such as kaizen and lean production, can be replicated for Japanese leadership as well.

REFERENCES

Charan, Ram, Drotter, Stephen and Noel, James (2001) *The Leadership Pipeline: How to Build the Leadership-Powered Company*. San Francisco, CA: Jossey–Bass.

Hall, Edward T. (1976) *Beyond Culture*. New York: Anchor Books.

Hamaguchi, E. (1977) *Nihon Rashisa no Saihakken* [The Re-Discovery of Japanese-ness]. Tokyo: Nihonkeizaisinbunshan.

Hirshman, Albert.O. (1970) *Exit, Voice, and Loyalty: Responses to Decline in Firms, Organizations, and States*. Cambridge, MA: Harvard University Press.

Kanai, T. (2005) *Riidaashippu-Nyumon* [Introduction to Leadership]. Tokyo: Nikkei-bunko.

Meyer, E. (2014) *The Culture Map: Breaking Through the Invisible Boundaries of Global Business*. New York: Public Affairs.

Nakane, Chie (1970) *Japanese Society*. Oakland, CA: University of California Press.

Watsuji, T. (1966 [1935]) *Ningen no Gaku toshiteno Rinrigaku* [Watsuji Tetsurō's Rinrigaku – Ethics in Japan], trans. S. Yamamoto and R.E. Carter. Albany, NY: State University of New York Press.

13
MEXICO
The Essence of Leadership in Mexico

Maria Fonseca Paredes: Dean and Professor of the Business School at Tecnologico de Monterrey (ITESM), State of Mexico Campus, Mexico

Fernando Sandoval Arzaga: Director of Entrepreneurship and head of the Centre for Entrepreneurial Families of ITESM, State of Mexico Campus; Member of the Faculty of Tecnologico de Monterrey, State of Mexico Campus, Mexico

INTRODUCTION[1]

Mexico is a country of over 120 million people, mostly distributed in small towns and villages across its varied landscapes. It has six cities of over a million inhabitants, and over 20 million people who reside in the vast, sprawling and rapidly growing metropolis of Mexico City. Economic and political power is concentrated there, and the tensions between rural and urban, rich and poor, are key to understanding the populism that characterizes political leadership contests. The economy is characterized by a persistence of public monopolies and private oligopolies in key economic sectors – such as energy and telecommunications, respectively – concentrating political and economic powers in spite of the need for rules and mechanisms to protect and enforce consumer rights, and promote and make competition viable.

Mexico has a rich history of native traditions and legends, as well as of Spanish and other cultures. Over time, these traditions have mixed and then evolved independently. Yet, regardless of where you are in Mexico today – in the northern, central or southern states – native traditions and values are common: a festive spirit, a strong spirituality and common occurrences of kindness and hospitality. To understand leadership in contemporary Mexico it is helpful to know something of the history and traditions that have developed in Mexico over the centuries, and how they have influenced the way leadership has been adopted, and more importantly enacted.

Various kinds of leadership have existed in Mexico. During the Aztec Empire (1325–1521), before Mexico was conquered by the Spanish, the Emperor Moctezuma led his people from adverse political entities to develop the largest politically coherent territory in ancient times. Moctezuma organized the empire in various provinces, created a strong central government and regulated the tax system. There was also an important military expansion initiated by his predecessors, and although he could not subdue the enemies in the end, he was considered to be a transformational leader, whose impact is still talked about to this day.

In 1523, the Roman Catholic Church's influence was evidenced in the region when its missionaries began arriving. The Church built monasteries and converted millions of native Mexicans to Roman Christianity. Religion has influenced the value system of average citizens of Mexico and the actions of its political elites, and it continues to be a vocal if not overly influential voice today.

Over the past two centuries, Mexico has gone through revolutionary periods where power was centred in and with various 'leaders'. Some leaders acted mostly to protect the

---

[1] In writing this chapter, we are indebted to Dean Behrens, Viseslav Simic, Gale Moore and Joe Smith for their thoughtful and diligent help in guiding us to have a better picture of Mexico from the outside.

poorest against adversity and corruption; but Mexico has also had leaders who sought their own personal benefit. This characteristic of seeking personal benefit, instead of acting for the benefit of others, has resulted in common myths of corruption as necessary for political and/or economic success in Mexican society.

Some 'leaders' illegally enriched themselves and left the Mexican people to pay the consequences of high levels of social insecurity, as well as living with the increasing gap between the richest and the poorest in the country. Thus, Mexico struggles with the influence of 'leadership' for the actual benefit of the people, versus 'leadership' that may only pose to benefit the common person, but results in, or is blatantly focused on, the personal betterment of a few. The question, thus, becomes important: when will Mexicans awaken?

Mexico, a country rich in natural resources and human capital, with an extraordinary geopolitical position, is an interesting place to understand and examine leadership from various perspectives. Our culture of fatalism, whereby many Mexicans focus on spiritualism, or the influence of the powerful and the mighty, allows for an exploration of how leaders gain power, utilize power and promote or limit change. By studying these issues, we can gain a better insight into how Mexico can become a nation with a better present, a more promising future and with greater participation of average citizens.

Leadership in Mexico was influenced by our Hispanic/colonial roots that left us with a paternalistic residue; on the other hand, cohabitation with other non-Hispanic cultures has developed a form of leadership that focuses more on results than on people as individuals. Leadership in politics, society, education, business, has several faces but a clear vision is still missing, leaving a new generation of Mexicans searching for strong, ethical and charismatic leaders to deliver clarity. Arguably, this desire for a 'saviour leader' results in co-dependent followers. This culture of dependency emerges from Mexico's colonialism, paternalism and the Roman Catholic Church's hierarchical structures that have been internalized by its citizens. Breaking this pattern is a key challenge for Mexican leadership and followership, but, as we will see, this may be changing, and in spite of this general dependency on strong leaders, there are also examples of more democratic movements that are fighting for social justice.

THE MAIN INFLUENCES ON LEADERSHIP

Leadership in Mexico has been impacted by various elements from its culture such as: (1) machismo and sexism; (2) paternalism and male dominance; (3) rigidity and hierarchy, all of which are expressed and reinforced in the social structures of education, family dynamics and religion.

Over the past two centuries Mexicans have been exploited and oppressed by others (e.g. Spain's subjugation of Mexicans and more recently, America's threat of wall building while still wanting cheap labour). Mexicans may be viewed as a poor and suffering people, one frequently defeated and conquered. It might be seen today in the inadequate geopolitical status of Mexico in spite of its extraordinarily advantageous position between North and South Americas, and its having ports on the shores of the world's greatest oceans – to many it seems that it has been the USA rather than Mexico that has reaped those benefits through the North American Free Trade Agreement (NAFTA), and might do that in the future through the Trans-Pacific Partnership (TPP).

The stereotype of masculine supremacy, social oppression and authoritarian politics pervade the arena of leadership and politics. Mexican men (almost exclusively in positions of power) often have very archaic beliefs about women in leadership roles, suggesting that motherhood is the supreme duty of a woman, and that it is an obstacle to a woman's career rather than a motivation to succeed.

Alternatively, Mexico has a very strong identity and culture that resists colonization and some even speculate about a reverse colonial process taking place, as Mexicans increasingly make their presence felt in the USA in terms of political and cultural influences. Within Mexico itself, artists and architects have shown avant-garde leadership in different times, developing new political art forms that embraced both indigenous and modernism (e.g., Frida Khalo, Diego Rivera and the muralists José Clemente Orozco and David Alfaro Siqueiros).

There exists a very sharp and distinct division in Mexican society between clusters of very postmodern intellectual elite, mixed in with a highly skilled and capable internationalist precariat, and an undereducated, almost preindustrial lumpenproletariat and finance-starved peasantry – a social gap thus created is very difficult to bridge, especially when the political elites are often corrupt, socially disconnected and incompetent in terms of modern public policy practices.

SYMBOLICALLY IMPORTANT MEXICAN LEADERS

To help understand Mexican leadership, here are a few examples of men and women who have influenced the social and political realms in Mexico's past and symbolize aspects of Mexican leadership.

Miguel Hidalgo: national identity leadership

After 300 years of colonial rule, a 'progressive' priest and leader named Miguel Hidalgo became the Father of Mexican Independence. He promoted an uprising against landowners and foreign aristocrats and declared war against the colonial government, issuing the famous call to action, the 'Grito de Dolores', on 16 September 1810 (16 September is now marked as Mexico's Independence Day). The nascent revolutionary force decided to strike for independence and marched on Guanajuato, a major colonial mining centre, marking the beginning of the fight for Mexican independence and a cultivation of a truly unique Mexican identity. In January 1811, Spanish forces fought and defeated the insurgent army, forcing the rebels to flee towards the US border; they were intercepted by the Spanish army and Miguel Hidalgo and his remaining soldiers were captured.

During the struggle for independence, Mexico lost one-tenth of its citizens. In the decades following separation from Spanish rule, Mexico saw a radical decline in its gross domestic product, per capita income and amount of foreign trade. America's Monroe Doctrine too, from the time of its declaration in 1823, considerably limited Mexico's free exchange with contemporary European powers and Russia. An increasing and considerable amount of conflict prevailed along the US–Mexican border for more than five decades, leaving a legacy of distrust and fear toward the USA, and a fear of further loss of sovereignty.

Porfirio Diaz: authoritarian leadership

Mexican president Porfirio Diaz was considered a dictator, a controversial figure, whose term is known as the Porfiriato. Between 1876 and 1911 an economic boom occurred when Diaz and his followers promoted foreign investments and reduced the effects of the US Monroe Doctrine. The economy boomed and many miles of railway tracks were laid to connect all of the important cities in the country. The peace that prevailed during the government of Porfirio Diaz allowed for the development of culture (e.g. literature, painting, music and sculpture) and science in Mexico. It was then when institutes, libraries, scientific societies and cultural associations were founded. There is a unique mix of pre-Colombian and European neoclassical style sculptures along the Porfiriato's great urban project of the main Reforma Avenue in Mexico City. His example of leadership reveals how authoritarian control may sometimes produce stability that allows growth and development but often at the expense of personal freedoms, which thereby creates resistance. The *guerrilleros* fought Porfirio Diaz and power shifted into the hands of their popular leaders.

Emiliano Zapata: revolutionary leadership

This was the period of the Mexican Revolution, a movement of middle-class protest against the Porfiriato that also aimed to ensure a fairer way of living for the poorer classes. Zapata led the villagers of Morelos on a crusade to recover the lost lands. Zapata remained a man of the people, indifferent to formal ideologies, aligned with traditional Roman Catholicism and as loyal to his Morelos followers as they were to him. He was a charismatic leader who became a martyr and continues to inspire those fighting for social justice.

Lazaro Cardenas del Río: reforming leadership

Lazaro Cardenas del Río became President in 1934. His symbolic action of halving his salary and moving from the grandiose presidential palace signified his leadership approach and values. During his administration, he carried out major land reforms that benefited the Mexican people and brought the country's oil industry back under Mexican control, thus restoring the people's faith in the revolution, and Mexico's declaration of economic independence.

Today, almost a century later, Mexico is experiencing a political and economic struggle at its highest levels due to neoliberal pressure to amend Article 27 of the 1917 Constitution (interpreted by Cardenas in a declaration of 1938 to mean that all petroleum reserves were the property of Mexico's government) to allow the private sector to invest in the nation's oil industry. A true political dialogue in Mexico is lacking involvement by the country's weak and almost invisible civil society.

Don Eugenio Garza Sada; Rafael Rangel Sostmann: leading via education

Don Eugenio Garza Sada was a successful businessman and philanthropist, born in 1892 in Monterrey. He was a socially minded and entrepreneurial leader, who was gradually promoted at his family business, the Cuauhtemoc Brewery. In 1943 he founded the Tecnologico de Monterrey, his most relevant contribution to Mexican society, since this private university has led the education system in Mexico. It was a modernizing force focusing on entrepreneurial philosophy, modernizing technology, educational innovation and a global vision.

Rafael Rangel Sostmann followed Sada and contributed to the education system in Mexico. As Tecnologico de Monterrey's president for more than 25 years (1985–2011) Rafael transformed and influenced not only the private educational system in the country, but also the greater government-financed nationwide education system by imposing higher standards. Under Rangel's leadership, the Tecnologico de Monterrey became one of Latin America's leading universities.

Elba Esther Gordillo: social justice and corrupt leadership

Elba Esther Gordillo was the leader of the National Education Workers' Union (SNTE) – Latin America's largest labour union. She fought for social justice and had huge influence, yet while officially working for Mexico's education system improvements, she was suspected of financial improprieties and accused of appropriating funds for personal benefit and buying political support with the teachers' union money. She was indicted, and has been under arrest since February 2013. Thus, fell one of Mexico's most powerful women.

Although workplace opportunities for women are increasing, gender inequalities, particularly in leadership roles, are still being perpetuated by social structures in both business and politics.

El Subcomandante Marcos: social movement leadership

We cannot explain contemporary leadership in Mexico without referring to El Subcomandante Marcos. In the mid 1990s, El Subcomandante Marcos was an intellectual *guerrillero* who led a collective movement of the indigenous groups in Chiapas (one of the poorest states in Mexico). Marcos wore a mask and nobody knew his identity; the media at that time said that 'he characterized the face of many oppressed groups in the country, tired of the individualism of many leaders who never helped to bring better conditions to the native people'. After a few years of conflict, El Subcomandante Marcos became a rock star of the politically correct (Castañeda, 2011) and internationally celebrated by anticapitalist movements for his engagement in new forms of postmodern resistance.

Andrés Manuel Lopez Obrador. contemporary leadership

Finally, in 2000, a leftist leader, Andrés Manuel Lopez Obrador started to create a political maelstrom by using the media to create chaos and by becoming the new victim: 'I am the legitimate President of Mexico, and everything is against my rights.'

Mexican leadership is a story of revolutionary struggle, modernizing leaders with progressive programmes, authoritarianism and corruption. All aforementioned leaders certainly experienced some successes but often through nineteenth and twentieth centuries methods of social struggle – armed insurrections, blockades of public thoroughfares and occupation of public spaces – rather than using modern technologies, civil society organizations and the democratic political systems that are quite well established in Mexico. The historical evolution of Mexican society provides a useful framework for understanding cultural values which are prevalent in Mexico today (Howell et al., 2008). These cultural values reflect its heritage and they strongly affect the behaviour of Mexico's leaders and in government, business, social movements and other contexts.

LEADERSHIP TODAY AND IN THE FUTURE

Mexicans believe that collectivism is part of their values as a society. Apart from a strong belief that we are a warm people, a nation of solidarity and unity, Mexican leaders have demonstrated that we are also an individualistically oriented culture. Mexican people want self-confident, strong and trusted leaders, who go beyond moving speeches and can mobilize actions that bring Mexico forward, towards new and improved development, regardless of political parties and ideologies. To succeed in this, Mexican leaders need to build a broader support base in order to develop a future with opportunities for all.

It is easy to exaggerate the importance of an influential leader in the imposing social edifice of Mexico. What could make Mexico particularly is the existence of opportunities and conditions to develop prosperity without giving up either transparency or sustainability. When things deteriorate, a nation requires leadership that transforms not only the context but also the culture and the vision of the country.

Tried and true strategies may be used, but new concepts and insights should be attempted and experimented with, in order to change directions. Environmentally we are deteriorating and society is suffering from more conflict and less and less social cohesion and compassion. Ancient, colonial era classism and racism, officially suppressed but internalized and subconsciously present, cause, for example, among many other problems, traffic jams and suburban sprawl. Mexican society is becoming increasingly divided, symbolized by growing gated communities. Yet, a belief in social justice drives many leaders to push for changes in Mexico, even if confronted by the system and its structures many of them feel that leadership is impossible.

Many traditions and cultural values from Mexico's past influence leadership in Mexico today. However, Mexicans are, as ever, learning different ways of facing life and solving unique Mexican problems. Whether in politics, business or social movements, leadership in Mexico requires a shift from a 'salvation' individualistic leader with compliant followers, to a more collectivist, grass-roots, collaborative and fellowship-oriented leadership. Complex problems require leadership that builds partnerships and creates agreements.

Mexico is a young, vibrant and dynamic society. If it manages to overcome negative patterns and if it finds new forms of leadership and new followership that draws on its rich cultural heritage, and if it harnesses the huge talent and dynamism of its young population, the potential for achieving change may be huge.

REFERENCES

Castañeda, Jorge G. (2011) *Mañana o Pasado: El Misterio de los Mexicanos*. Mexico: Aguilar.

Howell, J.P., de la Cerda, J., Martinez, S.M., Bautista, J.A., Ortiz, J., Prieto, L. and Drofman, P. (2008) 'Societal culture and leadership in Mexico – a portrait of change', in Jagdeep S. Chhokar, Felix C. Brodbeck and Robert J. House (eds), *Culture and Leadership Across the World: The GLOBE Book of In-Depth Studies of 25 Societies*. London: Taylor & Francis.

14
POLAND
Swaying Between Functionalism and Humanistic Management

Beata Jałocha: Assistant Professor at Jagiellonian University, Faculty of Management and Social Communication, Krakow, Poland

Michał Zawadzki: Assistant Professor at Jagiellonian University, Faculty of Management and Social Communication, Krakow, Poland

THE ESSENCE OF LEADERSHIP

Leadership in Poland is associated primarily with the ability to lead an organization to economic success. This state of affairs was undoubtedly affected by the relatively short duration of the capitalist economy that replaced the centrally planned communist economy in 1989. The initial phase of capitalism in Poland, correctly termed by Bolesław Kuc as 'amateur capitalism' (Kuc, 2004: 171), promotes the universal tendency to use neoliberal solutions in conducting organizational activities (including public organizations, such as universities), which impinges on management and leadership consciousness.

The development of leadership in Poland resembles the process of amalgamation, i.e. accumulation, mixing different elements borrowed from various concepts of leadership. Changes in social and political systems over recent decades (and even centuries) have also had a significant impact on leadership and followership development.

Polish leadership is dominated by the trait theory: leaders are expected to have charisma, the personality and capability to be a leader, the ability to motivate others and the determination exhibited in pursuing objectives. The dominant myth of leadership assumes the existence of a 'hero', a person who alone is able to solve very complex problems. The transactional approach to leadership also is present and is associated with creating an asymmetrical relationship between the leader and followers as natural and desirable. A leader has to decide, control and take strictly rational social actions – followers should listen, imitate and follow the leader into the fire.

Deviations from these expectations, especially in the private sector, are sometimes defined as pathologies that should be eliminated using management processes. The main objective of a leader is to achieve a high level of follower imitation: conformism is a desired value in many Polish organizations and a necessary condition for the implementation of economic efficiency and is identified as the prime objective of management (Zawadzki, 2014; Sułkowski and Zawadzki, 2015). However, as research shows, shared leadership is becoming more visible in many Polish organizations, usually civic organizations, cooperatives and NGOs. This is a recent and an optimistic and promising phenomenon (Bogacz-Wojtanowska and Jałocha, 2016).

It is common to follow populist leadership texts written by management gurus, particularly from the West (Zawadzki, 2015). Admiration of great individuals especially from the USA is commonplace, with Jack Welch being the most popular heroic leader character. This creates unrealistic expectations in relation to leadership. The discourse on leadership in Poland is shaped also on consultant reasoning, based on highlighting the careers of well-known figures from the business world as examples to follow (see Drzewiecki et al., 2015).

The functionalist approach, exalting conformism and treating organizational culture as a 'social glue' (Alvesson, 2013) dominates Polish management sciences as well as university business schools (but, of course, it is not only the Polish case, see Izak et al., 2017;

Magala and Zawadzki, 2017). Management education delays the transfer of knowledge because of outdated theory and populist books and theories being used uncritically. The curricula are still dominated by the outdated Edgar Schein and Geert Hofstede and favourites from the 1980s such as *In Search of Excellence* (Peters and Waterman, 1982) or *The One Minute Manager* (Blanchard and Johnson, 1982) are still having a great time in Poland, and are often objects of uncritical affirmation.

Despite the strong involvement of functionalism, the Polish management discourse includes many examples of alternative, humanistic approaches to leadership. The concept of a trustworthy guardian, by Tadeusz Kotarbiński (1987), the personalistic leadership of Bronisław Bombała (2010), leadership based on democratic coordination, by Czesław Sikorski (2006), the concept of limited leadership, by Andrzej Koźmiński (2013) and *The Three Faces of Leadership: Manager, Artist, Priest* by Hatch et al. (2005) join the international, humanistic leadership trends while maintaining Polish specificity.

THE MAIN INFLUENCES ON LEADERSHIP

By far the dominant paradigm of leadership in Poland is the charismatic leader, which applies in both business and politics. Longing for a leader-saviour has deep cultural, social and historical roots. First, the history of Poland is one of subordination to other powers. Several centuries of partition ended in 1918, and created a mythical image of a leader, the saviour of the nation. An example is Józef Piłsudski, a Polish statesman, soldier and prime minister during the interwar period, whereby followership meant total subordination to the leader's vision. After only 20 years of independence, World War II ended this and was followed by communism imposed by the Soviet Union.

The Soviets attempted to introduce their cults of the mythical Soviet leaders, exemplified by the cult of Stalin. This monstrous cult, 'the inspiration of millions', touched various spheres of social life; from poetry, which celebrated the acts of a 'great leader', to the changes of names of cities in honour of this communist tyrant. The emerging independence movement that resulted in the creation of Solidarity also needed a charismatic leader – Lech Wałęsa, the shipyard worker from Gdansk, who led Poles to regain their independence. Also, the Catholic Church, led by the Polish hero Pope John Paul II, had a huge impact on the resistance movement against communism.

For over 1000 years the Catholic Church has been present in Poland and despite the ongoing social changes, including the secularization of society, it still has a huge impact on the Polish people. The Church played a key role in the collapse of communism in Poland, supporting dissidents and helping internees. At the same time, the Catholic Church, especially its dominant right wing, is one of the least democratic organizations in the world. The followership is based on total submission to visions of the leaders of the Church, with the Pope understood as the personification of St Peter, the apostle of Christ.

This influence is visible in the Polish leadership in several ways, including dependence of political leaders on the Church (the Church's support helps to win elections) or lack of women's leadership.

A centuries-old tradition of strong, individual leadership has become the perfect ground to implant neoliberal concepts of leadership that brought to Poland multinational corporations in the early 90s. The ultraconservative government elected in 2015 supported strongly by the conservative part of the Polish Catholic Church with its emphasis on nationalism has become grist to the mill of further neoliberalization of the public sphere, including the organizational reality (see Harvey, 2007).

Neoliberal leadership trends are visible not only in Polish management theory but also in management practice (Koźmiński, 2013). The myth of success, striving for creating hyperconformity, treating resistance from others as a manifestation of one's own weakness or an organizational dysfunction, the desire for continuous control over others or motivating based on the trivial application of penalties and rewards, create a dramatic image of Polish leaders who cannot go beyond the Taylor–Fordist schemes in their thinking and acting.

Leadership in Poland is well illustrated in the currently popular book *Good Leadership: The Best Practices of Polish Business Leaders* (Drzewiecki et al., 2015), which reflects the concept of 'corporate cultism' described by Peters and Waterman in *In Search of Excellence* (1982) and critiqued by Hugh Willmott (1993). Its crux is the positive valuation of monocultures in organizations based on the homogenization of the beliefs of their members and conformism with reference to the actions of leaders (Zawadzki, 2015). Management processes are to be based on the use of individual autonomy as a means aimed at achieving financial targets: behind the mask of a lofty rhetoric of empowerment and giving the freedom to make decisions, there is the Orwellization and dehumanization of organizational cultures (Gabriel, 2015).

Humanistic and critical trends, however, resist the populist trends, mainly due to the humanistic management environment at the Faculty of Management and Social Communication in Krakow, at the University of Warsaw, at the Gdansk University of Technology and the University of Leon Koźmiński (but not only; see Nierenberg et al., 2015). Also, the rise of civic movements and the development of the 'third sector', derive from a more democratic concept of leadership. Leadership in these organizations is shared, and the values are not based on profit and organizational effectiveness.

LEADERSHIP TODAY AND IN THE FUTURE

In the social discourse, longing for a Messiah leader (Western, 2013) who will lead the nation, who will take care of the people and solve their problems, is still present. However, it is hard to believe that this promise could ever be fulfilled in the face of the huge changes taking place in the world around us. Undoubtedly, as shown by the recent parliamentary elections in Poland, won by the nationalist party led by a right-wing leader, these dreams are very strong. Polish society at large does not seem to be ready for a new paradigm, a new model of leadership. It was very interesting to observe a clash of two completely different concepts of leadership during the campaign that preceded the last parliamentary elections in Poland, a clash of the nationalist PiS (Law and Justice) party and the left-wing Partia Razem (Together Party). Razem is a young party created by activists coming from left-wing circles, urban activists, academics and activists of the third sector.

Razem, as opposed to PiS, has no single leader; leadership lies in the hands of democratically elected representatives and it aligns its ideals with other European social movements and activist groups. However, the lack of a leader was too much for both the media and the voters who expected a leader for the Razem party and it was not until one of its representatives appeared as a leader in a TV discussion that the party began to gain electoral points. This new party shows that a new generation of civic activists, in touch with wider social change, is active in Poland and will offer a different ideal of leadership to the messianic forces of conservative social actors.

The relatively frequent evocation of the example of Jack Welch as the ideal leader in the Polish discourse is very symptomatic. The attempt to imitate American business solutions in Polish organizations is, in turn, the aftermath of a deeper cultural phenomenon: the Americanization of Polish society. The *American Dream* is still deeply rooted in the Polish mentality. Polish managers seem to be obsessed with this seductive ideal, which is as old as the reforms of Margaret Thatcher and the neoliberal dream of a free market that will provide an effective regulation of all spheres of social life.

It is also worth mentioning that entry to the European Union in 2004 had implications for Polish leadership in several ways. For instance, it creates a dependency on the other, and Polish leaders are overseen by a powerful technocratic system. Although the independence of the Polish public bodies is guaranteed by the constitution, the mass projectivization (execution of hundreds of thousands of projects financed by the EU) means that developmental objectives of public organizations, regions and even the whole country, are subordinated to the overarching goals imposed by an entity that provides financial resources (EU). Hence, the role of public sector leaders is also changing under the influence of these transformations.

What remains largely ignored in Poland, what does not appear in the leadership discourse, is women's leadership. Probably the biggest (though not the only) impact is the right wing of the Catholic Church, which sees a woman as a mother, a wife, a person for whom the family is the primary goal. Women are not encouraged to take leadership roles and in the majority of Polish organizations there is no equality. Nowadays, many Polish women embrace the 'Western' life; they dream of careers, self-fulfilment, however they still hit the glass ceiling. Research shows that business organizations recruit the same number of men and women, but sadly symmetry in the development of their careers ends at the recruitment stage.

As the Women Leadership in Business Foundation report indicates, in 2014 there were women on the boards of 11.6% of the companies listed on the Polish stock exchange, but they held the function of CEO in only 6.5% of these companies.

Polish leadership today is caught in a socially constructed, political and economic fog. There are the influences of the past, great sufferings, loss of borders, heroic national struggles still very fresh in the minds. There are the post-communist neoliberal reforms, the influences of idealized oversimplified 'Messiah' American leadership models. The influence of the EU and its meta-models of bureaucratic leadership and there is the digital age and globalized forces that make all feel disorientated.

Contemporary organizational leadership leans towards 1980s American models of transformational leadership and conformist cultures, mixed with a heady conservative nationalism that draws on the strength of the Catholic Church and particularly the memory of the Polish Pope, Saint John Paul. As Ukraine falls apart, and the EU struggles with refugees the leaders of Poland are becoming polarized towards conservative nationalist and Messiah forces. In parallel to this, the new emerging humanistic leadership ideas and the political and social movement forces that are experimenting with leaderless and new democratized forms of leadership.

Polish leadership is in flux and there will be ideological, political and economic struggles ahead to define how Polish leadership emerges in the future.

REFERENCES

Alvesson, Matt (2013) *Understanding Organizational Culture*, 2nd edn. London: Sage.

Blanchard, Ken and Johnson, Spencer (1982) *The One Minute Manager*. New York: William Morrow and Company.

Bogacz-Wojtanowska, E. and Jałocha, B. (2016) 'The bright side of social economy sector's projectification: a study of successful social enterprises', *Project Management Research and Practice*, 3, 5043.

Bombała, Bronisław. (2010) *Fenomenologia Zarządzania: Przywództwo*. Warsaw: Difin.

Drzewiecki, A., Chełmiński, D. and Kubica, E. (eds) (2015) *Dobre Przywództwo: Najlepsze Praktyki Polskich Liderów Biznesu* [Good Leadership: The Best Practices of Polish Business Leaders]. Warsaw: Wolters Kluwer.

Gabriel, Y. (2015) 'The caring leader – what followers expect of their leaders and why?', *Leadership*, 11 (3): 316–34.

Harvey, David (2007) *A Brief History of Neoliberalism*. Oxford: Oxford University Press.

Hatch, Mary J., Koźmiński, Andrzej and Kostera, Monika (2005) *The Three Faces of Leadership: Manager, Artist, Priest*. Malden–Oxford–Carlton: Blackwell.

Izak, Michal, Kostera, Monika and Zawadzki, Michal (eds) (2017) *The Future of University Education*. London: Palgrave Macmillan.

Kotarbiński, T. (1987) *Pisma Etyczne*. Wrocław: Wydawnictwo Zakładu Naukowego im Ossolińskich.

Koźmiński, Andrzej K. (2013) *Ograniczone Przywództwo: Studium Empiryczne*. Warsaw: Poltext.

Kuc, B.R. (2004) 'Fenomen przywództwa', in W. Kieżun (ed.), *Krytyczna Teoria Organizacji: Wybór zagadnień*. Warsaw: Wydawnictwo Wyższej Szkoły Przedsiębiorczości I Zarządzania im Leona Koźmińskiego. pp. 165–86.

Magala, S. and Zawadzki, M. (2017) 'Performing academics: return to meritocracy?', in C. Cannavale, F. Maimone and P. Malizia (eds), *Evolution of the Post-Bureaucratic Organization*. Hershey: IGI-Global Publisher. pp. 88–104.

Nierenberg, B., Batko, R. and Sułkowski, Ł. (eds) (2015) *Zarządzanie Humanistyczne*. Krakow: WUJ.

Peters, Tom and Waterman, Robert (1982) *In Search of Excellence: Lessons from America's Best-Run Companies*. New York: HarperCollins.

Sikorski, Cz. (2006) *Organizacje bez Wodzów: Od Przywództwa Emocjonalnego do Koordynacji Demokratycznej*. Warsw: C.H. Beck.

Sułkowski, Ł. and Zawadzki, M. (2015) 'Critical discourse in the contemporary management science', *Folia Philosophica*, 34. Special Issue: Forms of Criticism in Philosophy and Science, ed. D. Kubok. Katowice: University of Silesia. pp. 19–230.

Western, Simon (2013) *Leadership: A Critical Text*, 2nd edn. London: Sage.

Willmott, H. (1993) 'Strength is ignorance: slavery is freedom: managing culture in modern organizations', *Journal of Management Studies*, 30 (4): 515–52.

Zawadzki, M. (2014) *Nurt Krytyczny w Zarządzaniu: Kultura, Edukacja, Teoria*. Warsaw: Sedno.

Zawadzki, M. (2015) 'Smuggling panaceas by management gurus: a critical approach', in A. Örtenblad (ed.), *Handbook of Research on Management Ideas and Panaceas: Adaptation and Context*. Cheltenham: Edward Elgar. pp. 313–26.

15
RUSSIA

Leadership in Russia: Between Hero and Victim

Ekaterina Belokoskova-Mikhaylova: President of the Psychoanalytic Association of Psychologists, Coaches and Consultants of Organizations (Russia), Supervisor and Training Analyst of European Confederation of Psychoanalytic Psychotherapies, Member of ISPSO

Konstantin Korotov: Associate Professor and Director of the Centre for Leadership Development Research at ESMT – European School of Management and Technology, Berlin, Germany

Irena Izotova: psychoanalytically oriented executive and leadership team coach, organizational consultant and lecturer, Higher School of Economics, Russia; Member of ISPSO, Member of Board, Association of Psychoanalytic Coaching and Business Consulting (Russia)

INTRODUCTION

Leadership behaviours in Russian politics, businesses, education and other fields of life seem to have very similar foundational principles. This chapter presents Russian leadership within the context of Russian sociohistorical legacy. It explores the main factors contributing to the expectations of leaders and followers in Russia, and sheds light on the associated challenges and opportunities. This chapter is based both on research by international and Russian leadership and organizational scholars, and the authors' extensive practice of working with Russian leaders in educational, coaching, and therapeutic settings.

KEY PRINCIPLES OF RUSSIAN LEADERSHIP PRACTICE

Russian leadership rhetoric has been traditionally based on the themes of overcoming hurdles (e.g. building the city of St Petersburg on marshland, costing thousands of lives), responding to external attacks (e.g. defending the country against Nazi Germany in World War II), or reacting to unfriendly environmental developments (e.g. developing new economic models under conditions of Western sanctions imposed on the country in 2015). Russian mythology carries on those themes through official historic accounts, fiction and popular folk discourse. Shekshnia et al. (2009) argue that this mythology, supported and perpetuated by the societal elites, legitimizes the leadership styles prevalent in the country in the eyes of the followers. Seen in broad terms, it is particularly focused on the past and on the indebtedness of the current generations to the previous ones for their sacrifice. This orientation towards the past in the Russian leadership discourse has been of paramount importance in both domestic and international attempts at understanding Russian leadership (Kets de Vries et al., 2004; Grachev and Bobina, 2006; Khapova and Korotov, 2007).

The Russian leadership mythology posits that overcoming of seemingly unsurmountable difficulties through mobilizing followers for struggle, fight and potential suffering for the sake of victory in the name of defeating the perpetrator or achieving some abstract better good (e.g. organizing the world's most luxurious Olympics) is the main perceived task of a leader. The leader is expected to mobilize the troops for sacrifice. The cause of the sacrifice has to be positioned in noble terms. Rational exploration of alternatives, cost–benefit analysis, or a choice of not going into a battle are not the leadership traits explicitly expected by the majority of the followers. As historically leaders have been associated with military actions (expansion of the country's territories or defending its borders in the light of external threats), military vocabulary is paramount in Russian leadership parlance.

At the same time, Russian leadership practices have been concerned with defining and defending the right for existence of Russia's own way of dealing with daily societal or economic challenges, cautiously looking at examples and patterns from the outside world, but still believing in the special circumstances surrounding the country and thus substantiating a call for developing something unique and different, suitable for Russia only. This search for differentiation has been frequently justified in Russian theorizing and lay people's conversations about the uniqueness of the Russian history, culture, psychosocial archetypes, and position between Eastern and Western civilizations. Both Russians and Westerners (e.g. Puffer and McCarthy, 2001) trying to explain what it takes to lead in Russia typically refer to a poem by a renowned Russian poet Tiutchev, which states 'Russia cannot be understood with the mind alone, no ordinary yardstick can span its greatness: She stands alone, unique – In Russia one can only believe!' This metaphor of impossibility of application of rational analysis to the country at large propels the charismatic side of leadership to the forefront in the expectations of the followers and serves as a powerful defence mechanism against the periodically emerging question of whether it makes sense to invent everything (including the leadership approaches) locally.

The Russian tradition to see the world is connected with perpetual everlasting fight between light and darkness, the spirit and matter, good and evil. It splits the world into two parties: 'we' and 'they'. 'We' are always the ambassadors of good and light and 'they' are ambassadors of darkness, enemies. A person lives his or her life feeling as if he or she were submerged into a hostile dangerous world, where his or her life consists of suffering and heavy burden only. In the domestic history of Russia there is a chronology of recurrent sociocultural crises with alternating manic and depressive stages or phases: reforms – counter reforms, enthusiasm – stagnation (Yakovenko and Muzykantskiy, 2011). Part of domineering social strategy reproduces the patterns of lameness, historical guilt and social despondency.

Obsessive drive for uniqueness or differentiation is connected to claims of superiority of Russia and its ways of living and working commensurate with the size of the country and its ambition on the world stage. The leadership role is to achieve a unique position, causing awe and admiration, with the cost being of secondary importance. Moreover, the leader is perceived to hold the final accountability for success or failure, and the heroic nature of leadership persists in the perception of the population. The heroic side of leader–follower interactions can also be demonstrated by driving achievement under conditions of supposedly limited resources. An important caveat here is that the personal physical and psychological resources of the people are seen as limitless. The perpetuated need to suffer and sacrifice for a greater cause is in action here again.

The socioeconomic changes following the collapse of the Soviet Union called for an accelerated development of leadership talent capable of responding to the new reality, and particularly to the growing connection of Russia with the rest of the world. The past quarter of a century offered multiple opportunities for learning from other nations, including leadership patterns (Kets de Vries et al., 2004), and Russians have embraced those opportunities wholeheartedly (Korotov, 2008). However, learning does not mean automatic translation of the intellectual understanding into life and work practices.

SOCIOHISTORICAL CONTEXT

The critical exploration and evaluation of the developmental options for Russia goes far back in the history of this large country with challenging natural conditions. Russia, willingly or unwillingly, experimented with application of foreign governance models, societal organization, religion and ways to reproduce or challenge values through generations. The urge for exploration of what the external world can offer has often been related to overcoming a particular set of challenges and has been combined with a critical assessment of the propositions made by the external parties. For example, Russian tribes in Novgorod chose to invite Scandinavians to reign in the region that was being torn apart by tribal rivalry in the ninth century.

While acknowledging the mandate of the invited external rulers, the people of Novgorod managed, however, to keep a level of independence, critical assessment and influence that would allow them to challenge the authority figures. A similar example is the choice of religion for the then pagan population of Russia: in the twelfth century Prince Vladimir of Kyiv invited representatives of various religions to make a value proposition that would suit best the need to unite the people. In an equivalent of what may resemble today's tender of a consulting service, the choice was made for the Greek variant of Christianity.

For leaders of the developing Russian state, the Byzantine Empire offered an attractive model to follow, including a dream or vision of taking a leading civilizational position that has been driving Russia up to the present day. However, despite accepting the religious proposition, Russia eventually developed its own version of Byzantine Christianity, culminating in the Russian Orthodox version of the religion. Since that moment the Russian Orthodox religion has in a way strengthened the concept of autocracy: submission, the suffering, the canonical 'Life for the Tsar'. Orthodox ideas such as humility, compassion and acceptance of the authority coming from the above, are closely connected with the approval by religious institutions of the acts of the Russian rulers and later modern Russian political figures.

For centuries Russia was under the Mongol yoke, an involuntary political and tribute dependency of Russian princedoms on the Mongol Empire. It lasted on the basis of Mongol military power up to the end of the fifteenth century. This time has been interpreted differently in terms of its influence on the development of the Russian state: some historians believe that it was the reason for Russia's alienation from Europe and subsequent falling behind in terms of socioeconomic development. Others suggest that it became a critical predecessor of the future Russian Empire which allowed the establishment of order, law and coordination of various parts of the vast country.

In the early eighteenth century the Russian Tsar Peter the Great went to learn from the Europeans, particularly the Dutch, about the ways they built warships. Having mastered the craftsmanship by rolling up his sleeves and working incognito, he then transferred the shipbuilding skills, and together with them quite a few management and governmental organization principles, to Russian soil, overcoming the resistance to the new methods with rather brutal force. Connecting education with coercion in Peter the Great's way of modernizing the country may have contributed to one of the persistent expectations followers have of the Russian leaders: he (or less often she) has to be an accepted authority or subject matter expert in order to demand compliance from the followers. Once the mastery is demonstrated, sovereign power of the leader can ignore the positions of others, and can legitimately serve as a foundation for demanding compliance. A consequence of this is that up until today leaders believe in the expert foundation of their power, and do not want to express the vulnerability of not knowing something in their domain. Demonstrating personal expertise often reinforces the leadership position, particularly its charismatic side.

Vladimir Yakovlev in his interview for Radio Svoboda (2015) says this of recent dramatic events in Russian history: 52 million people were killed during last 100 years in Russia one way or another, i.e. during World War I, the communist revolution, civil war, Stalin's repressions, World War II, post-war repressions and annihilation of people captured during the war. According to Yakovlev (2015), we have to acknowledge that Russia has been the most terrible point of genocide and torturing people which has ever existed in the world during the whole story of humankind. The country may still fail to fully understand how much this still influences the population. Modern Russian leaders are largely silent about that period, as if they avoid the possible psychological effects of talking directly about the events. After 1917 Russia became split in time as Soviet Russia refused to return the debts of tsarist Russia – these were just two different states. Bolsheviks (Soviet) leaders made the denial of international norms and the denial of ideas of continuity from the Russian Empire the basis of the Soviet system.

This unexamined trauma has a profound influence on the development of the country. The arrival of capitalism in Russia, coupled with the increased power of the state in the early twenty-first century, have created a peculiar system where private entrepreneurial initiative has to adjust to the conditions imposed from the top. As a result, business leaders behave in a pattern resembling a constant fight. Business leaders are vulnerable as they work in an environment where they may lose everything in one moment because of the actions of state officials. The ineffectiveness of the law creates a dependency on the goodwill of people in authority positions. In modern Russian business, the ambivalence of followers towards leadership becomes apparent. On the one hand is the collective sacrifice and a willingness to give their lives for the common cause; on the other, individual survival strategies in a situation of conflict of values.

Gender diversity in leadership also has its own peculiarities in Russia. Leadership discourse uses primarily masculine forms of the language, and many leadership practices are dominated by explicit demonstration of machismo and patriarchal values. Still, female leadership is increasingly present in Russian organizational and societal lives.

Since the 1917 October revolution it was proclaimed that men and women had acquired equal rights, opportunities and accountability, and during the Soviet Union period women were granted certain space for labour and career advancement. The world's first female astronaut was Valentina Tereshkova, who made the flight into space at the age of 26 years. Not least of the selection criteria for first flight was the ability of female candidates to lead an active social life, to be a leader, an authority figure – to speak in public strongly demonstrating the advantages of the Socialist system of values. There even were official standards for the representation of women in government. In 1984 35% of the Supreme Soviet of the USSR were women. After the collapse of the Soviet Union in the murky 1990s when the former social system collapsed it was women in many families who had to become breadwinners. That gave a boost to women's entrepreneurship and set the route for the most ambitious of them. According to a 2016 report by Grant Thornton entitled 'Women in Business', Russia now boasts the highest proportion of women in senior management roles worldwide (45% versus 23% in the USA, 21% in the UK, Japan ranking lowest with only 7% of senior positions held by women).[1] Despite the generally sexist environment in Russia, women can be successful enough in their movement forward.

CURRENT AND FUTURE CHALLENGES

The restriction of personal freedom has been a dominant theme of psychological development through Russian history. One of the key tasks for the future leadership at all levels in Russia will be supporting society in working through the trauma of past generations and

[1]www.grantthornton.global/en/insights/articles/women-in-business-2016/ (accessed 24 November 2017).

overcoming the fear of personal responsibility and civil activity – a foundation of a strong civil society. Allegiance to a leader who personifies supreme power has been an important psychological mechanism, that lies deep within Russian culture and it will be difficult to displace. Structural and cultural changes will need to take place to challenge the current norms of lawlessness that inhibit positive change. Clear expectations of, and trust in the implementation of law and order will be needed to allow new leadership to emerge in more distributed ways.

It is difficult to identify patterns in the Russian protest movement. There are examples of new leadership coming from a new generation of political activists that challenge supremacy of current Church, business and political leadership. At the same time, it would be an exaggeration to speak of a serious resistance to the authoritarian norms from the new generation Since *perestroika* in the 1990s and until 2010 there was a vibrant protest movement, which was followed by stricter laws and prosecutions. Russian implicit leadership theories may stand in opposition to the realities of the fast-changing world relying on cooperation, adaptive and mutual learning, and utilizing the expertise of others. Globalization has certainly touched Russian realities. Internet technology helps to get any news from anywhere in the world, as opposed to the state-controlled television channels. The global business environment influences the style of leadership and values adopted by foreign companies operating in Russia. Nevertheless, it is important to remember that in general Russia is very conservative, and having vast territories covering one-sixth of the globe contributes to the fact that leaders of different areas may behave somewhat independently, and even anarchically. The percentage of people who regularly travel abroad is very low compared to the total population of the country, and many people have no access to exploration of alternative leadership models. Therefore, the majority of Russians are very slow to change their attitudes and followers remain compliant to expert leaders. If leaders are still expected to be experts in every aspect of their work, efficiency and effectiveness will surely be lost. Moreover, the development of new forms of leadership and new forms of organization necessary for the twenty-first century will be restrained and will limit Russian progress and development.

The sacrifice-demanding approach to leadership connected to the military discourse and based on the notion of indebtedness to previous generations is unlikely to be effective with a new generation who have access to information about other leadership models and practice.

Change in leadership models cannot happen without significant modifications in the implicit leadership theories of majority of the population, and this means a big change in culture. As a result, one of the critical tasks of the new leaders for Russia will be to simultaneously work on their own leadership approach and vitally also on the needs and expectations of their followers. This may be a daunting task.

REFERENCES

Grachev, M.V. and Bobina, M.A. (2006) 'Russian organizational leadership: lessons from the GLOBE Study', *International Journal of Leadership Studies*, 1 (2): 67–79.

Kets de Vries, M.F.R., Shekshnia, S., Korotov, K. and Florent-Treacy, E. (2004) *The New Russian Business Leaders*. Cheltenham: Edward Elgar.

Khapova, S.N. and Korotov, K. (2007) 'Dynamics of Western career attributes in the Russian context', *Career Development International*, 12 (1): 68–85.

Korotov, K. (2008) 'Citius, Altius, Fortius: challenges of accelerated development of leadership talent in the Russian context', *Organizational Dynamics*, 37 (3): 277–87.

Puffer, S.M. and McCarthy, D.J. (2001) 'Navigating the hostile maze: a framework for Russian entrepreneurship', *The Academy of Management Executives*, 15 (4): 24–36.

Russian Association of Political Science (2012) 'The human capital of the Russian political elite'. in E.B. Shestopal and E.V. Selezneva (eds), *Political and Psychological Analysis*. Russian Political Encyclopedia (ROSSPEN).

Saab, M. (2014) 'The surprising countries with more women in corporate leadership than in the US', *The Times Magazine*, 14 June.

Shekshnia, S.V., Puffer, S.M. and McCarthy, D.J. (2009) 'Cultural mythology and global leadership in Russia', in Eric H. Kessler and Diana Wong-MingJi (eds), *Cultural Mythology and Global Leadership*. Cheltenham: Edward Elgar. pp. 325–42.

Yakovenko, I. and Muzykantskiy A. (2011) *Manikheystvo i gnostitsizm: kul'turnyye kody russkoy tsivilizatsii* [Manichaeism and Gnosticism: Cultural Codes of Russian Civilization]. Moscow: Russkiy put.

Yakovlev, V. (2015) 'Bežat' ot terrora, vojny i niŝety [Fleeing from terror, war and poverty]'. Interview, 1 December 2015. www.svoboda.org/content/article/27399883.html (accessed 9 November 2017).

16
SCANDINAVIA
Scandinavian Leadership and the (E)Quality Imperative

Johan Grant: executive coach, leadership consultant and assistant professor

Yngve Magnus Ulsrød: executive coach and business consultant

INTRODUCTION

The Scandinavian region, consisting of Norway, Denmark and Sweden, is among the wealthiest, happiest and most peaceful parts of the world (Helliwell et al., 2016).

There is no unified conception of Scandinavian leadership but some studies have been carried out revealing some differences in the leadership culture between the Scandinavian countries (Grenness, 2003). However, we think there are important similarities and an ongoing convergence in our region driven by what we will call the (E)quality imperative. 'We' the authors are a Swedish organizational psychologist and a Norwegian corporate executive, both with long experience with Scandinavian organizations operating globally.

THE (E)QUALITY IMPERATIVE

Fusing *equality* and *quality* is our way of describing a composite of two deeply held assumptions or systems of thoughts shaping Scandinavian leadership. The first is an *instrumental belief* that democratic leadership based on equality, inclusion, empowerment, consensus, competence, work–life balance and safety, creates productive workplaces with high-quality output. The second is a *normative value* that equality is the pinnacle of Western civilization, and as such equality is an end in itself. The complementary, intertwined and covariant nature of the belief and value systems makes it very compelling but also problematic. The reasoning tends to get closed and difficult to challenge because of its inherent morality making it socially unacceptable to question it (at least from inside our cultural sphere): 'Equality, which is in itself good, *also* leads to quality of output, which leads to wealth, which fosters more equality leading to an increasing spiral of equality, quality and wealth.' It is not just (yet) another theory or value that could be replaced by any other (less ethical) theories or value of what constitutes a good and productive workplace or society.

The belief: equality fosters quality

The atmosphere of the typical Scandinavian workplace is gentle, informal and relaxed. The boss is not expected to have the corner office, but to be close to the team, acting in different roles as a member, coach and reinforcing supporter. Power distance, privileges and coercive leadership are subject to resentment since it threatens to rip the social fabric of equality. Lars Rebien Sørensen, the previous CEO of Novo Nordisk, a Danish global healthcare company, was named the top of HBR's 2015 ranking of the best-performing CEOs in the world (but also the lowest paid among the top candidates). Highlighted in the HBR article was Mr Sørensen's modest approach to leadership, focusing on consensus, humbleness and a 'team stronger than the individual' attitude described as *'atypical for Americans but, not necessarily in Scandinavia'* (Ignatius and McGinn, 2015: 2).

In general, the Scandinavian workforce is highly educated and workers are trained to 'think for themselves'. As such, they are expected to be self-motivated and able to make decisions without detailed instructions. Command-and-control leadership is not working with Scandinavians, who associate it with primitive or disturbed minds, systems or cultures with a lack of trust and respect for people's freedom and discretion. Another important part of the belief system is that if democratic, participative practices and consensus are used, employees will speak up before decisions and willingly execute them since they both understand the rationales behind the decisions and respect them since their perspectives have been considered. Managers from other cultures are often challenged by the Scandinavian culture which may seem vague, conflict-avoidant and with lack of control. American, German and French managers often get into trouble managing Scandinavians because they tend to interpret the independence as lack of discipline and respect for hierarchy which in turn makes Scandinavians lose respect since they experience a 'lack of trust'.

The value: equality as an end in itself!

The value part of the Iquality imperative is strongly expressed in the 'Law of Jante' created by the Dano-Norwegian author Aksel Sandemose in his novel *A Fugitive Crosses His Tracks* (Sandemose, 1933). The first two commandments of the Law of Jante are: *'You are not to think you are anything special'* and *'You are not to think You are as good as We are'*. The rest of the commandments follow the same theme: the individual is less than the group. The Law of Jante is typically used to describe a repressive social pattern holding the individual back. No doubt that the Law of Jante is deeply ingrained in our culture. It is celebrating the virtues of modesty and suppressing displays of wealth and success. The Law of Jante is often attacked as something solely negative. However, we think that it should be understood and appreciated as a counterforce balancing our highly individualistic culture preventing it from becoming egotistical. The problem is when it is not understood in this way, but rather as an imperative, it becomes authoritarian and suppressive against healthy competition and winner instinct. This is something the renowned assertive and bold Swedish soccer player Zlatan Ibrahimovic (of Croatian/Serbian decent) experienced in his early career. Today, Zlatan's success has been appropriated as 'Made by Sweden' but the social pressures to quell his extraordinary talent was strong and sports journalists seriously debated whether Zlatan was good or bad for the Swedish national team even though his individual brilliance was obvious. Also, in our school systems we see strong expressions of the Law of Jante. Tuition is free (from kindergarten to university), but elite-type private institutions are very few.

IKEA of Sweden is a strong symbol of the (E)quality imperative. It was founded by Ingvar Kamprad in 1943, and is the world's largest furniture retailer. The vision of IKEA is to *'Create a better everyday life for the many people'* and the culture is deeply founded in the (E)quality imperative and Swedish welfare politics. This is reflected in Kamprad´s *'The Testament of a Furniture Dealer'*, IKEA's most important cultural artefact, where he describes how all employees should be encouraged to take initiatives and act as responsible members of *'the IKEA family'*. The family culture of IKEA and the skilfully crafted corporate narrative have cultish dimensions built around myths about Kamprad's (supposedly) thrifty lifestyle. The strength of IKEA as a symbol for the (E)quality imperative is so strong that no critique or revelations about tax evasion, copying, use of child labour or Kamprad's own Nazi sympathies (as a young man) seem to harm the brand (Kristoffersson, 2014).

HISTORICAL AND CULTURAL FOUNDATIONS

We will describe in what follows two historical and sociocultural foundations of the (E)quality imperative: *peaceful collaboration* and *economic and individual freedom.*

Peaceful collaboration

Today, harmony, 'gentle' and peaceful ways of dealing with conflicts are very important ingredients in the Scandinavian culture. The Nobel Peace Prize, awarded to 101 individuals and 24 organizations, for accomplishing fraternity between nations and reduction of war stands as a strong expression of this. However, Scandinavia has a bloody history based on great power ambitions. In 1397, it was agreed, in the Kalmar conference (famous as the most decisive Nordic meeting for a Nordic union) (Lönnroth, 1934), to establish a Nordic Union (1397–1523) consisting of Denmark, Norway and Sweden. The initiator and true ruler was Queen Margarete I (1353–1412) of Denmark and Norway. In the Union Letter from 1397, Queen Margarete emphasized that

> there shall be one king, and no more than one, for all three kingdoms, and the kingdoms will never be separated again, with the will of God. (Danstrup, 1946)

This ambition was problematic and what was called for was actually not collaboration between equals but one kingdom or state (Harrison and Eriksson, 2010). A lot of blood was then shed in fights for the dominance of the Baltic sea and rebellions against politics, election of the ruling king and higher taxes. It was not until the end of the Napoleonic wars, when it was evident that Scandinavia would not become a great Nordic power, a more peaceful mindset based on each country's sovereignty began to emerge.

The realization that we Scandinavians would never become a unified great power took the edge off our fighting spirit and replaced war with negotiations. We realized that, being small countries at the outskirts of Europe, we would need to cooperate to channel our international ambitions. The cooperation between our countries had a 'corporate' pragmatic ideological flavour with 'strategic intents' of creating synergies and/or economies of scale. Today, peace-making in the international arena is important for the Scandinavian identity, sometimes treated as an 'export trade' in which we invest huge political efforts and money, promoting Scandinavian peacemakers and envoys in areas of conflict around the world.

In the labour market, peaceful collaboration has been instituted by strong labour unions balancing the power of the employers. Approximately 70% of Swedish and Danish employees and 50% of Norwegian employees are members of a labour union. Since the 1930s the unions have been a major power base and important influencer setting the political agenda with symbiotic bonds with the social democratic parties. The majority of workplaces have Collective Agreements between unions and employers regulating wages and working conditions including the sociopsychological working environment. In 2003 Norway adopted the law on a minimum of 40% representation of both sexes on the boards of state-owned and private public limited companies. For companies of a certain size (25–35 employees), in all three countries, it is mandatory to have employee representatives on company boards. Workplace representation for employees in Sweden is through the local union at the workplace. There is no other channel. Legislation requires the employer to inform and negotiate with the unions at the workplace before making major changes, and many of the practical arrangements for doing so, which elsewhere in Europe are fixed by law, are left in Sweden to local negotiations. The domain of influence of the unions moved from psychosocial and physical work environment to also include the domain of business management and investment. Albeit controversial when introduced, today there is a consensus that these laws and regulations have fostered a gentle and responsible partnering attitude curbing militant union behaviours.

Economic and individual freedom

The Scandinavian countries are often described as 'socialist', allowing a 'soft market economy'. However, we think the opposite is truer. Our wealth has been built on the market economy and a strong economic freedom for 'the many' that has later been 'civilized' or tamed by pragmatic social-democratic politics and the policies of the welfare state.

The Vikings of Norway, Denmark and Sweden (800–1060 AD) established Scandinavia as a great power by settlement and establishing influential trading places around the European coasts. The Vikings had few ideological aspirations. They were simply looking for wealth and used a unique combination of skills in war, trading and farming.

Again, like with peaceful collaboration, the Vikings' raids were pragmatic and skilful, carrying some resemblance with today's Scandinavian businesses with export of farm products, engineering, raw material and art. The Vikings' raids were large-scale projects, with a clear 'business objective', a well-crafted strategy and power of implementation.

Serfdom was abolished in Sweden and Norway by the twelfth century (Denmark after 1450), long before other European countries. Since a large number of farmers owned their land they became traders and gained strong political influence, which they still have. In the middle of the nineteenth century liberal politics unleashed a strong wave of innovations with entrepreneurs who created an explosive increase in wealth, transforming Scandinavia into one of the richest regions in the world. The wealth paved the way for the social democratic projects of the welfare state, providing equal opportunities and distribution of wealth and public responsibilities for those who are unable to avail themselves of the minimal provisions of a good life.

The Scandinavian version of social democracy is more influenced by the German sociologist Weber's ideas about modernity and Lutheran work ethics, than Marxist materialism. According to the World Values Survey (WVS, 2015) the Scandinavian countries are by far the most individualistic and secular and postmodernist countries in the world. And, our shared belief is that in order to be *truly* independent the individual has to be economically and socially independent. The role of politics is to create a context that breaks down barriers to independence, which explains (with a little help from the Law of Jante) our tolerance and acceptance of societal regulations that restrict the influence of religion, the family or any other collective, seen as obstructive to individual freedom whether it be in choice of partner, occupation, political, religious or sexual preferences.

THE FUTURE OF THE (E)QUALITY IMPERATIVE

Simply put, Scandinavians both enjoy and gain from equality. The combination of soft leadership practices on the one hand and the focus on hard quality and results on the other is a conundrum, especially for many outsiders who debate causality: Are the gentle practices and social security a result of, or the cause of wealth? However, within Scandinavia there is a consensus, perhaps with the exception of the political far right, that there is an interaction of effects and circular causality involved. The far right-wing populist parties started their journey in the 1970s and 80s, ending up in government positions in both Denmark (the third largest party in the 2001 election), Norway (the second largest party in the 2005 election and since 2013 with key ministerial roles in the government) and Sweden (the third largest party in the 2014 election). We believe that the far-right populist movement with its quest for nationalism and 'a new authoritarian settlement' (Western, 2015), for better or for worse, challenges the value-driven aspect of the (E)quality imperative. However, from a global and 'mainstream' perspective the interest in Scandinavian leadership is on the rise. The quest for a new sustainable capitalism creates a demand for our combination of pragmatism and social ethos and pathos. Scandinavia can play an important role in peace-making and global politics as well as in the world of business where were pioneers in building a pragmatic, yet sustainable capitalism, combining economic growth with ecological and social sustainability.

Given its strengths, we think that Scandinavia should continue to develop its role as an integrator, fostering peaceful cooperation, respect and understanding for the importance of economic and individual freedom. We think that the opportunity for such a role has never been greater as the world is becoming more and more connected, interdependent and vulnerable. On the other hand, the prosperity and freedom from hardship can cause Scandinavians to embrace a somewhat naïve and unrealistic worldview, with an inability to deal with threats to our lifestyle and values. The political unrest, terrorism, extreme political and religious movements, the refugee situation, increased xenophobia and environmental problems, all pose real challenges to our societies and the egalitarian leadership ideals. Another concern is that the (E)quality imperative can also become its Achilles' heel. If true defence of equality is substituted by politically correct and naïve politically correct authoritarians who deny the complexity of the global society, this will undermine the success and will fuel further reactions from the far right and other discontents.

A key leadership challenge will be how to balance the new globalized quest for individualism, that also infiltrates Scandinavian culture, and which may undermine the social 'collectivism' that allows high tax and high welfare provision, and underpins the (e)quality values. The task for Scandinavian leadership is to enable an inclusive individualism to flourish while holding on to our (e)quality values that have been so successful for us in the past.

REFERENCES

Danstrup, John (1946) *Danmarks historia* [History of Denmark]. Malmö: A.B. Allheims Förlag.

Grenness, T. (2003) 'Scandinavian managers on Scandinavian leadership', *Journal of Value-based Management,* 19: 9–21.

Harrison, Dick and Eriksson, Bo (2010) *Sveriges historia* [History of Sweden], *1350–1600.* Stockholm: Norstedts.

Helliwell, J. Layard, R. and Sachs, J. (2016) World Happiness Report 2016. www.worldhappiness.report (accessed 9 November 2017).

Ignatius, A. and McGinn, D. (2015) 'Novo Nordisk CEO Lars Sørensen on what propelled him to the top', *Harvard Business Review on Leadership*, November issue. https://hbr.org/2015/11/novo-nordisk-ceo-on-what-propelled-him-to-the-top (accessed 24 November 2017).

Kristoffersson, Sara (2014) *Design by IKEA*. London: Bloomsbury.

Lönnroth, E. *(1934) Sverige och Kalmarunionen* [Sweden and the Kalmar Union]. Göteborg: Elanders Boktryckeri och Aktiebolag.

Sandemose, A. (1933) *En flyktning krysser sitt spor. Fortelling om en morders barndom* [A Fugitive Crosses His Tracks]. Oslo: Tiden Norsk Forlag.

Western S. (2015) 'Political Correctness and Political In-correctness: A psychoanalytic study of new authoritarians'. academia.edu. 16 September 2015.

WVS (2015) World Values Survey. www.worldvaluessurvey.org (accessed 9 November 2017).

17
SOUTH AFRICA
A Racialized and Gendered Leadership Landscape

Peliwe Mnguni: Associate Professor at UNISA School of Business Leadership, Gauteng, South Africa

Jeremias J. De Klerk: Professor in Human Capital Management and Leadership at University of Stellenbosch Business School, Cape Town, South Africa

INTRODUCTION

South Africa has many ethnic, racial, political and business 'realities' and these are inextricably linked to how leadership is practised and understood. South African organizations, in both the private and the public sectors, are heated crucibles within which many opposing leadership models, perspectives and ideas meet and mix. Inherent polarities in South African society render a uniform perspective on leadership impossible.

Historically, leadership in South Africa had two main influences: the indigenous African worldview and the Western perspective. Under the African perspective, traditional leadership played an important role in society and local governance (Khunou, 2012). Chiefs were, and in some instances still are, at the top of the hierarchy and reigned paramount over their tribal areas. Leadership was practised in a fairly autocratic manner with the assistance of community elders. While not formally recorded, traditional boundaries and the chief's authority were generally known to the tribe (Ndlela et al., 2011). Even today, and despite the weakening of the traditional leadership system due to democratization, most Africans, particularly those residing in rural areas, have much respect for the chiefs and the chieftain hierarchy. The Western influence on South African leadership came with the colonization of Southern Africa, first by the Dutch and later the British. The Western view of leadership dominated the apartheid regime's politics and became the leadership model in most private and public organizations. From 1948 up to 1994, white Afrikaner men dominated political leadership in South Africa. Rooted in a strong Protestant heritage, the boundaries between the Church and politics became completely blurred and these leaders tended to see their leadership role as a Godly instruction and duty.

To appreciate the current leadership practice and discourse in South Africa also requires that one take into account the country's political and historical context. This includes interrogating both the apartheid and the ANC (African National Congress) exile authority systems. These two systems continue to influence how authority and leadership are understood and enacted across various institutions in the country. While the two systems might be expected to be different, they actually had much in common. Both were characterized by heightened anxiety, of a persecutory kind. Mutual hatred and suspicion meant that both systems put authoritarian and oppressive authority structures in place. Totalitarian forms of control emerged within both groups as fear of the 'other' was actively propagated and used as a rationale for demanding complete submission to authority. As the struggle against apartheid gained momentum, traditional leadership within black communities was gradually joined and at times overtaken by revolutionary political leadership. Within the white society, persecutory and paranoiac leadership emerged to fend off (prevent the occurrence) the *'swart gevaar'* (black threat).

In a manner that parallels infant development (Klein, 1959), unresolved issues from the moment of birth of the new South Africa in 1994, seem to inform regressed societal and organizational leadership dynamics. This includes destructive leadership and followership behaviours, characterized by authoritarianism, an over-reliance on positional authority, bullying and harassment. Paranoid anxiety is evident in people's ambivalence about relatedness outside their in-groups, and their willingness to authorize only those they consider to be similar to themselves. Mutual splitting and projective dynamics that dominate South Africa's societal and organizational leadership experience include mutual mistrust, and the splitting off of such inherently human foibles as incompetence, greed and corruption. A dominant narrative within some sections of South African society is that black leaders are weak, corrupt and incompetent. There is, concomitantly, a tendency to valorize whiteness and to presume efficiency and effectiveness on the part of white leaders, especially white male leaders. There is a tendency in South Africa to over-scrutinize the predominantly black public leadership and to turn a blind eye to many a corporate misdemeanour by whites.

HOW IS LEADERSHIP GENERALLY UNDERSTOOD IN SOUTH AFRICA?

It is within this historical context that a politicized, racialized and gendered leadership discourse has emerged in South Africa. South African workplaces have not been spared the politicization and racialization of leadership. Consistent with this historical context, leadership in South Africa is both admired and feared, is both despised and venerated. This ambivalence, like other South African dynamics, tends to follow racial lines. For the most part, one would argue, black South Africans seem to reject, or at least to struggle internalizing 'white' authority (the majority of leaders in corporate South Africa are still white men). They (black followers) both fear and loathe this situation. For black South Africans, white forms of taking up leadership and exercising authority are often experienced as persecutory. In contrast, white South Africans tend to reject black authority and project black leaders to be incompetent, corrupt and weak. They concomitantly idealize leadership of white males in particular. While black South Africans tend to aspire for positional authority, white people, and Afrikaners in particular, tend to defer to it.

When the new democratic government came into power in 1994, progressive legislation was passed to reverse the injustices of apartheid. At an organizational level, this meant that black South Africans, and black women in particular, had to be fast-tracked into leadership positions. In a racially polarized society like South Africa, where paranoid anxiety holds sway, such measures were and continue to be experienced as taking away from white South Africans. One finds a situation whereby a number of white South Africans feel 'done to' by 'reversed discrimination'. Opportunities for mutuality get lost as black South Africans, on the other hand, feel that the negotiated settlement by their leaders, and the 'rituals and symbolisms' around it, short-changed them. A polarized societal and organizational leadership landscape thus emerges, whereby all sides of the race divide choose only to see themselves as victims and the 'other' as perpetrator. Disowned and not worked through, destructivity is driven underground, and gets enacted by various sections of society. Within South African organizations, it manifests as abusive working relationships and as oppressive authority relations. Superficial and instrumental forms of relating dominate, including between leaders and followers.

Blacks and whites in top leadership positions become ideological idols to those lower in the organization. From idealized fantasies, blacks and whites become blind to the fact that their respective idols may also have 'feet of clay'. When both black or white executives are not able to perform, and are then replaced, non-performance is denied and removal projected to result from racially discriminatory practices. Projections of white men as the only partly responsible for the inhumane legacy of apartheid now negate their ability to take up decisive leadership positions, especially if opposed by women or people of colour.

Too often in the name of political redress, leadership is seen as a position that must be filled in ways and by people to rectify past injustices, rather than the act of providing good leadership. Simultaneously, there appears to be a lack of focus to develop fast-tracked black and female leaders' competencies in order to make them successful in these positions. As result, too many people in high positions are set up for failure, just to be replaced by new ones who are again set up for failure. It is tempting to attribute such failures to general incompetence of black and/or women leaders. As systems psychodynamics inform us, however, it is never just about the individual or a particular group. The fact that their white male counterparts seem to do well enough invites us to consider the possibility that alleged '(in)competence' is due to unconscious systemic factors that serve to defend fantasies of white supremacy.

There is also, a palpable gender dynamic in South African leadership. While South Africa prides itself as having one of the most gender-transformed parliaments and government institutions, women continue to be under-represented in senior corporate leadership. The few women who make it to the apex of business leadership tend not to finish their contracts and often leave to set up their own businesses. Anecdotal stories from senior women leaders in both the public and the private sectors point to an oppressive, masculine organizational culture in South Africa. This includes the sexualization of women by both senior and junior male colleagues, as well as women being targets and victims of bullying. Problematic gender dynamics within South African organizations are also confirmed by the authors' experiences of working with women leaders from across industries. A common experience is that men do not listen to women, and that men are always regarded as more powerful and influential, even if they are on a lower job level than a female colleague. Anecdotal evidence also suggests that men appoint women, or allow women to be appointed in leadership positions, to maintain the fantasy of gender equality, but silently still lead from behind. The fact that women 'allow' this to happen is a matter for further leadership research and ongoing conversations.

In public and political leadership, idealization dominates people's thinking about leadership. It is more the party affiliation of a specific leader that plays a role in how he or she is seen as a leader, than his or her leadership abilities or competencies. This extends from the far right to the far left of South African politics. A clear example of this is the unconditional support for President Jacob Zuma by Julius Malema, then leader of the ANC Youth League (ANCYL). In 2008, Malema infamously claimed 'we will kill for Zuma.[1] This was part of concerted efforts by ANC-linked formations, including the ANC Women's League, to get the charges of corruption and rape against Zuma thrown out of court. This was done in order to facilitate his appointment as President of South Africa.

This dynamic is not restricted to only one race or one side of the political arena. Leaders of an extremist 'white' political party, the Freedom Front Plus (FF Plus) are revered for keeping 'apartheid nostalgia' alive. The main appeal of FF Plus leaders to their conservative white Afrikaner followers is their ability to feed this nostalgia in the name of preserving an imagined purity of the white Afrikaner culture, as if this culture can be ring-fenced from other cultures. It is only recently, after a black man took over leadership of the Democratic Alliance (DA), which is the main opposition party, that the DA started to transform its image as a 'white' political party. However, it now struggles to maintain the support of many white voters who only supported the DA as white opposition in the fight against the predominantly 'black' ANC.

For political leaders, leadership has become confused with narcissistic entitlement and hierarchical rights and privileges, rather than the actual leadership role with accountability to serve and deliver. The responsibility of leaders to provide hope and future direction to a nation in turmoil seems to be lost to many. Political leaders are exploiting the 'we-ness' in more collectivistic cultures for their personal and political gain, to the extent that leadership competency in political leadership is fast deteriorating (Hofstede et al., 2002). Primitive dynamics are evident as leaders seem to be elected on the basis of their ability to help various South African constituencies defend against persecutory anxiety. At a time when the country and its institutions need to build on the gains

[1]'We will kill for Zuma' (2008, June 17), retrieved 4 November 2015 from IOL News: www.iol.co.za/news/politics/we-will-kill-for-zuma-1.404646#.VjtlYlhd7bY; 'Zuma is corruption "champion"' – Malema (2015, February 13), retrieved 4 November 2015 from News 24: www.news24.com/SouthAfrica/Politics/Zuma-is-corruption-champion-Malema-20150213.

made during the transition period, one witnesses political leaders increasingly assuming leadership positions to advance narrow personal and political party interests.

ADDITIONAL FACTORS TO UNDERSTANDING LEADERSHIP IN SOUTH AFRICA

In the midst of this polarized discourse, one often gets a sense that a leadership vacuum exists in the country, as no one can be sufficiently authorized by all societal and organizational stakeholders. As a defence against the relational tensions that attend complex societal and organizational landscapes such as ours, the tendency to over-rely on formal authority comes as no surprise. Unnecessarily cumbersome organizational processes, rules and processes are often relied upon, as if to monitor and keep in check the untrustworthy other. Evidence of this in corporate South Africa can be found whereby, as part of the transformation imperative, black men and women are often placed in senior positions, including CEO positions, only to find themselves constrained by organizational processes. This includes creating a special position of Co-CEO, typically filled by a white male, as soon as a black CEO is employed. Simphiwe Tshabalala of Standard Bank and Bongani Nqwababa of Sasol are recent examples of this trend. The leadership role is thus reduced to signing off on committee decisions, which the leader may or may not agree with, but are consistent with 'policy'. This management by the committee system serves the same purpose, and ensures that organizations have in place impotent leaders who lack both positional and personal authority. Within public sector organizations, appointing leaders on short-term contracts and/or in acting positions serves to de-authorize them.

CONCLUSION

After more than 20 years of democracy, it seems that neither leaders, nor followers are able to delink the historical political struggle, and contributions made for or against the struggle, from the need to provide effective leadership. The dilemmas that seem to paralyse leadership practice in South Africa are as baffling as they are to be expected. Twenty years ago South Africa was at the forefront of providing excellent political leadership, not only to our own population but also to the world. The leadership example set by Nelson Mandela somehow got lost. Perhaps current leaders continue under the fantasy that they are still covered under the halo of Madiba's magic and have the fantasy that proverbially they still wander in his footsteps? However, this can at best be a short-term fantasy, a denial and self-deception in defence against the disillusion of the reality.

Currently, Western conceptualizations dominate leadership theory, practice and education in South Africa. This begins with, and extends to, leadership education curricula in business schools relying heavily on Western texts and theories. Even case studies used in business and leadership education tend to be those developed elsewhere, typically the USA. Perhaps the time has arrived for an Africanization of leadership. More concerted effort is needed to make sure that while leadership theory and practice in South Africa draws and builds on Western conceptualizations that it is also infused with African sensibilities.

To conclude, the main leadership issue in South Africa currently is to de-politicize, de-racialize and de-gender leadership and to refocus on basic principles of competent leadership.

REFERENCES

Hofstede, G., Van Deusen, C.A., Mueller, C.B. and Charles, T.A. (2002) 'What goals do business leaders pursue? A study in fifteen countries', *Journal of International Business Studies,* 33 (4): 785–803.

Klein, M. (1959) 'Our adult world and its roots in infancy', *Human Relations*, 12: 291–303.

Khunou, S.F. (2012) 'A legal history of the institution of traditional leadership in South Africa, Botswana and Lesotho: A comparative study', *Recht in Afrika,* 15 (2): 163–86.

Ndlela, R.N., Green, J.M. and Reddy, P.S. (2011) 'Traditional leadership and governance in Africa', *Africa Insight,* 40 (3): 1–18.

18
TURKEY
Thriving on Uncertainty: Leadership in Turkey

Serdar Karabatı: Associate Professor of Management at the Faculty of Business, Istanbul Bilgi University, Turkey

Beyza Oba: Professor of Management and Organization at the Faculty of Business, Istanbul Bilgi University, Turkey

INTRODUCTION

In this chapter, we aim to describe the dominant leadership model and its antecedents in Turkey. This dominant leadership model is characterized by a belief in the role of an authoritarian, typically male leader with full command to organize the private and the public, a model that can be articulated as a form of 'paternalistic leadership' (Aycan, 2006; Pellegrini and Scandura, 2008). We speculate that the roots of paternalist leadership can be traced back to certain historical developments and the role assumed by political actors, especially the state. We will thus provide a summary of major historical turning points and societal tensions and also direct readers' attention to current debate on leadership and political participation in Turkey in the closing sections. We also want to put forward the activism in the Gezi protests which may offer the development of an alternative Turkish leadership model, following other contemporary leadership patterns that challenge top-down and elitist practice.

HISTORICAL DEVELOPMENTS

Turks' emergence in world history dates back to late sixth to early seventh centuries. Originating from shamanic and nomadic roots, Turkic clans, in their quest for a great nation, migrated westward, mixing with, fighting, being inspired from and influencing other cultures on their path. Two significant sociopolitical outcomes occurred over this 500-year period that led to Osman forming the Ottoman Empire in 1302 (Inalcik, 2009): first, the conversion to Islam and second the entry into eastern Anatolia in 1071. The Ottoman Empire was an absolute monarchy during much of its existence and its peoples have been treated as subjects (*kul*) of the sultan (Inalcik, 2009), which is a form of Messiah leadership (Western, 2013). Subjects followed a tradition of obedience and deference (*biat*) as the sultan acted in political, military, judicial, social and religious capacities under a variety of titles. This patrimonialism was partly based on the sultan's power as head of the Muslim community, later his status as caliph, but the real power of the centre derived from a large military and administrative machine staffed by 'slave' officials (Mardin, 1998). The Ottoman society was, of course, never purely homogeneous. The empire witnessed many instances of civil resistance and internal conflicts, such as the long-ranging *Celali* revolts (between 1519 and 1648), especially during periods the bureaucratic apparatus failed in meritocracy and wealth distribution.

Roughly 500 years after its foundation, the Ottoman elites started embracing the idea of a constitutional regime, largely as a necessary response to decline in military and political power. Legal and social reforms realized by Mahmud II during his *Tanzimat* ('reorganization') period of 1839–76 not only slowed down the Ottoman Empire's demise but they also set the path towards industrialization and modernization. Despite various measures that were taken, however, the decades spanning the late nineteenth century were characterized by increased turmoil and wars. The turn into the twentieth century saw tax revolts in 1906–07, which further augmented the attention to civil liberties (Kansu, 2002) and led to the settlement of a second constitutional period in 1908. The 1908 Revolution was largely the work of the Committee of Union and Progress (CUP), which started as an underground movement and later evolved into a political movement (Zürcher, 1995: 139–48). CUP was able to confront and pressurize the Sultan and the government but could not fully take over the regime, partly due to the Sultan's stronghold in Istanbul. The period of 1908–09 was characterized by political power plays and tensions and eventually led to an uprising against CUP. On the night of 12 April 1909 armed groups led by certain religious leaders and students of religious schools took to the streets demanding an Islamic regime.

After decades of political and military struggle, modern Turkey was established in 1923. The founding fathers of the new regime, led by Mustafa Kemal (later Atatürk, meaning 'Father of the Turks'), mostly came from the ranks of the late Ottoman military and were inspired largely from the ideas of the sociologist Ziya Gökalp. They envisioned a new secular Turkish Republic, a classless society based on solidaristic nationalism. Progress would be achieved through harmonious relationships and interests were to be expressed by different occupational groups. This new Turkish state was an authoritatively secular one and developed its own definition of the proper citizen. The founding fathers underlined that the people were sovereign but they also believed that they, as the saviours of the state, had to act as a vanguard of the people in order to mobilize them (Mardin, 1998). These nationalistic goals were pursued under a single party regime until 1946, the year first democratic elections were held. As we can see, Turkish history of leadership shifts from sultans with dependent and subservient followers to new modernizing secular forces again led by a charismatic powerful individual who was seen as the 'father of Turkey'.

MAJOR TENSIONS IN TURKISH SOCIETY

Current Turkish society is faced with several dilemmas, some of which are deep-seated. One major polarization is between secularists and Islamists. This tension based on the secular–Islamic divide has been so dominant that 'it has acquired the quality of a national obsession in Turkey' (Kandiyoti, 2012: 514). The divide has been pervasive, shaping the everyday lives of ordinary people on such issues as dressing, schooling and entertainment. One of the major explanations of this deepening divide and tension has been anchored to the modernization efforts during the Republican era. In a radical effort to secularize, fundamental changes were realized in the realm of bureaucratic, legal and legislative spheres, and central institutions of Islam were weakened. Furthermore, Republican elites in line with Western notions of positivism enforced new practices (like banning Islamic head coverings for state officials, using the Latin alphabet, changing weekly holidays from Friday to Sunday) which aimed to transform existing cultural patterns (Kandiyoti, 2012). The Republican political elites tried to accomplish this transformation by restraining the political role of religion and relegating it to the practices of private life. However, these moves were not a rigid segregation between Islam and secular state matters but rather a regulation of public appearance of Islam by 'state fiat' (Gulalp, 2005: 357). For example, on the one hand, religious schools were closed, but on the other, Imam Hatip schools were established to train preachers who would conduct their services in line with the priorities of the new establishment.

Later, with the initiation of a multiparty system in 1950s, the conservative right-wing, following a populist stance, made various moves to integrate key Islamic figures into Turkish politics. Establishment of the Islamist National Salvation Party and its coalition with the Republican People's Party (founded by Ataturk) in 1973 was largely an outcome of the inclusion of these new actors in the political arena. During this period, the number of Imam Hatip schools and their enrolment increased drastically (Kandiyoti, 2012). The graduates of these schools were employed by the state as bureaucrats and by state universities as academics. State cadres that were once occupied with bureaucrats educated in secular schools were increasingly being replaced by individuals raised with a 'state-approved' religious formation. The ensuing military coup of 1980 created a political milieu where resistant voices found an additional base to mature in the name of religion (Tugal, 2009). According to a report on national culture published by the State Planning Organization in 1983, three pillars of the Turkish culture were determined to be 'family, mosque and the military'. Thus, an official transition was made from secularism to 'religion-based nationalism' (Kandiyoti, 2012: 520). Structural adjustment programmes and neoliberal policies further promoted Islamist elites who, countering the secularist elites, slowly penetrated into various aspects of economic, political and social life.

Largely related to the secular–Islamist divide, we observe another ongoing tension over the status of women in Turkish society. Women were integrated to the national project of the early Turkish Republic, in efforts towards Westernization and modernization. In this vein, a series of legal reforms were realized and new civic and criminal codes were introduced to replace the Islamic Law, and women were given equal rights with men, regarding issues of marriage, inheritance and politics. They were given the right to education (Toprak, 2005), and a culture that favours a more Western dressing style was promoted. Women were considered to have a pivotal role in the reinvention of the national culture and efforts to empower women were instrumental in cultivating Turkish nationalism. However, this transformation in the role of women within the society has been realized 'under the strict discretion and monopoly of the Kemalist elites' and an independent women's movement was not allowed (Arat, 2000: 111).

Although the secular system secured women's equality and professionalism in the public sphere, patriarchal practices and mindsets prevailed in the private realm, more so among conservative circles, in particular in rural Turkey. Authoritarian control over women's sexuality, gender roles and childrearing practices has increased during the last decade, with the implementation of a political agenda based on religion under the ruling Justice and Development Party (AK Party) led by yet another all-powerful male Turkish leader, Recep Tayyip Erdoğan. This party promotes patriarchal religious values that foster traditional roles for women (Eslen-Ziya and Erhart, 2015). As control over women's lives deepens, domestic violence, sexual harassment and honour killings tend to increase (Toprak, 2005). Thus, a severe gender divide has been re-introduced to a society reversing the secularization process that did a lot to challenge such a divide.

CONCLUSION AND DISCUSSION

The roots of the current leadership approach in Turkey can be attributed to the existence of a powerful and benevolent state tradition and to the state-created uncertainties which deem the presence of a fatherly leader necessary to resolve tensions, exert control and provide stability. At the national level, differences and tensions are largely promoted by state policies and have been instrumental in legitimizing the political actions taken. As the divisions between secular–religious, men–women, Turk and non-Turk deepen, the tensions encountered by citizens deem necessary a leadership model that incorporates a fatherly figure with full authority to organize public and private affairs, and to reduce uncertainty through authoritarian means. The coup attempt on 15 July 2016[1] by a breakaway military group with allegiance to a religious cleric has added another angle to these divisions and paved the way to self-proclaimed legitimacy for the government in taking further authoritarian measures.

Workplace leadership

These issues are not only relevant for the political sphere; they are deeply ingrained in daily lives and workplace cultures. As verified by various cross-cultural studies in management, an authoritative, paternalistic leadership and its indicative dimensions prevail in the Turkish corporate and public environments. Reflections of paternalism on workplace lead to a work culture that emphasizes the importance of fulfilling obligations to one another (and the leader) and an absence of initiative-taking (Aycan, 2006).

[1]See http://live.aljazeera.com/Event/TURKEY_COUP_ATTEMPT?Page=0 (accessed 24 November 2017) for a summary of events.

Furthermore, as the GLOBE study (Den Hartog et al., 1999) indicates, Turkey is characterized by comparatively lower scores on participation and relatively higher scores on leader charisma. In such workplaces, participation usually emerges as a top-down process rather than as a collective decision (Ascigil, 1994) and directive leadership is endorsed (Euwema et al., 2007).

Old versus new leadership

Turkish leadership has a genealogy: from Sultan and Caliph, to Atatürk, founder of the Republic and described in the Turkish Constitution as 'immortal leader and unrivalled hero', and today President Erdoğan offering himself as a new embodiment of the Father of the Turks, building an unsteady bridge between modernity and Islam and nationalism and global politics. Yet there are new leadership shoots also appearing in Turkey.

Turkey is experiencing a new wave of social movements that questions the authority of the 'old' paternalist leadership model. These developments are in line with the characteristics of 'Autonomist' leadership described by Western (2014). Rooted in the deepening social-political tensions, these movements challenge the dominant leadership logic and, as incidences of *'fearless speech'* (Foucault, 2001), bring in counter-voices on environment, biopolitics and urbanization. One example is the Gezi protests that started spontaneously in late May 2013, when a small group of protesters gathered to start a camp at a public park in Taksim Square, Istanbul, in protest against an urban regeneration project. The Gezi protest developed into a social movement leaving a serious hallmark on Turkish politics. Gezi has been instrumental in challenging the dominant leadership model and providing an example of an alternative model of distributed and autonomist leadership, decentring the leader to provide a milieu where leadership is practised collectively. The Gezi protests, as with other leaderless, anti-hierarchical social movements, organize by consensus-based decision-making mechanisms and through cooperation rather than the iron hand of a single, powerful, heroic leader. This process of organizing was also facilitated by individual information-sharing across social media. Utilization of social media and digital platforms like Twitter (Varol et al., 2014) and *Ekşi Sozluk*[2] (Furman, 2015) enabled an efficient way of information-sharing and also has been an important instrument in shaping the dynamics of the social movement by the demands, grievances, hopes and personal stories of the participants.

An investigation of the characteristics and behaviours of Gezi protestors reveal further clues about differences in Turkish society. Roughly 73% of the Gezi protestors are below

[2]*Ekşi Sozluk* (English: Sour Dictionary) is a crowdsourced hypertext dictionary and Who's Who compilation.

the age of 30 (KONDA, 2014) and are highly educated, approximately 56% of them hold a university degree or above (this is strikingly different from 12%, the overall figure for Turkey). Although most of Gezi protestors were not members of a political party (membership around 21%), they were found to be somewhat politically active. Two top choices of Gezi protestors, when asked about self-identification categories, were *liberal* and *secular* (Bilgiç and Kafkasli, n.d.). Gezi protestors mostly come from a segment of the population, representing 25% of younger adults, who are anxious that their liberties will be taken away.

It can be argued that Gezi had an impact on politics and certain conventions, the effects of which might be more observable in later years. Gezi is considered a new way of engaging with democratic practices with its emphasis on collective work, peaceful solidarity and free exchange of goods, services and ideas (Ors and Turan, 2015). The emergence of volunteer groups like *Oy ve Otesi*[3] is proof that practices based on mutual responsibility are finding a significant place. These and similar developments are likely to influence the ways autonomist leadership becomes more pervasive, despite uncertainty stemming from Turkish politics. What is clear is that there has been a very strong past tendency throughout Turkish history to turn to Messiah leaders, particularly when the country is under threat or destabilized. This destabilization is both a cause and effect of such leadership. Turkey is regionally placed at a nexus of political and social activity, bridging Europe and Asia, on the border of the warring Middle East, in tense relations with Russia. Turkey is experiencing social, religious and political change internally and having to engage with a fast-changing environment externally. It is unlikely that the model of Sultan or Messiah is a sustainable or desirable leadership approach for the near future. Whether democratic forces alongside Gezi's 'digital natives' (the young, educated, urban young activists who use social media with great effect) will have a big enough influence to offer more dispersed and democratic leadership options for Turkey is the challenge.

REFERENCES

Arat, Y. (2000) 'From emancipation to liberation: the changing role of women in Turkey's public realm', *Journal of International Affairs*, 54 (1): 107–23.

Ascigil, S.F. (1994) 'Turk endustri firmalarinda katilimla ilgili beklentiler: Is ile ilgili inanclarin etkisi', *ODTU Gelisme Dergisi*, 21 (3): 323–40.

---

[3]*Oy ve Otesi* (English: Vote and Beyond) was founded on 24 April 2014 and attracted over 30,000 volunteers in a few months. The main goals of the organization are to promote participation in the elections and to ensure transparency in the observation of ballot counts.

Aycan, Z. (2006) 'Paternalism: towards conceptual refinement and operationalization', in Uichol Kim, Kuo-shu Yang and Kwang-kuo Hwang (eds), *Scientific Advances in Indigenous Psychologies: Empirical, Philosophical, and Cultural Contributions*. London: Sage. pp. 445–66.

Bilgiç, E.E. and Kafkasli, Z. (n.d) *Gencim, Ozgurlukcuyum, Ne Istiyorum?* Istanbul: Istanbul Bilgi University. www.bilgiyay.com/Content/files/DIRENGEZI.pdf (accessed 31 October 2014).

Den Hartog, D.N., House, R.J., Hanges, P.J., Ruiz-Quintanilla, S.A. and Dorfman, P.W. (1999) 'Culture specific and cross-culturally generalizable implicit leadership theories: are attributes of charismatic/transformational leadership universally endorsed?', *The Leadership Quarterly*, 10 (2): 219–56.

Eslen-Ziya, H. and Erhart, I. (2015) 'Toward postheroic leadership: a case study of Gezi's collaborating multiple leaders', *Leadership*, 11 (4): 471–88.

Euwema, M.C., Wendt, H. and Van Emmerik, H. (2007) 'Leadership styles and group organizational citizenship behaviour across cultures', *Journal of Organizational Behaviour*, 28 (8): 1035–57.

Foucault, Michel (2001) *Fearless Speech*. Los Angeles, CA: Semiotexte.

Furman, I. (2015) 'Alternatif medya olarak akranlararasi uretim: 2013 Gezi Parki eylemlerinde Ekşi Sozluk'un rolu uzerine bir inceleme', in Baris Coban and Bora Ataman (eds), *Direnis Caginda Turkiye'de Alternatif Medya*. Istanbul: Kafka.

Gulalp, H. (2005) 'Enlightenment by fiat: secularization and democracy in Turkey', *Middle Eastern Studies*, 41 (3): 351–72.

Inalcik, Hali (2009) *Devlet-I 'Aliyye Osmanli Imparatorlugu Uzerine Arastirmalar: Klasik Donem (1302–1606)*. Istanbul: Is Bankasi Kultur.

Kandiyoti, D. (2012) 'The travails of the secular: puzzle and paradox in Turkey', *Economy and Society*, 41 (4): 513–31.

Kansu, Aykut (2002) *1908 Devrimi*. Istanbul: Iletisim.

KONDA (2014) 'Public perception of the "Gezi protests": Who were the people at Gezi Park?' 5 June 2014. http://konda.com.tr/en/raporlar/KONDA_Gezi_Report.pdf (accessed 9 November 2017).

Mardin, S. (1998) 'Some notes on normative conflicts in Turkey', in Peter Berger (ed.), *The Limits of Social Cohesion*. Boulder, CO: Westview Press. pp. 207–32.

Ors, I.R. and Turan, O. (2015) 'The manner of contention: pluralism at Gezi', *Philosophy & Social Criticism*, 41 (4–5): 453–63.

Pellegrini, E.K. and Scandura, T.A. (2008) 'Paternalistic leadership: a review and agenda for future research', *Journal of Management*, 34 (3): 566–93.

Toprak, B. (2005) 'Secularism and Islam: the building of modern Turkey', *Macalester International*, 15: 27–43.

Tugal, Cihan (2009) *Passive Revolution: Absorbing the Islamic Challenge to Capitalism*. Stanford, CA: Stanford University Press.

Varol, O., Ferrara, E., Ogan, C.L., Menczer, F. and Flammini, A. (2014) 'Evolution of online user behaviour during a social upheaval', in Proceedings of the 2014 ACM Web Science Conference. Association for Computing Machinery. June. pp. 81–90.

Western, Simon (2013) *Leadership: A Critical Text*, 2nd edn. London: Sage.

Western, S. (2014) 'Autonomist leadership in leaderless movements: anarchists leading the way', *Ephemera: Theory & Politics in Organization*, 14 (4): 673–98.

Zürcher, Erik (1995) *Modernlesen Turkiye'nin Tarihi*. Istanbul: Iletisim.

19
UNITED KINGDOM
Dis-United Kingdom? Leadership at a Crossroads

Richard Bolden: Professor of Leadership and Management, University of the West of England, Bristol, UK

Morgen Witzel: Fellow at the Centre for Leadership Studies, University of Exeter, UK

THE ESSENCE OF LEADERSHIP IN THE UK

The United Kingdom (UK) is an English-speaking nation in North-West Europe, comprised of four countries – the mainland nations of England, Scotland and Wales (collectively called 'Great' Britain) and Northern Ireland (which was formed in 1921 by an Act of the British Parliament that split the nation of Ireland into two). In June 2015, the overall UK population was estimated at 65.1 million, of which 54.8m lived in England, 5.4m in Scotland, 3.1m in Wales and 1.9m in Northern Ireland (Office for National Statistics, 2016).

Britain was formerly the centre of a major colonial empire, with Queen Elizabeth II (the current British monarch), remaining the titular head of the Commonwealth – a partnership of 53 nations, including many former members of the British Empire. In 1973 the UK joined the European Economic Community (now the European Union) and following a referendum in June 2016 (in which the public voted by a margin of 51.9% to 48.1% to leave the EU) is now negotiating the terms of its exit (colloquially termed 'Brexit').

Lewis (2006: 115) describes the UK as having a 'casual' leadership style – with a preference for tact, diplomacy, informality, compromise and fairness. He also notes the British tendency for self-deprecation and humour (where leaders may be frowned upon for taking themselves too seriously) alongside a desire to appear 'business-like' (with a clear demarcation between personal and professional life).

Hofstede's latest figures (Hofstede Centre, n.d.) characterize the UK as high on 'individualism' and 'masculinity', low on 'power distance' and 'uncertainty avoidance', and moderate on 'long-term orientation'.[1] This profile suggests a preference for meritocratic leadership and management practices, a willingness to cope with uncertainty and ambiguity, and a tendency to recognize and reward 'masculine' leadership and management behaviours.

The GLOBE study of leadership and cultural differences in 62 societies (House et al., 2004) captured separate empirical data for England and Ireland[2] – placing both within the 'Anglo cluster' alongside the USA, Canada, Australia, New Zealand and White South Africa. A similar framework to that of Hofstede was used to assess cultural differences, with Anglo societies scoring in the mid-range on all dimensions other than 'power distance' (which was high) and 'gender egalitarianism' (which was low).[3] In terms of societal values (i.e. views on how things *should be* rather than how they necessarily *are*) performance orientation, humane orientation, family collectivism and future orientation were

[1]This is a similar profile to the USA, with the exception of uncertainty avoidance, which is lower in the UK, and long-term orientation, which is lower in the USA.

[2]Although the Irish data refer only to the Republic of Ireland, which is not part of the UK.

[3]Note this is different from Hofstede, who put power distance as low for the UK.

all ranked highly and power distance relatively low, with all others in the mid-range (Ashkanasy et al., 2002).

In addition to cultural practices and values, the GLOBE study explored leadership preferences. Respondents from Anglo societies showed strongest preference for 'charismatic', 'team-orientated' and 'participative' styles, with ratings for 'humane' leadership also relatively high and 'autonomous' and 'self-protective' leadership relatively low. In a detailed analysis of GLOBE findings for England, Booth (2008) highlighted a strong focus on leading change through inspiration, vision and clear direction. He also highlighted a tendency for employees in England to be critical of leaders who were perceived to be autocratic, bureaucratic or driven by status. Evidence from the 2012 CIPD Annual Survey supports this claim, with 72% of organizations in England reporting an overall deficit of appropriately skilled leaders and managers, 65% reporting a paucity of leadership and management skills among senior managers and 85% reporting poor leadership and management skills among line managers and supervisors.

Together these findings suggest a somewhat ambivalent approach to leadership in the UK – with individuals and organizations demonstrating both an appetite for clear and inspiring leadership and a healthy scepticism of bureaucracy and power, with a preference for participative decision-making and teamwork. Given the large and diverse population of the UK, however, any attempt to characterize national leadership styles and/or preferences is inevitably prone to substantial generalization. In particular, how far the findings for England can be generalized across the rest of the UK is a moot point. It is likely, for example, that leadership in Northern Ireland might share at least as many characteristics with the Republic of Ireland as with England.[4] National analyses also mask significant differences within and between regions – with substantial variation across major cities such as London, Birmingham and Manchester (reflected through a heterogeneity of affluence, culture and ethnicity) and between urban and rural areas. As with almost any country, overall generalizations about leadership, though valuable, must be understood within the context of potential regional and temporal variation.

MAIN INFLUENCES ON LEADERSHIP

In his analysis of the GLOBE data for England, Booth (2008) concluded, 'if a characterization of England is possible, at the heart of it would be an understanding of the fundamentally divided nature of society'. He described this as a tension between the values and practices of traditionalism and liberalism.

[4]In analysis of the GLOBE data for the Republic of Ireland, Keating and Martin (2008) suggest, 'the fundamental difference between the Irish and English historical experience is that the English have been a conquering people, the Irish a conquered'.

Many British leadership and management practices have their roots in traditional institutions. Notably the UK is one of the few Westernized nations that retains both a monarchy and a democratically elected parliament. Many industries also have long histories – with Great Britain[5] initiating the Industrial Revolution in the late eighteenth century.

The concept of leadership has long been associated with the English language.[6] The etymology of the verb 'to lead' can itself be traced back to the Old English word *lithan* ('to travel') which was introduced in around 800 AD and revised around 400 years later to mean 'to guide' (Grace, 2003). The term 'leader' was coined in around 1300 to acknowledge the role played by politicians and statesmen but was not applied to other organizations until the nineteenth century when the term 'leadership' emerged to describe the activity undertaken by 'leaders' (Grace , 2003). Bass (1990) thus describes 'leadership' as a concern mainly of people of Anglo descent, used since the twentieth century to promote concepts of democracy and shared purpose, particularly in the USA (Rost, 1991).

For a relatively small nation, the UK has had a huge impact on how leadership is understood and enacted globally – a fact that can be largely traced to its colonial legacy. At its peak, Britain's empire covered almost a quarter of the Earth's total land area and one-fifth of its population. While all but a very few of Britain's overseas territories have now been granted independence, many retain key aspects of the infrastructure that was put in place by the British. This is perhaps most obvious in the transport infrastructure, with many former colonies retaining the British tradition of driving on the left-hand side of the road, but extends much further into the structure of public and private sector institutions. Lange (2004) identifies significant differences in the political and economic development of former British colonies depending on whether or not they were directly governed by European settlers or indirectly governed by indigenous populations on behalf of the British. His findings demonstrate 'that there is a negative and robust relationship between the extent of indirect rule and political stability, bureaucratic effectiveness, lack of state regulatory burden, rule of law, and lack of government corruption even controlling for other factors' (2004: 906).

While the previous point highlights one important aspect of 'postcolonialism' (the enduring legacy of colonization following the end of colonial rule) another, and perhaps even more significant legacy, is the impact on culture and identity. As Dutton et al. (1998: 7) argue:

[5]Note that it was not until 1801 that the Kingdom of Great Britain and the Kingdom of Ireland were united to create the UK.

[6]While the national language of the UK is English, recognized regional languages exist in Wales, Scotland and Ireland.

> The countries of the West ruled the peoples of the non-western world. Their political dominance had been secured and was underwritten by coercive means – by conquest and in blood. It was further underwritten by narratives of improvement, of the civilizing mission and the white man's burden, which were secured in systems of knowledge which made sense of these narratives, and were, in turn, informed and shaped by them ... the administration and exploitation of the colonies shaped the West's sense of self, and created new forms and regimes of knowledge.

From this perspective, the British sense of political, military, economic and cultural strength and superiority that emerged through its dominance over large parts of the world continues to bolster its sense of significance and place in global events. Throughout the nineteenth and early twentieth centuries Britons perceived themselves as being 'leaders' in an intellectual and spiritual sense, as Dutton et al. suggest, with a responsibility to set an example that the rest of the world would follow. Correspondingly, many of those who were colonized developed a sense of inferiority and an aspiration towards the values and priorities of their oppressors, traces of which are still evident today. This latter point is significant in terms of conceptualizations of 'leadership' given that this concept is so closely linked to English language and values. Hence, it is perhaps unsurprising that the British tendency towards individualism and masculinity, as described in the previous section, remains embedded in much leadership theory and practice around the world.

Since the end of the colonial era Britain has retained its sense of being a proud, strong and independent nation – a perception at least partly sustained through its experience of World War II. While other nations of Europe were either occupied by and/or in allegiance with the Nazis, Britain remained free. While Britain's ability to resist invasion was dependent on a range of factors, including the support of its allies (many from former British colonies), its island geography and failures of Nazi military strategy in other regions (particularly along the Eastern Front), popular stories and recollections focus mainly on the defiant approach of the British people. This is exemplified by Prime Minister Winston Churchill, who topped a 2002 BBC poll of the '100 Greatest Britons' with 28.1% of the vote, demonstrating his continuing significance as a national exemplar of strong leadership.[7]

In the years since World War II Britain has seen significant socioeconomic change – with a trend towards liberalism as highlighted by Booth (2008). A growing consumerism, fuelled by economic prosperity, has brought into question many traditional divisions in society and the values that underpin them. There has also been a diversification of the

---

[7]Other people in the Top 10 included Isambard Kingdom Brunel (24.6%), Princess Diana (13.9%), Charles Darwin (6.9%), William Shakespeare (6.8%), Sir Isaac Newton (5.2%), Queen Elizabeth I (4.4%), John Lennon (4.2%), Horatio Nelson (3%) and Oliver Cromwell (2.8%). For further details see http://news.bbc.co.uk/1/hi/entertainment/2509465.stm (accessed 8 November 2017).

population, with an overall increase in other ethnic groups in proportion to white British and Irish.[8] Along with this are changes in religious affiliations. While 2011 census data from England and Wales indicate that Christianity remains the dominant religion (59% of the population), 25% claim no religious affiliation and a significant minority (5%) are Muslim (Office for National Statistics, 2012).

The UK has a reputation as a tolerant and inclusive society. However, a number of factors, including immigration, an ageing population, a government policy of public-sector austerity following the 2008 financial crisis, and the results of the controversial Brexit vote, highlight a tension between the principles of individualism and collectivism. Despite the cultural dimensions approach of Hofstede and GLOBE suggesting an either/or position there is much evidence to suggest a coexistence of both factors within British society. Alongside a popular fascination with 'heroic' leaders such as Churchill, Wellington, Nelson or Cromwell, for example, people of the UK have a long history of championing the fight of ordinary people against the elites – such as the medieval peasant leader Wat Tyler, the abolitionist William Wilberforce and the Tolpuddle Martyrs. The tension between individualism and collectivism was illustrated particularly well by the miners' strike of 1984–5, when two alternative leadership 'heroes' emerged. For some, the hero was the individualist Prime Minister Margaret Thatcher who 'stood firm' against the miners; for others, the heroes were the miners themselves, who exhibited strong leadership and courage in the struggle.[9]

A final observation for this section is the role of UK-based leadership research, theory and development. Given the links between leadership and the English language it is perhaps unsurprising that, alongside the USA, British academics and authors have had a disproportionately large impact on the field of leadership studies. While systematic research on leadership really only began in the mid-twentieth century the origin of trait-based, behavioural and charismatic approaches can be traced back to the 'great man' approach advocated by Thomas Carlyle (a Scotsman) in his book *On Heroes, Hero-Worship, and the Heroic in History,* first published in 1840. While leadership research from the USA tends to take a positivist or realist approach, underpinned by large-scale statistical analysis of quantitative data, there remains a strong tradition of interpretivism in UK leadership studies, informed by critical, qualitative and inductive approaches.

This alternative approach to leadership studies tends to be featured in journals such as *Leadership, Human Relations* and *Organization Studies* and is exemplified by the emerging field of 'critical leadership studies' (CLS) (Alvesson and Spicer, 2012; Collinson, 2014). While mainstream approaches tend to present leadership as an inherently positive and desirable phenomenon CLS seeks to expose and explore underlying assumptions about

[8]For a summary of trends from 2003 to 2013 see http://bit.ly/1NbGgOE (accessed 8 November 2017).

[9]The miners' experience is depicted memorably in the film *Brassed Off.*

leadership and its potential for perpetuating abuses of power and authority – in effect tapping into the British tendencies towards scepticism, equality and independence.

LEADERSHIP TODAY AND IN THE FUTURE

In many regards the UK stands at a crossroads in terms of its relationship with, and experience of, leadership. Following many centuries as a leading world power its position is somewhat less certain than it once was. A Russian official at the G20 Summit in 2013 famously dismissed Britain as a 'small island no one listens to' (*Daily Telegraph*, 2013) yet it was recently ranked 5th in the world for GDP (World Bank, 2014) and 1st for 'soft power'[10] (Portland Communications, 2015).

What happens to leadership in the UK next is partly dependent on the outcome of two major changes to the constitution and makeup of the nation. First, there is the issue of the UK's vote to leave the European Union. The outcome of the referendum took many by surprise, highlighting widespread dissatisfaction with the culture of public and private sector leadership over recent years. Alongside the political and economic ramifications of the UK's departure from the EU is a fundamental need to re-evaluate its sense of national identity and place in the world. Following four decades of ever-closer union with its European neighbours, Britain is now going it alone and seeking new alliances and opportunities. Second, there is the question of the nature of the relationship between UK member countries. In September 2014, the Scottish people voted 55.3% to 44.7% to remain in the UK, however, since the Brexit vote it seems quite possible that a second referendum may be called in the future, which may ultimately lead to the break-up of the United Kingdom.

The government's response to these challenges is likely to be further devolution of powers from England to Scotland, Northern Ireland and Wales, alongside devolution of powers from Westminster (the seat of UK central government) to different regions of England. Such changes will have an impact on the sense of national unity, and is likely to accelerate the emergence of different local leadership cultures and practices, making research into regional variations an increasingly important area for further research.

As the UK reviews and renegotiates its sense of national identity and its relationship with the rest of the world – navigating a path through traditionalism and liberalism – the British tendency towards informality, self-deprecation and tolerance of ambiguity may work to its advantage. To understand British stoicism, it helps to understand something of the infamous British weather. As the American author Bill Bryson (1996) eloquently expressed it:

---

[10]The concept of 'soft power', coined by the Harvard professor Joseph Nye, focuses on the ability to shape the attitudes and behaviours of others through non-coercive means, such as positive attraction and persuasion. At a national level, it is enacted through political values, culture and foreign policy.

> Sometimes it rained, but mostly it was just dull, a land without shadows. It was like living inside Tupperware.

Britons are renowned for weathering the storm – they've done it before and they'll do it again. To understand leadership in the UK it is important to understand its culture and history. There is much fine writing to be found on the subject – far too much to cover in this short chapter. Rather than relying solely on leadership textbooks for answers, however, next time can we encourage you to try some British literature, comedy, drama, music or art? Shakespeare, Byron, Bowie, Banksy and Monty Python all have much to say about leadership.

REFERENCES

Alvesson, M. and Spicer, A. (2012) 'Critical leadership studies: the case for critical performativity', *Human Relations*, 65 (3): 367–90.

Ashkanasy, N.M., Trevor-Roberts, E. and Earnshaw, L. (2002) 'The Anglo cluster: legacy of the British Empire', *Journal of World Business*, 37 (1): 28–39.

Bass, Bernard M. (1990) *Bass and Stogdill's Handbook of Leadership: Theory, Research and Managerial Applications*, 3rd edn. New York: Free Press.

Booth, S. (2008) 'Inspirational variations? Culture and leadership in England', in Jagdeep S Chhokar, Felix C. Brodbeck and Robert J. House (eds), *Culture and Leadership Across the World: The GLOBE Book of In-depth Studies of 25 Societies*. New York: Lawrence Erlbaum. pp. 335–60.

Bryson, B. (1996) *Notes from a Small Island*. London: Black Swan.

CIPD (Chartered Institute of Personnel and Development) (2012) *Learning and Talent Development: Annual Survey Report 2012*. London: CIPD.

Collinson, D. (2014) 'Dichotomies, dialectics and dilemmas: new directions for critical leadership studies?', *Leadership*, 10 (1): 36–55.

Daily Telegraph (2013) 'Russia mocks Britain, the little island'. http://bit.ly/1QcptS4 (accessed 5 January 2016).

Dutton, M., Gandhi, L. and Seth, S. (1998) 'Postcolonial studies: a beginning', *Postcolonial Studies*, 1 (1): 7–11.

Grace, M. (2003) 'The origins of leadership: the etymology of leadership'. Paper presented at Annual Conference of the International Leadership Association, Guadalajara, Mexico.

Hofstede Centre (n.d.) 'Country comparison: What about the UK?' http://geert-hofstede.com/united-kingdom.html (accessed 4 January 2016).

House, Robert J., Hanges, Paul J., Javidan, Monsour, Dorfman, Peter W. and Gupta, Vipin (eds) (2004) *Culture, Leadership and Organizations: The GLOBE Study of 62 Societies*. Thousand Oaks, CA: Sage.

Keating, M. and Martin, G.S. (2008) 'Leadership in the Republic of Ireland', in Jagdeep S. Chhokar, Felix C. Brodbeck and Robert J. House (eds), *Culture and Leadership Across the World: The GLOBE Book of In-depth Studies of 25 Societies*. New York: Lawrence Erlbaum. pp. 361–96.

Lange, M.K. (2004) 'British colonial legacies and political development', *World Development*, 32 (6): 905–22.

Lewis, Richard D. (2006) *When Cultures Collide: Leading Across Cultures*, 3rd edn. London: Nicholas Brealey.

Office for National Statistics (2012) Religion in England and Wales 2011. www.ons.gov.uk/ons/dcp171776_290510.pdf (accessed 4 January 2016).

Office for National Statistics (2016) Population Estimates. http://bit.ly/28IITPF (accessed 27 July 2016).

Portland Communications (2015) Soft Power Index. http://softpower30.portland-communications.com/ranking (accessed 5 January 2016).

Rost, Joseph (1991) *Leadership for the Twenty-First Century*. Westport, CT: Praeger.

World Bank (2014) GDP Rankings. http://data.worldbank.org/data-catalog/GDP-ranking-table (accessed 5 January 2016).

20
UNITED STATES OF AMERICA
Mourning in America: Leadership in the Divided States of America

Zachary Gabriel Green: Professor of Practice, Leadership Studies, University of San Diego and Executive Leadership Coach, World Bank, USA

Cheryl Getz: Associate Professor and Director of Leadership Minor, Department of Leadership Studies, University of San Diego, USA

TRIUMPH VERSUS INSTABILITY: TWO VIEWS OF AN EMERGING AMERICA

The year was 1984. Economic prosperity was present once more in the United States. President Ronald Reagan adopted the theme of 'morning in America' in his re-election campaign as a powerful metaphor to express what many at the time saw as the dawning of a renewal in the nation. Winning the election in a landslide, the legacy of leadership in the Reagan years became cemented in his second term with the iconic words, 'Mr Gorbachev – Tear down this wall.' With the subsequent liberation of East Berlin, the breakup of the Soviet Union and the end of the Cold War, many considered the USA the pre-eminent superpower in the world (Robinson, 2007).

Less discernible during this same period was the dark night of dreams deferred for another America (Hughes, 1959). Millions of the most vulnerable, disproportionately from poor, urban communities, largely African American and Hispanic, accrued few benefits and little liberation from their situation through the trickle-down economics policies of the era (Frank, 2007). This America also included a growing white underclass that inhabited arid post-industrial landscapes and inhospitable urban centres, locked away – literally and metaphorically – in cycles of poverty. Meanwhile in the Middle East and beyond, the presence of extremist sentiments began to be expressed. Violence and volatility from uncertain sources became the new norm. In places like Libya, Lebanon and Lockerbie, ambiguous faceless and stateless agents of 'terrorism' launched a boundless age of war against the infidels representing US interests. Still oceans away, this complex and contentious transformation was not yet visible to most Americans (Dabla-Norris, 2015). As such, the strong belief in meritocracy where anyone from anywhere could achieve the 'American Dream' through hard work and self-reliance persisted. Leadership across all sectors in the USA remained emblematic of these beliefs. Few noticed how the fissures of structural inequality, systemic discrimination, economic disparity and global antipathy would decades later reveal a divided state and *mourning* in America.

Signs of a divided country became most evident in terms of economic disparity. The contrast between the millions who live in despair and poverty and the fact that the USA continues to produce world-leading companies and billionaires is one telling marker of this trend. Charismatic and energetic innovators who demonstrated leadership by working tirelessly created new organizational forms and business models that embraced the growing digital age. Leaders like Elon Musk provide one of the examples of how the USA still integrates 'educated immigrants' and offers a context in which amazing success is achieved. Musk, a South African educated in Canada, became a US citizen and is CEO of Tesla (electric car manufacturer). He also holds other leadership roles with innovative companies, including one devoted to exploring private space travel. His mission is humanitarian and environmental while being matched by phenomenal business success (Vance, 2015).

Yet, leadership in the USA today is also divided along political lines. Stories like that of Musk, as well as the founders of Google and Apple, an immigrant and a child of immigrants respectively, are walled away narratives as the nation lurches towards isolationism in a quest for security. These leaders represent parts of the country that have performed exceptionally well (e.g. Silicon Valley). In such areas leadership is dynamic and innovative while other sectors continue to suffer post-industrial decline. Many minority communities in some urban centres face deteriorating conditions. Yet, unnamed and hidden leadership at the grassroots level continues unabated. Community activists and religious advocates show amazing resilience, even in the face of a dramatic change in political circumstance.

Historically, the Protestant work ethic and the revolutionary capacity to integrate diverse communities produced US leadership in business and civil society. These values nurtured a young nation towards developing the exceptional capacities needed over the next two centuries to become the world's leading economic and military force. Yet, today the position of the USA in the world is in question given the 2016 presidential election results. There is no longer a political or social consensus that the American Dream is alive and well. With potential signs of decline, an American identity crisis is expressed through the polemics of the contemporary political debate and revealed through the leaders and leadership it produces today. Indeed, this growing divide inspires leadership in the form of a Trump presidency; one that can be termed protectionist but can as readily be characterized as regressive, inward looking and defensive (Zakaria, 2017).

HISTORICAL SEEDS OF SEPARATION

Leadership in the USA today reflects aspects of the nation's founding and the settling of the land by the first Europeans. When Puritans established the Plymouth Colony in the New World, they sought to escape religious persecution and brought with them ideals that separated them from European established churches. These early pilgrims believed God's favour was afforded and revealed through those who acted with individual initiative and effort. With the fervour of a *chosen people*, they believed that they were God's instruments in this 'promised land'. The indigenous people they encountered were *the other* and considered uneducated heathens who could readily be placed aside, removed or killed as needed. Such beliefs and practices meant that the *chosen* could live into promise of what God provided. In the years to come, the march of 'Manifest Destiny' that would stretch to the Pacific alongside the growing slave trade across the Atlantic set the stage for an America where the privileged few would retain wealth and power in *these* United States of America.

The Declaration of Independence composed by Thomas Jefferson inscribed life, liberty and the pursuit of happiness as unalienable rights for individuals of the nascent nation. The Enlightenment greatly influenced Jefferson's writing. He was also inspired by egalitarian and non-conformist liberal sects such as the Quakers who left England under persecution for their radical beliefs, such as equality for women and the right to worship freely (Meacham, 2012). Thus, a split occurred that has survived centuries of debate, between the Puritans who believed in American exceptionalism that evolved from being of the *chosen* people, and a more liberal tradition that believes in equal opportunities, and freedom of expression and religious beliefs. Both sides of this split lay claim to be inheritors of the Founding Fathers' aspirations.

Equality of *men* was enshrined into the fibre of what the country would become. As the nation grew, leadership was expressed by the ideals of self-reliance, a more secular expression of earlier Puritan principles. Individual authority, coupled with a consistent questioning of institutions, was seen as the means through which material success was attained, achievement gained and a life of liberty assured. In this respect, leadership and the rights of the individual were essentially synonymous with the founding of the country. Yet, what is shared even in the face of these divides is a near reverence for charisma as a core characteristic for the representatives of this leadership. A Trump presidency and the clarion call of 'Make America Great Again' harkens to a mythic lost horizon that denies the demographic realities of a changing nation and the nature of global interdependence. A closer examination of these narratives may help to highlight the tensions as well as reveal the nature of the divided states.

THE DIVIDED *NOT UNITED* STATES

Abraham Lincoln is perhaps one of the most iconic representations of 'Great Man' leadership in US history. President during the Civil War, he is remembered for a pragmatic and strategic approach to a conflict that preserved the Union and emancipated millions of slaves of African ancestry. Though he lived to see the unconditional surrender of the Confederacy, he would be assassinated well before his leadership could be tested in the process of healing the nation and unifying the country. In many respects, the USA continues to fight the Civil War. Now, more than 150 years later, the divisions that tore the country asunder continue in proxy political wars along geographic, economic, religious, social identity and racial lines. The old Confederacy has experienced resurgence in being solidly what are called *red states*, which vote consistently for conservative, often Evangelical Christian, and Republican candidates. The cause of the South has been further emboldened by a Supreme Court that sharply reduced the impact of landmark Civil Rights era legislation that had largely ended practices that suppressed the vote of African

Americans. The Court ruled that the laws unduly burdened these states, with arguments that in the 50 years since the legislation these discriminatory practices had come to an end (Liptak, 2013).

Additional challenges represented by the ascendancy of Barack Obama, the defeat of Hillary Clinton and the prominence of Apple's openly gay CEO, Tim Cook, highlight the centrality of the tension that sexuality, gender and race represent in this national discourse. Additionally, recent Supreme Court rulings that extend marriage rights regardless of sexual orientation, and other laws protecting transgender people have further challenged the social cohesion of the country. It is evident that the changing face of political and business leadership in the USA is being met with an unconscious backlash in conservative areas where a desire to return to white male, heterosexual dominance as the norm resulted in the election of Donald Trump. The escalating and contentious discourse on these social issues brings into question the pace of change, the role of government and the nature of leadership.

The American psyche was notably influenced by the events of 9/11, the terrorist attacks that bought down towering symbols of American identity, and created fear that has yet to abate. The corresponding financial crisis and Great Recession of 2008 added to the uncertainty about what was once believed to be the solid financial foundation of the nation. Shaken and suddenly questioning the capacity of an irrefutable military to keep Americans safe, coupled with unprecedented economic hardship, the USA entrusted its leaders to exchange liberties for security. Followers motivated by fear now seek to keep those who represent difference, and thereby threat, from entering across the boundaries of the country. Whether these people are from the US southern border and dream of economic opportunities or are international asylum seekers who live in hopes of finding refuge from war, the response from many corners of America and authorized by the Trump administration is to keep *the other* out. At the other liberal extreme are those that see intrusions on privacy and policies that exclude as draconian and xenophobic. They tend to demonize conservative Americans, labelling their fellow citizens as intolerant and equating their views with all forms of 'ism's' and bigotry. The vehement entrenchment held in these polarized narratives largely mutes whatever voices of moderation there may be. Thus, those who hold leadership roles become mirrors of these views and merely reflect the polarity.

CHARISMATIC LEADERSHIP AND BEYOND

Leadership in the USA is often synonymous with charisma. While research does suggest that charisma is an important component of leadership, in the American context this trait is also associated with a persistent messianic call (Western, 2013). The wish for relief from social and economic ills is projected onto the charismatic figure. Through much of American history, formal and informal leadership roles are afforded to such persons for the illusion of protection and order these leaders are believed to offer (Heifetz, 1999). In the USA, the inevitable dependency and disappointment leads to literal and symbolic assassination of the leader. From Abraham Lincoln, to John F. Kennedy, to Malcolm X, to Martin Luther King, elements of what they envisioned were silenced with the bullets that took their lives. With their deaths, the fragility of their followership and the agenda they represented were often systematically dismantled and diluted, leaving the core vision of their leadership lost.

In these instances, the American character is revealed where person and role are conflated. In other words, the underlying values of self-reliance are challenged by the ease with which charismatic leadership in politics, the Church, business and popular culture is embraced time and time again – and then rejected. Those who fear they have the most to lose in the emerging world embrace a leadership that is primitive, unfiltered, bigoted and xenophobic. When African Americans and women can hold the highest office in the land, the white underclass, living in post-industrial landscapes of desperation, no longer see themselves as represented, and sense a loss of power and privilege. As such, many of these same voters who embraced a message of hope in twice electing Obama succumbed to fear and turned to a new president. In Trump, they see a leader who offers to save and protect the land from those who would attack the country and steal their jobs (Tyson and Maniam, 2016).

In contrast, there is another America that recognizes its role of leadership in the world. This America acknowledges the devastation brought by its recent military actions and the nation's disproportionate use of global resources to fuel its economy. These citizens argue for greater equity, transparency and fairness in how the country takes up its superpower status. Leadership is then expressed differently; more nuanced and networked than the competing and polarized visions of America (Ibarra and Hunter, 2007). Hence, the USA faces the challenge of whether this period of deep division will represent the continued descent into darkness of a once great nation or the dawn of opportunity for immense united renewal. In particular, advances in technology offer a parallel metaphor for leadership, producing more distributed networks of leaders and emergent theories and practice that are adaptive to new contexts.

LEADERSHIP AND TECHNOLOGY

At the turn of the twentieth century with the industrial revolution came migration from rural to urban life in the USA. The names Carnegie, Rockefeller and Ford were synonymous with these advances and also became the faces of philanthropy. In the twenty-first century, the revolution is technology. Apple, Microsoft and Facebook are among the largest and most influential global businesses. The nature of their leadership practices shapes how Americans and much of the world interacts. Among the founders of these technology companies are Steve Jobs, Bill Gates and Mark Zuckerberg. They, and others like them, are the new faces of wealth, influencing how leadership is represented and practised in the USA. We saw in Steve Jobs the continuation of the self-reliant leader, willing to stand alone with ideas that broke paradigms of business. The iconic introduction of the Macintosh computer literally demonstrated the need to smash the conventions of the time to introduce a new understanding of what was possible technologically. The blend of transforming, charismatic and situational leadership with true messianic force is why Apple is the dominant personal technology corporation in the world. We see these practices replicated throughout Silicon Valley and beyond. In contrast, Bill Gates and Mark Zuckerberg represent the renaissance of the great American tradition of philanthropy. They model servant leadership in that they have committed the vast majority of their lifetime wealth to address issues in the nation and the world.

Yet beyond these individuals, another factor much more core to leadership is linked to the role of technology in the lives of the rest of the world. Access to personal digital devices has become an extension of the person in the USA. Pew Research indicates that 91% of Americans own and regularly use a cell phone, tablet, or other digital device, and 65% are making use of smartphones (Anderson, 2015). These *digital natives* are as accustomed to communicating with their devices as they are face-to-face, and will soon occupy the majority of US leadership positions. As such, it can be argued that the digital persona is increasingly as important as who people present themselves to be when they physically meet another person. The corresponding impact on leadership becomes as much about how one presents their latest tweet or post at a social networking site as it is about direct personal presentation, darkly mastered by Trump. The challenge of the emerging future is in how the USA will make use of this liberty and opportunity.

CONCLUSION

In the final analysis, leadership in the United States of America may well be at a crossroads that requires addressing and holding complexity. Managing the current and historic tensions creates the opportunity for the nation to reach once more towards a fuller expression of its identity. With cultural diversity and information technology as rich resources for a different leadership interface, the USA is faced with a choice. If the nation continues to perpetuate a narrative dominated by a Messianic view of leadership that drives followers to action based in fear and polarity, the discourse will be incomplete and destructive to the fibre of the country. Likewise, messianic leadership that presents the fantasy of salvation and hope is problematic. This hyper-optimism can occasionally produce outstanding results but more often produces dependent followers who give up their autonomy and fall in love with the idealized leader until the inevitable failure occurs, and the leader is crucified. While such a pattern is part of the American psyche and may well continue into the near future, a more integral vision of leadership that embraces the potential of what the United States may yet become is needed to overcome the contemporary mourning in America.

REFERENCES

Anderson, M. (2015) 'Technology device ownership: 2015'. Pew Research Center. 29 October. www.pewresearch.org/data-trend/media-and-technology/device-ownership/ (accessed 9 January 20017).

Dabla-Norris, E., Kochhar, K., Suphaphiphat, N., Ricka, F. and Tsounta, E. (2015) 'Causes and consequences of income inequality: a global perspective'. International Monetary Fund. 15 June. www.imf.org/external/pubs/cat/longres.aspx?sk=42986.0 (accessed 15 January 2017).

Frank, R.H. (2007) 'In the real world of work and wages, trickle-down theories don't hold up', *New York Times*, 11 April. www.nytimes.com/2007/04/12/business/12scene.html (accessed 15 January 2017).

Heifetz, Ronald A. (1994) *Leadership Without Easy Answers*. Cambridge: Harvard University Press.

Hughes, Langston (1959) *Selected Poems*: New York: Vintage Classics.

Ibarra, H. and Hunter, M.L. (2007) 'How leaders create and use networks', *Harvard Business Review*, January issue. https://hbr.org/2007/01/how-leaders-create-and-use-networks (accessed 12 January 2017).

Liptak, A. (2013) 'Supreme Court invalidates key part of Voting Rights Act', *New York* Times, 25 June. www.nytimes.com/2013/06/26/us/supreme-court-ruling.html (accessed 21 December 2016).

Meacham, Jon (2012) *Thomas Jefferson: The Art of Power*. New York: Random House.

Robinson, P. (2007) 'Tear down this wall', *Prologue Magazine*, Summer, 39 (2). www.archives.gov/publications/prologue/2007/summer/berlin.html (accessed 4 January 2017).

Tyson, A. and Maniam, S. (2016) 'Behind Trump's victory: divisions by race, gender, education'. Pew Research. 9 November. www.pewresearch.org/fact-tank/2016/11/09/behind-trumps-victory-divisions-by-race-gender-education/ (accessed 25 January 2017).

Vance, Ashlee (2015) *Elon Musk: How the Billionaire CEO of SpaceX and Tesla is Shaping Our Future*. London: Virgin Books.

Western, Simon (2013) *Leadership: A Critical Text*, 2nd edn. Thousand Oaks, CA: Sage.

Zakaria, F. (2017) 'Trump's protectionism reversing 70 Years of American foreign policy'. Newsmax 27 January. www.newsmax.com/FareedZakaria/trump-protectionism-foreign-policy/2017/01/27/id/770737/ (accessed 9 November 2017).

PART TWO

Analysis

21
UNRAVELLING LEADERSHIP: INTRODUCTION TO ANALYSIS AND METHODOLOGY

Simon Western

INTRODUCTION TO PART TWO

Part One of this book offered rich and diverse accounts of how leadership has emerged through specific national and regional contexts, revealing how historical, social and cultural contexts inform how leadership is conceptualized and practised today. In editing this book, our guidelines to authors (see Appendix) gave them the task to 'unravel leadership' by offering insights, examples and explanations as to why leadership in their country/region is textured, how it has a particular essence, flavour and way-of-being perceived and enacted. We invited authors to reflect on the tensions between global and local forces that shape leadership practices (which include followership expectations) and to highlight the sociocultural and historical influences that shape leadership perceptions and practices in their region.

Part Two of this book now offers an analysis and reflection on the data found in these 20 chapters. My aim is to unravel leadership further by undertaking two approaches to analysis of each individual chapter and then looking at what the findings reveal as a collective overview. Leadership across the following chapters is explored by looking for common and uncommon factors and patterns.

The first analysis looks at 'insider-leadership' patterns, by undertaking a discourse analysis that looks for insider or common leadership factors, present in the dominant theories and practices found in the Western literature. To this end, a dominant leadership discourse framework (Western, 2013) is used for the methodology (see Chapters 22 and 23). This allows exposure of the discourses that underpin leadership assumptions and practices, while noting that within these shared discourses diverse and nuanced differences exist. This analysis is not attempting to discover or create a universal leadership theory, nor is it aiming to integrate leadership across these diverse chapters. The opposite is closer to the truth. For instance, in Chapter 24, I explore outsider-leadership perceptions and practices by identifying leadership that is uncommon and sits outside of the dominant discourses. This outsider-leadership analysis attempts to identify differences, nuances and hidden forms of leadership that are submerged (sometimes crushed) under the weight of the dominant and normative accounts of leadership that are imposed from the most powerful leadership voices.

The dominant leadership discourses are shaped, taught and marketed mostly from Westernized sources, in particular from the dominant US university business schools and their publications such as the Harvard and Sloan Business Reviews. Also, the big consultancy companies who sell executive education and whose consultants publish populist books, e.g. Peters and Waterman (1982), Collins and Porras (2000), Laloux (2014). These leadership approaches are utilized and further promoted to dominate the global arena, by large global corporations who pay for much of the research, directly and through participating in very expensive MBAs and executive education at universities. The corporations then buy the trainings and act upon the latest leadership products – the fads, rhetoric and leadership mantras espoused by the business schools and consultancies. Together these three forces – university business schools, the big consultancy companies and global corporations – create a self-referencing and financing network that shapes global thinking and practices about leadership at a rhetorical level and perhaps in practice as well (Sahlin-Andersson and Engwall, 2002).

These purveyors of leadership offer a homogenous and 'vanilla'-flavoured leadership, that dominates the leadership narrative with fetishized and repetitive individualistic accounts of heroic leadership (Tourish and Pinnington, 2002) delivered in different tropes and guises. New leadership fads are constantly invented or recycled (Western, 2013) to sell new training courses, books, magazines, consultancy products and services. These leadership fads also happen to support existing power elites. For example, individualized accounts of charismatic and transformational leaders reinforce and legitimize the outlandish rise of CEO pay, and it is the CEOs who buy in the leadership training. The 'superhuman CEO' and their superhuman pay rises coincided with the emergence of the Messiah leadership discourse (Western, 2005, 2008, 2013) that arrived in the 1980s championing charismatic and transformational leaders (e.g. Bass, 1985, 1998; Conger and Kanungo, 1987; Burns, 2003).

> In 1978, CEOs earned 30 times the take of the average employee; now, according to the Economic Policy Institute, they get 276 times as much. These numbers betray an attitudinal upheaval. Time past, a CEO's pay was set on a scale with others in the same organization. This was dubbed 'internal equity.' But in the 1980s, a consultant named Milton Rock sold the idea of 'external equity.' Now, as if CEOs belong to a tribe of superhumans, they are paid on a scale with only their 'peer CEOs'. (Lowenstein, 2017)

Patrick Foulis (2016), writing for *The Economist*, compared how medieval Christianity controlled the discourse of its time, and how management theory (leadership theory sits within this body of work) does the same today. He argues for a reformation:

> The similarities between medieval Christianity and the world of management theory may not be obvious, but seek and ye shall find. Management theorists sanctify capitalism in much the same way that clergymen of yore sanctified feudalism. Business schools are the cathedrals of capitalism. Consultants are its travelling friars. Just as the clergy in the Middle Ages spoke in Latin to give their words an air of authority, management theorists speak in mumbo-jumbo. The medieval clergy's sale of indulgences, by which believers could effectively buy forgiveness of their sins, is echoed by management theorists selling fads that will solve all your business problems. Lately, another similarity has emerged. The gurus have lost touch with the world they seek to rule. Management theory is ripe for a reformation of its own.

This analysis is part of the reformation that is desperately needed. It reveals a plurality and diversity of leadership approaches that transcend and resist the dominant and increasingly homogenized leadership practices and rhetoric.

To summarize, the aim of this Part of the book is to offer insights, patterns and emergent leadership approaches that arise within the chapters discussed in Part One.

The analysis objectives are threefold; to discover:

1. *how the dominant insider-discourses of leadership appear in each country or region;* to identify which dominant 'insider-leadership' discourses emerged in each of the 20 chapters, and in which weightings they appeared, i.e. which were dominant and which weaker, and how they interacted in each country/region.

   To achieve these findings a discourse analysis is undertaken utilizing the four dominant leadership discourses identified through research of the mainstream leadership literature over the past century and through observing practice (Western, 2005, 2008, 2013).
2. *patterns, commonalities and differences in insider-leadership discourses found across the 20 regions/countries.*

   Using the findings of the insider-leadership analysis above, the analysis identifies leadership patterns that emerge in the collective leadership findings across all countries/regions. It then takes a continental picture: an income-based analysis and an education-based analysis.
3. *'outsider-leadership' approaches, i.e. uncommon, hidden and emergent leadership approaches found within specific regions/countries.*

   A novel methodology is used to search for leadership approaches that sit outside of the normative and dominant 'insider-leadership' discourses found in the mainstream literature.

Finally, I reflect on the analysis and data findings, drawing also upon the overall experience of working (with Éric-Jean) with the authors and editing the chapters, to share insights and thoughts on the leadership issues and themes that have arisen throughout Part One of the book.

ANALYSIS METHODOLOGY

The aim of the methodology is to deliver heuristic learning rather than empirical data that produce absolute knowledge. This research methodology is designed to develop explanatory theory rather than predictive theory (Fleetwood, 2005; Reed, 2005).

The analytic methodology employed has four parts:

1. *Allowing the chapters to speak for themselves.* In Part One of the book the chapters exist without interpretation or analysis to allow multiple readings, interpretations and learning.

Each reader can bring their unique experience, cultural background and insights to apply their own analysis and interpretations. Each reader can then make what sense they can of the leadership that emerges in the chapters, and then reflect on how it applies and sheds light onto his or her own perceptions and practices of leadership.

2. *Critical theory approach.* The second part of the methodology applies a specific critical theory approach (Western, 2012, 2013) – to *look awry, depth analysis, network analysis, emancipatory analysis* – to take a critical reading of each chapter. Analysing the text by 'looking awry and cross-wiring' questions normative accounts and looks for what might be hidden within the texts or what speaks through the texts. Reading the texts with a critical lens is looking both for what the authors are trying to consciously convey in their work, and also utilizing an applied psychoanalytic/critical theory approach to interpret and hypothesize what is unconsciously written into these chapters, in the forms of discourses and gaps that appear. This analysis is also paying close attention to leadership issues that open up or close down the potential for workplaces to be emancipatory, i.e. to provide spaces for employees to be autonomous and flourish rather than feel oppressed and inordinately controlled.
3. *Insider-leadership discourse analysis* This discourse-analysis methodology analyses the texts to locate how the four dominant leadership discourses play out in each country/region. There was no certainty of finding all four discourses in each chapter, yet they all emerged in each chapter albeit that some were very marginal, and the way they showed up had very local applications.

This analysis is written with full awareness of a Westernized bias. The author is British and the discourse analysis emanates from researching mainstream Westernized leadership literature and practices. This acknowledged bias informed the research methodology. Insider-analysis consciously looked at what leadership could be identified as being similar enough to fit into one of the four dominant Western leadership discourses.[1]

The analysis then identified what was left outside of these dominant Westernized leadership discourses. This freed me from feeling obliged, consciously or unconsciously, to become biased and to try to make leadership approaches fit into the four discourses where they didn't. This part of the methodology was very important in terms of feeling free and creative, to look awry and capture outsider-leadership approaches that did not fit into normative approaches. Readers from internationally and culturally diverse backgrounds will see things in these chapters that are missed in this analysis, due to different sensitivities and perspectives, and any insights and communications to add to future research is welcome. This is a work in progress.

---

[1]The discourses identified in these chapters were not 100% the same discourses that emerged in my earlier work. I had to adapt my understanding of them to accommodate regional and cultural differences, in order to make sense of leadership in non-Westernized cultures, while maintaining the integrity of the discourses and methodology. This was not too arduous, as the four discourses are umbrella categories that hold together many diverse leadership approaches anyway. Reading them through the lens of a different perspective, region and culture was exciting and expanded my own learning about each discourse, as well as about leadership in each country.

4. *Corroboration of research:* Finally, the discourse analysis findings were tested and corroborated by asking some chapter authors and also some leaders in different regions to complete a leadership discourse questionnaire (answering as if they were a 'typical leader' speaking on behalf of their country/region). This leadership questionnaire reveals the respondents' hidden perceptions of leadership, reflected in the same four discourses used in this analysis. Testing whether these respondents were closely aligned to the discourse analysis findings allowed us to further explore any big discrepancies and get clarity when necessary. To see the questionnaire, go to www.hiddenleadership.com.

OUTSIDER-LEADERSHIP ANALYSIS: IN SEARCH OF LACK

Having analysed the chapters for insider-leadership discourses, the methodology turned to focus on looking for gaps, for what is left out, what is lacking and what is left over, 'the remainder' after the discourse analysis is complete. This draws on Lacanian psychoanalytic theory, that suggests there is always a remainder, a gap or a lack that exists which does not fit into the Symbolic realm (Boxer, 2014a, 2014b; Lacan, 2017). In this analysis, the gap exposes a lack in normative accounts of leadership. This lack points to what Lacan calls 'the Real', which is unnameable and yet points to a subjective truth (Lacan, 1982).

The Real in this analysis is the Real of leadership that cannot be confined to knowledge and is beyond being symbolized into language. In psychoanalysis, this lack can reveal to the client their symptom which points to the very essence of who they are. Arnaud and Vidaillet (2017) write:

> In the Lacanian approach, the symptom is considered to be a unique construction of the subject, a construction that must be handled in such a way as to preserve its uniqueness while minimizing or, if possible, eliminating its dimension of suffering or destructive potential.

This outsider-analysis aimed to discover, or more correctly to get a hint of, a leadership symptom of the country or region; in terms of a 'symptom' that contains a kernel of subjective truth, an essence around which leadership circles and repeats itself. This is a radically different formation of leadership than the individualized competency model.

The leadership that exists in the gap, which is left out of insider/normative accounts, identifies a lack that points to unconscious desire and to the Lacanian Real. These outsider-leadership themes and approaches are 'a remainder' from the discourse analysis, they are what is left out. These fragments of leadership are given names that partially capture the leadership that is hidden, or not fully realized. This is 'the Real' of leadership, i.e. how leadership really works in its singularity and peculiarity of each one of the diverse countries and regions. This approach differs from the discourse analysis that attempted to discover how leadership is perceived, conformed and performed, in order to fit into the dominant leadership language. These outsider-leadership approaches expose nuanced forms of leadership that speak (unconsciously) through the texts. It revealed leadership symptoms, and essences and delivered unexpected riches that require further exploration.

REFERENCES

Arnaud, G. and Vidaillet, B. (2017) 'Clinical *and* critical: the Lacanian contribution to management and organization studies', *Organization*, [online first] DOI 1350508417720021.

Bass, Bernard (1985) *Leadership and Performance Beyond Expectations*. New York: Free Press.

Bass, Bernard M. (1998) *Transformational Leadership: Industrial, Military, and Educational Impact*. Mahwah, NJ: Lawrence Erlbaum Associates.

Boxer P.J. (2014a) Blog post 'Minding the gap – three moments of time'. 19 March 2014. www.asymmetricleadership.com/2014/03/minding-the-gap/ (accessed 24 November 2017.

Boxer, P.J. (2014b) 'Defences against innovation: the conservation of vagueness', in D. Armstrong and M. Rustin (eds), *Defences Against Anxiety: Explorations in a Paradigm*. London, Karnac. pp. 70–87.

Burns, James MacGregor (2003) *Transforming Leadership: A New Pursuit of Happiness*. New York: Grove/Atlantic.

Collins, Jim C. and Porras, Jerry I. (2000) *Built to Last*, 3rd edn. London: Random House Business Books.

Conger, J.A. and Kanungo, R.N. (1987) 'Toward a behavioural theory of charismatic leadership in organizational settings', *Academy of Management Review*, 12: 637–47.

Fleetwood, Steve (2005) 'Ontology in organization and management studies: a critical realist perspective'. *Organization*, 12 (2): 197–222.

Foulis, Patrick (2016) 'Management theory is becoming a compendium of dead ideas', www.economist.com, Schumpeter column, 17 December 2016 (accessed 9 November 2017).

Lacan, Jacques (1982) 'Le symbolique, l'imaginaire et le réel' [The symbolic, the imaginary, and the real]', *Bulletin de l'Association Freudienne*, 1: 4–13.

Lacan, J. (2017) *Formations of the Unconscious. The Seminar of Jacques Lacan: Book V* (ed. Jacques-Alain Miller; trans. Russell Grigg). Cambridge: Polity Press.

Laloux, Frederic (2014) *Reinventing Organizations: A Guide to Creating Organizations Inspired by the Next Stage in Human Consciousness*. Brussels: Nelson Parker.

Lowenstein, Roger (2017) 'CEO pay is out of control. Here's how to rein it in', www.Fortune.com, 19 April 2017 (accessed 9 November 2017).

Peters, Tom and Waterman, Robert (1982) *In Search of Excellence: Lessons from America's Best-Run Companies*. New York: HarperCollins.

Reed, Michael I. (2005) 'Reflections on the "realist turn" in organization and management studies', *Journal of Management Studies*, 42 (8): 1621–44.

Sahlin-Andersson, K. and Engwall, L. (eds) (2002) *The Expansion of Management Knowledge: Carriers, Flows and Sources*. Stanford, CA: Stanford University Press.

Tourish, D. and Pinnington, A. (2002) 'Transformational leadership, corporate cultism and the spirituality paradigm: an unholy trinity in the workplace?', *Human Relations*, 55 (2): 147–72.

Western, Simon (2005) 'A critical analysis of leadership: overcoming fundamentalist tendencies'. Doctoral Dissertation: Lancaster University Management School.

Western, Simon (2008) 'Democratising strategy', in D. Campbell and D. Huffington (eds), *Organizations Connected: A Handbook of Systemic Consultation*. London: Karnac. pp. 173–96.

Western, Simon (2012) *Coaching and Mentoring: A Critical Text*. London: Sage.

Western, Simon (2013) *Leadership: A Critical Text*, 2nd edn. London: Sage.

22
THE FOUR DISCOURSES OF LEADERSHIP

Simon Western

This chapter offers a brief overview of the four dominant leadership discourses that are used in the insider-leadership discourse analysis. These discourses emerged at different times over the past century in the West, and are all mainstream leadership discourses that remain present today: Controller leadership, Therapist leadership, Messiah leadership and Eco-leadership (Western, 2008, 2013). Figure 22.1 shows when each discourse emerged and dominated, and how each still exists today.

AN OVERVIEW

The leadership discourses are used as a heuristic device to promote further enquiry and learning, rather than fixing leadership in a particular way. Each leadership discourse is not 'good' or 'bad' and the discourses are not exclusive. One discourse can dominate but others are always present in different weightings within a given leadership setting. Discourses are not neat and succinct categories and boundaries blur as leadership is fluid, not fixed.

What is a discourse?

Over the past century, four key discourses have emerged that dominate leadership thinking. A discourse in this sense is an underlying set of assumptions that becomes accepted as the norm. It affects and shapes our views about something. For many people, leadership means a heroic charismatic figure, but there are other discourses of leadership. These determine how leadership is enacted and spoken about, but they are not always explicitly known to us. Discourse is related to power, as a way to control and normalize ways of thinking and being; as Judith Butler says, discourse defines the 'limits of acceptable speech' (2004: 64). A discourse determines what can be said and also what cannot be said, it impacts on our views, our self-perceptions and it is not possible to escape discourse.

This method of discourse analysis provides a way of thinking about leadership rather than a way of defining how leadership is, or how a leader should or does act. It is a heuristic way of opening leadership up for reflection. This discourse analysis method has been tried and tested in practice across multiple international settings, in diverse sectors and with different levels of leaders and followers. Each time it has been used the results have provoked deep thinking and reflection, which is the purpose of the methodology. When applied to the country chapters in this book, the discourses were used with more openness to variants in culture than as described in the original research findings. This was to enable non-Westernized applications of leadership to find their own expressions where possible. Leadership approaches that did not fit or sat

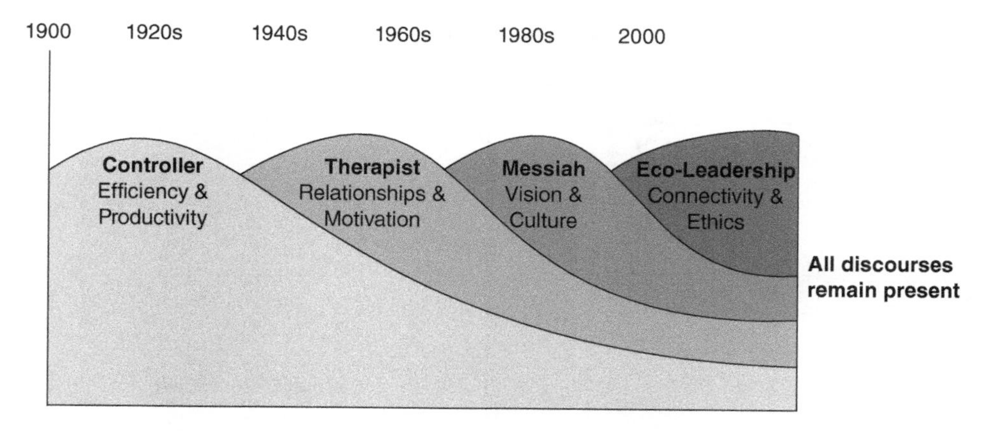

Figure 22.1 The discourses of leadership

outside of these normative Westernized discourses, were put in the following section, 'outsider-leadership approaches'.

TIME LINE

Controller leadership discourse reflected the industrial leadership at the turn of the twentieth century that utilized science and rationality to improve productivity. Therapist leadership became more dominant in post-war Europe and the USA, reflecting a democratization of the workplace, a re-focusing of leadership on motivation rather than coercion and control of employees, and a focus on individuality and emotions at work. It became dominant after the post-1960s counter-culture heralded in therapy culture and the workplace became a key site for self-actualization and personal development (Maslow, 1968). Due to an economic slump and the rise of the Asian economies, the dominance of Therapist leadership gave way to Messiah leadership, focusing on how transformational leaders could inspire employees with grand visions, and create strong loyal and committed cultures that would challenge the Asian economies who relied on collectivist culture as a way of leveraging success (Bass, 1985, 1998). Finally, at the beginning of the new millennium the rise of a new Eco-leadership discourse emerged. This reflected the network society (Castells, 2000, 2012) and the realization that we were entering a new paradigm whereby the machine metaphor for organizations in the twentieth century was giving way to a new organizational metaphor, the eco-system. Globalization and new informational technology created a more interconnected and interdependent world, which demanded new organizational forms and new leadership.

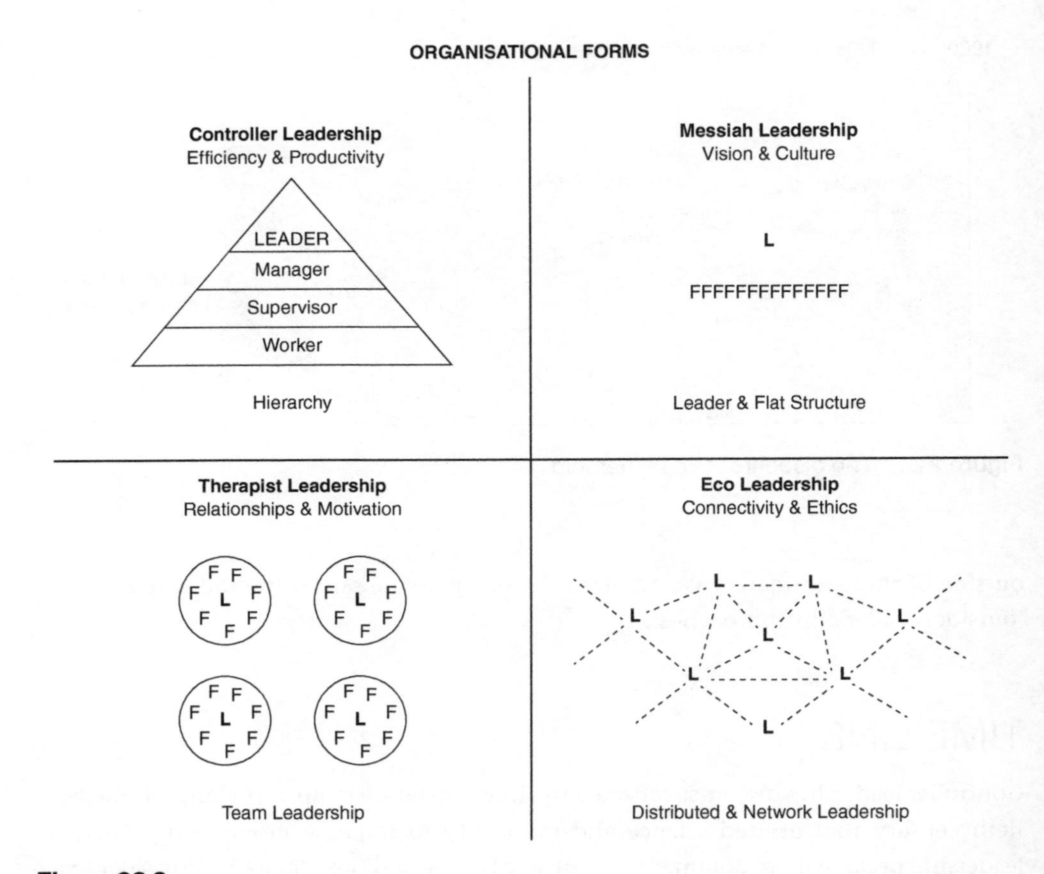

Figure 22.2

Figure 22.2 offers an image of the classic organizational structure that each leadership discourse produces.

I will now briefly offer an overview of each discourse.

THE CONTROLLER LEADERSHIP DISCOURSE

'Efficiency through control'

The first leadership discourse that emerged at the beginning of the twentieth century is that of the *Controller leader.* The Controller leadership discourse is born from scientific rationalism and the industrial revolution, standardization and mechanization creating the mass production of the factory. The Controller leader operates as a technocratic leader whose sole aim is to exert environmental control of both human and other resources in order to maximize production efficiency and effectiveness.

Traditionally in industrial settings employees were treated as replaceable human resources to be controlled and to act as 'cogs-in-the-wheel' of the efficient organizational machine. Time and motion studies and division of labour meant that unskilled labour was utilized on production lines which maximized efficiencies and enabled mass production of goods to take place. Cars and other consumer goods became available due to these practices and Controller leadership proved hugely successful. Industrial leaders introduced management control systems with great effect. According to Peter Drucker, 'management's greatest achievement of the century was to increase the productivity of manual workers fiftyfold' (cited by Crainer, 2000).

Controller leadership then migrated to the bureaucratic office with mixed success, where each employee knew their place and had set tasks to fulfil. After a period of demise, Controller leadership is on the rise again in new contexts such as the 'gig economy' due to computer technologies that produce vast data enabling us to measure much more and from a virtual place. This produces a new form of Controller leadership which imposes 'control by numbers' and creates audit culture (Power, 1997) target setting and in today's workplace employees can be surveyed/controlled through mobile technologies like never before.

While Controller leadership is vital, i.e. controlling finance and resources focusing on efficiency and utilizing scientific-rationalism is a vital part of leading an organization, the shadow side is that it can produce de-humanizing workplaces, that diminish individual autonomy and creativity. When target culture and short-term performance dominate leadership thinking, it can lead to a rigid organization that is unable to adapt, to be strategic and agile and this can be very problematic in today's fast-changing organizational context. When the efficient ends become more important than the means by which they are attained, serious problems arise.

Good examples of Controller leadership today are McDonald's, Starbucks, Ryanair and other budget airlines that focus on maximizing efficiency to reduce costs, and offer mass transport or food of a standardized and uniform quality at very cheap prices. The maxim for today's Controller leader is *'If you can't count it, it doesn't count'* shortening William Cameron's maxim 'Not everything that can be counted counts, and not everything that counts can be counted' (1963: 13).

Controller leadership is necessary in all organizations. The question is how much of this leadership approach is required, where in the organization is it needed most, and how can it integrate and work alongside other leadership approaches, without creating rigid organizations and dehumanizing conditions.

The four qualities of Controller leadership

1. *Efficiency:* Controller leaders are the direct descendants of Frederick Taylor's 'Efficiency Craze', when scientific management was applied to factory work to create mass-production techniques such as the production line. This leadership approach relishes the challenge of making the workplace more efficient, through use of technology, restructuring and work re-design. The focus is on increasing successful output using the minimal resources and costs, and success included quality control measures
2. *Task and target focus:* Controller leaders are very task-focused and less strategy-focused. They like to have clarity around tasks and know who is going to complete them. Setting clear output and performance targets and measuring the results is how Controller leaders like to operate. They don't like anything that gets between a workforce and completing its tasks.
3. *Clear systems, roles, processes and structures:* Controller leaders strive for clear accountability, systems, processes, roles, accountabilities and responsibilities. Clarity enables greater accountability and control for the leaders of organizations.
4. *Scientific rationalism:* Underpinning all of the above is the idea that scientific rationalism will deliver results. Controller leaders like to have facts, measurements and evidence-based results. Whether in a hospital, factory, bank or retail outlet, the Controller leader will rely on rationalism and science to deliver success.

The shape of a classic Controller-led organization is the hierarchical pyramid, but we should note that this is changing in contemporary Controller-led organizations that utilize Controller leadership by numbers.

THE THERAPIST LEADERSHIP DISCOURSE

'Happy workers are more productive workers'

Therapist leaders take a very humanistic approach to leadership; their focus is people, people and people. We call this the Therapist discourse, referencing how therapeutic culture permeates our lives in the West (Rose, 1990; Furedi, 2003), expanding its influence beyond the clinic. Therapist leaders are attracted to these underpinning therapeutic ideas and they work with employees in two main ways. First, they hold a philosophy of the 'Celebrated-self' (Western, 2012); they believe that each person has a huge untapped potential and if we overcome our self-doubts, inhibitions and psychological limitations (usually inflicted on us from childhood) we can fully celebrate our true selves and maximize our potential, thereby becoming more effective and productive workers. Second, they often work with the other side of the therapeutic human condition we call the 'Wounded-self' (Western, 2012). This relates to the perception that deep within us we are all injured souls, damaged by childhood or some event and that we crave caring for and reparation.

Therapist leaders often espouse a belief in the Celebrated Self but are quickly drawn to the Wounded-self in practice. Therapist leaders identify with the Wounded-self, they feel your pain, and they are sensitive to it and want to make it better. Therapist leadership emerged in the post-1960s, from the counter-cultural movement that celebrated individualism, emotional expression and privileging the search for happiness. In the workplace, the human relations and human potential movements flourished with Maslow's self-actualizing theories (Maslow, 1968) becoming mainstream for HR and leadership training. Today emotional intelligence and leadership coaching are symbolic of the continuing power of Therapist leadership.

There are two main challenges that Therapist leaders have to work hard to avoid:

- They can easily develop dependent followers, 'we love our leader, s/he is so caring'. This can limit the team's and individual's capacity to think independently and challenge the leader.
- They can be over-focused on individuals and their team and don't think strategically, missing the big picture.

Therapist leaders are very necessary in organizations; they can be very caring, insightful and skilful in their people leadership. They manage conflict well and they see problems arising before they explode. They develop loyal followers, and when working well really get the best from individuals and teams they lead.

The four qualities of Therapist leadership

1. *Self-awareness:* Therapist leaders have high levels of self-awareness, which is a key leadership attribute, enabling them to see their strengths and weaknesses, and not be afraid to acknowledge these and work on them and with them to get the best from themselves.
2. *Relational dynamics:* Having a good understanding of relational dynamics is important as Therapist leaders not only focus on individuals but also look at team dynamics, and try to get balanced teams. For example, many of such leaders choose team members on the basis that they are like them. This creates a dangerous scenario of groupthink, and limits the team by excluding creative difference. A skilled Therapist leader will have the confidence to work with differences, using their skills and understanding of team and relational dynamics to operate through tensions and get the very best from a diverse but strong group.
3. *Coaching skills:* Therapist leaders are naturally coaching leaders; they see the ability to coach and mentor their people as a vital part of their leadership role, and continually work on themselves to strengthen this ability.
4. *Developmental focus:* Therapist leaders are development addicts! They love training and development, and seek opportunities for themselves and their team at any opportunity. Investing in people, they believe, is the key to company success.

THE MESSIAH LEADERSHIP DISCOURSE

'Charismatic leaders and strong cultures'

The Messiah leadership discourse emerged in the early 1980s and became the dominant discourse until around 2000. The Messiah leadership discourse signified a new surge in leadership theory and practice as leadership became a very sought-after idea, pushing management into the background. During this period, the compensation of CEOs rose astronomically, reflecting the perception that they were Messiah leaders. It has two important components that separates it from the idea of the great hero leaders of the past. Messiah leadership combines individual charismatic leadership alongside the drive to create strong and aligned organizational cultures. This strong culture enables 'culture control' to take place.

The big idea of Messiah leadership was that employees followed the leader willingly because they had faith in him/her and in the company vision, so they were committed, loyal and worked hard with less need for supervision or coercion to produce results. At its best, this culture control works positively to produce engaged employees working collectively to produce the best outcomes. At its worst, it produces dangerous conformist and dependent cultures, which we will look at later. The word Messiah is evocative and comes from research analysis of the transformational leadership literature that made great claims for this new form of leadership, using prophetic and often messianic language. Messiah leaders are usually but not always charismatic extroverts; they can also be quiet leaders whose charisma shines through in less obvious ways.

The Messiah leadership discourse provides charismatic leadership and a vision of the future, often in the face of a turbulent and uncertain environment. The Messiah discourse has long appealed to individuals and collectively to society, especially in turbulent environments, promising salvation from the chaotic world in which a lack of control is experienced. New purpose and direction is felt under a Messiah leader. The great hero leader of the past was critiqued for creating dependency cultures, which created a non-thinking blind loyalty. Devoted soldiers following the charismatic leader into battle willing to give their lives for him/her offered a metaphoric model. Today's Messiah leader realizes that a dependency culture does not work in a modern organization that relies on employees bringing their knowledge, passion and adaptive thinking to the work. Today's Messiah leaders therefore attempt to create cultures whereby employees are loyal because they believe in the vision, but where they do not need hierarchical supervision. They work hard and are self-motivated because they have faith in the leader, and belief in the company vision. Hierarchical structures were flattened as the need to manage, motivate and control employees diminished.

These prophetic Messiah leaders initially were heralded as creating entrepreneurial and dynamic companies, yet in spite of their aims to avoid dependency cultures they often created highly conformist cultures. Peters and Waterman's (1982) best-selling book *In Search of Excellence* described the most successful companies as having 'cult-like cultures'. Perhaps the most successful example of a Messiah leader was Steve Jobs at Apple, whose employees retained inventiveness yet were fiercely identified with Jobs' vision and the Apple brand. Today's Messiah leaders in big companies need not only to present a vision to their employees but to customers, clients, shareholders and other stakeholders. They often act as a symbolic figurehead for the brand which can influence share prices more than income streams these days. Steve Jobs, like many charismatic visionaries, was hugely gifted but also a leader with many flaws (Ricks, 2012), just as with today's Messiah leaders such as Elon Musk and Jeff Bezos (Schwartz, 2015).

The dangers of Messiah leadership are clear. Messiah leaders when working well create strong dynamic cultures that inspire and energize the workforce. These cultures, however, often slide into becoming monocultures, whereby anybody who dissents or offers a different view from the leadership position is seen as being disloyal and is marginalized or pushed out of the company. This creates silent and compliant organizations and when this happens the company loses creativity and initiative, and mistakes or malpractice are not corrected. This can lead to catastrophic failures.

The other challenge for Messiah leadership is the gap between rhetoric and reality. Often employees and customers, shareholders and stakeholders like the idea of a Messiah leader taking them to great places so they can project onto an ordinary leader 'Messiah leadership' qualities and expectations. Everybody wanted a Messiah to turn the company around, to lead the public service sector back to a strong position, to change the company culture, and this was reflected in their huge salary hikes. Messiah leaders often have strong egos that can serve them well or not. If they get seduced by power, the financial rewards and internalize follower projections of being special, they can become grandiose and omnipotent and lose their good judgement. What may look like Messiah leadership may also be a mirage, a fantasy that all collude with until it comes crashing down.

All organizations need some Messiah leadership, especially start-ups, social entrepreneurs and those organizations going through great changes in the face of social and technological changes around them.

The four qualities of Messiah leadership

1. *Charisma and influence*: A Messiah leadership has charisma; others admire, have trust and confidence in the leader, enabling them to influence others.
2. *Vision*: Creating a strong vision of the future, setting clear purpose and mission enables Messiah leaders to set the agenda, to inspire and motivate and to raise both morale and material resource to achieve goals.

3. *Strong culture*: The Messiah leader is focused on creating strong and aligned cultures to produce a form of culture control, i.e. a group dynamic that binds people together in common cause. When working well it creates a dynamic and collective energy and sense of well-being and, when not so well, it creates dependency and conformist cultures.
4. *Faith in themselves*: Messiah leaders have strong egos and a strong sense of self and a faith in themselves expressed through their vision of the future, which becomes an extension of the self. When this becomes dysfunctional it can lead to omnipotence, grandiosity, narcissism and misjudgements on a grand scale. When working well, this is harnessed to great effect to drive positive change and mobilize others.

THE ECO-LEADERSHIP DISCOURSE

'Creating spaces for leadership to flourish'

In today's increasingly globalized and networked society there is an urgent need for new forms of organization. We all face a common underlying challenge, i.e. *how to adapt in today's extremely fast-changing and networked world*. To address this challenge takes new forms of leadership we call Eco-leadership (Western 2008, 2013).

The pre-fix 'Eco' is used because this form of leadership resonates with our understanding of eco-systems. However, Eco-leadership is not all about ethics and the environment, it is also about realizing that twenty-first-century organizations are better understood as interdependent and interconnected eco-systems. This new understanding replaces twentieth-century ideas of organizations as efficiency 'machines' run with clear hierarchies, structures and boundaries.

The Network Society[1] of today undoes the leadership theory of the past century. Hierarchies, fixed structures and static roles are not fit-for-purpose in this new work environment. Eco-leadership focuses on distributing leadership throughout the organization. Knowing your customers' or clients' changing needs and adapting to them locally and specifically requires leadership at the edges as well as the centre. Eco-leadership is not a luxury, it's a necessity!

Today, change takes place between connected peers, much more than the imagined top-down change led from a hierarchy. This change *from vertical power to lateral power* has taken politicians, economists and company leaders by surprise. Very few are adapting fast enough to keep up, and many are getting left behind, thinking in the old paradigm and not recognizing the new.

---

[1]The Network Society refers to how the Internet, computers, social media and globalization are changing the way we work, live and relate to each other. This is more than a technological advance, it is producing social change that may be a big as the last industrial revolution.

Successful leaders today are those who recognize this change and who nurture lateral connections, and distribute leadership and power as widely as they can. We call them Eco-leaders as they recognize that organizations are like *'eco-systems within eco-systems'* (Western, 2013). These are not biological eco-systems like a rainforest, but they act in similar ways. Organizational eco-systems are made up of people, technology and nature; interconnected networks that are interdependent on each other. These organizational eco-systems operate in the wider context of political, technical, social and natural eco-systems that influence all organizations. For far too long many organizations have acted as if they live in a closed system (the banking system for example) without accounting for wider influences that impact on the banks, and also the influences they have on wider society. We are all interconnected and interdependent, whether through climate change or the cost of our limited natural resources.

Eco-leaders look two ways: (1) Internally the organization is an interconnected web of activity, and leadership means influencing and nurturing these connections to produce positive change. (2) Externally, Eco-leaders look at the social, technological, political and environmental changes that are occurring that influence how their organization functions. Command and control leadership doesn't work in today's organizations as leaders can't control an eco-system or network, they can only influence it.

Take the examples of the financial crash of 2008, the Arab Spring revolutions that overthrew dictators and armies that held total power, or the fast rise of Apple, Google and Amazon, as world-leading companies. What they all have in common is they happened as result of today's networked, interconnected and interdependent world. Without the Internet, the digital economy, social media, mobile technologies, none of these events would have happened.

Another example is running a health system today: it is no longer about running an efficient 'factory-hospital' complex, i.e. getting patients diagnosed, treated and discharged. It is about recognizing that healthcare is also about well-being, and that public health and social care are interdependent, i.e. you cannot solve huge and expensive problems like the rise of diabetes or depression without looking at the connections to the other parts of the eco-system that produce these challenges.

Unless today's leaders recognize these networks of connections and our interdependencies, then they are working in the wrong paradigm! Whether solving environment or migrant challenges, financial service or manufacturing challenges, running healthcare and education systems, or whether working in a family business, we all have to turn to Eco-leadership (supported by other discourses) if we are to meet the social, political environmental and economic challenges and opportunities in today's networked society.

The four qualities of Eco-leadership

1. *Connectivity and interdependence:* Eco-leadership is founded on connectivity, recognizing how the network society has transformed social relations, and it also recognizes our interdependence with each other and the environment. Eco-leadership focuses on internal organizational ecosystems (technical, social and natural) and the external ecosystems of which organizations are a part.
2. *Systemic ethics:* Eco-leadership is concerned with acting ethically in the human realm *and* protecting the natural environment. Systemic ethics goes beyond company values and individual leader morality, which conveniently turns a blind eye to the wider ethical implications of their businesses, e.g. by ignoring social inequality, the downstream impacts of pollution and supply chain workers, world poverty and environmental sustainability.
3. *Leadership spirit:* Eco-leadership acknowledges the importance of the human spirit. It extends its values beyond material gain, paying attention to community and friendship, mythos and logos, the unconscious and non-rational, creativity and imagination. It draws upon the beauty and dynamic vitally within human relationships, and between humanity and the natural world.
4. *Organizational belonging:* To belong is to be a part of the whole, it is to participate in the joys and challenges faced by communities. Businesses and corporations, like schools, banks and hospitals, belong to the social fabric of community, and cannot operate as separate bodies. Eco-leaders commit organizations to belong to 'places and spaces', developing strong kinship ties. Place refers to local habitat and community, and space to the virtual and real networks that organizations also inhabit. Organizational belonging means ending a false separation, realizing that company interests and societal interests are interdependent. Organizational belonging is to rethink organizational purpose and meaning.

ADAPTIVE DISCOURSES FOR THIS GLOBAL ANALYSIS

The four discourses needed adapting to accommodate non-Western perspectives in this book. There was not a plan to adapt the discourses but the chapters revealed how they took on nuanced and morphed forms from how they first appeared in Westernized literature. In essence, the four discourses remained constant, representing the four core ways leadership is conceptualized and practised. Yet the reasons that underpin a discourse and how it plays out in practice changes in each particular context. This is also true in Westernized contexts, so the Messiah leadership discourse may look quite a bit different in a USA hi-tech business than it does in a UK bank for example. Messiah leadership paired with Controller leadership also will play out in a very different way than if it is paired with Therapist leadership.

This section will briefly highlight the key adaptions that stand out for each discourse in this book.

- *Controller leadership discourse* emerged from the Enlightenment values that privileged scientific rationality and reason in the West, and in the workplace, it was the industrialization and urbanization process that underpinned the dominance of the Controller leadership discourse. Industrial leaders invented a new managerial class, the factory system and imposed bureaucratic structures overseen by supervisors in factories and offices. The underpinning logic that led to the Controller discourse was the Enlightenment values of science and rationality applied to work, under the auspices of progress. In non-Western countries Controller leadership is not necessarily tied to the Enlightenment values and is enacted and conceptualized in more localized ways. What is common across these diverse ways, is that this discourse imposes control on resources, including human resources. This may be done in an authoritarian way where the leader utilizes fear and coercion to get things done. Or it can be the implementation of more subtle and nuanced control leadership that puts in place very tight control processes and systems to improve efficiency, or it can be the imposition of nuanced forms of culture control and/or 'control by numbers'.
- *Therapist leadership discourse* in the Westernized conception refers to the democratization of the workplace in post-World War II Europe/America, and the emergence of 'Therapy culture' and individualism following 1960s counter-culture. In Asian and other cultures, these factors were less dominant and yet the Therapist leadership discourse often seemed present in the chapters. In these more collectivist cultures, the Therapist leadership discourse emerged more from the long traditions of 'business through relationship' as described through 'wasta' in the Middle E and 'guanxi' in China.

  Like the guanxi which operates in the Chinese world, wasta involves a social network of interpersonal connections rooted in family and kinship ties that surround and frame specific leadership situations. Wasta involves the exercise of power, influence and information-sharing through social and politico-business networks and is intrinsic to the operation of leadership, central to the transmission of knowledge and the creation of opportunity. But just as guanxi has positive connotations of networking and negative connotations of corruption, so too does wasta.
- *Messiah leadership discourse* in the West was linked very closely to the 1990s rise of transformational leaders (e.g. Bass, 1985, 1998; Burns, 2003). These were championed to offer charismatic leadership (e.g. Peters and Waterman, 1982) that offered visions in order that they could engineer cultures (Kunda, 1992) using soft-power and influencing techniques. In non-Westernized cultures, Messiah leadership is less tied to the specific idea that a charismatic leader could get employee buy-in from developing visions that created strong cultures as strong cultural ties already exist in collectivist cultures and were successfully being harnessed in the Asian tiger economies of the 1980s and 90s. The Messiah leader therefore is more of a charismatic/powerful leader who utilizes position power to attain his or her goals, sometimes in a relational way (paired with the Therapist) at other times in a coercive/authoritarian way (paired

with the Controller). An unusual pairing in non-Western cultures are an authoritarian/controlling leader paired with Eco-leadership, which relates to a more holistic approach alongside a paternalistic one.

- *Eco-Leadership discourse* in the West emerges as a result of the IT explosion, the rise of the network society, hyperglobalization and environmental challenges and social resistance movements. The Western focus is on taking an ethical leadership approach and applying systems and network theory to distribute leadership with the aim of creating socially responsible, adaptive and dynamic organizational cultures. Eco-leadership in the East draws on a much longer tradition of holism, connectedness, how paradoxes can be worked within non-linear ways, and thinking anthropologically and ecologically together, i.e. about the human–nature relationship and drawing on natural and environmental metaphors to influence leadership and organizational behaviour.

These four dominant discourses that interplay with each other, are the basis of the discourse analysis in the following chapter.

REFERENCES

Bass, Bernard (1985) *Leadership and Performance Beyond Expectations*. New York: Free Press.

Bass, Bernard M. (1998) *Transformational Leadership: Industrial, Military, and Educational Impact*. Mahwah, NJ: Lawrence Erlbaum Associates.

Burns, James MacGregor (2003) *Transforming Leadership: A New Pursuit of Happiness*. New York: Grove/Atlantic.

Butler, Judith (2004) 'Gender regulations', in J. Butler (ed.), *Undoing Gender*. New York: Routledge.

Cameron, William B. (1963) *Informal Sociology: A Casual Introduction to Sociological Thinking*. New York: Random House.

Castells, Manuel (2000) *The Rise of the Network Society: The Information Age: Economy, Society and Culture*, I. Oxford: Blackwell.

Castells, Manuel (2012) *Networks of Outrage and Hope: Social Movements in the Internet Age*. Cambridge: Polity Press.

Crainer, S. (2000) *The Management Century: Critical Review of 20th Century Thought and Practice*. New York, NY: Jossey–Bass.

Furedi, Frank (2003) *Therapy Culture: Cultivating Vulnerability in an Uncertain Age*. London: Routledge.

Kunda, Gideon (1992) *Engineering Culture: Control Commitment in a High-Tech Corporation*. Philadelphia, PA: Temple University Press.

Maslow, Abraham (1968) *Toward a Psychology of Being*. New York: Van Nostrand.

Peters, Tom J. and Waterman, Robert (1982) *In Search of Excellence: Lessons from America's Best-Run Companies*. New York: Harper and Row.

Power, Michael (1997) *The Audit Society: Rituals of Verification*. Oxford: Oxford University Press.

Ricks, T. (2012) 'Steve Jobs: a great and toxic leader', Foreignpolicy.com, 14 September. http://foreignpolicy.com/2012/09/14/steve-jobs-a-great-and-toxic-leader/ (accessed 24 November 2017).

Rose, Nikolas (1990) *Governing the Soul: The Shaping of the Private Self*. London: Routledge.

Schwartz, T. (2015) 'The bad behaviour of visionary leaders', *New York Times*, 26 June. www.nytimes.com/2015/06/27/business/dealbook/the-bad-behavior-of-visionary-leaders.html (accessed 9 November 2017).

Western, Simon (2008) 'Democratising strategy', in D. Campbell and D. Huffington (eds), *Organizations Connected: A Handbook of Systemic Consultation*. London: Karnac. pp. 173–96.

Western, Simon (2012) *Coaching and Mentoring: A Critical Text*. London: Sage.

Western, Simon (2013) *Leadership: A Critical Text*, 2nd edn. London: Sage.

23
INSIDER-LEADERSHIP: A DISCOURSE ANALYSIS

Simon Western

The key findings from the discourse analysis are set out below. The discourse analysis rated how the four leadership discourses appeared in each individual chapter,[1] drawing on experience of having worked with these discourses in both theory and practice for over a decade. This analysis was not only done on the final chapter versions, but also while working closely with the authors during the editing and writing of them. Distinct references to particular discourses in the texts gave clear and obvious data for the analysis, yet a lot of subtle referencing took place which had to be reflected on and made sense of. As previously mentioned, the findings were corroborated with a leadership questionnaire taken by some authors and other leaders in the countries, and discussions took place with authors to dig deeper when more clarity was required. It is important to reiterate here that the aims of this analysis are to provoke thinking and learning; it is a heuristic piece of research. It is not aimed at delivering hard replicable or empirical data, but acknowledging that subjectivity was alive both in the discourse analysis process and in the choice of authors and the experience they brought and left out, as revealed in the unique way each chapter is written.

The discourse analysis considers the following data, shown in a graph with a brief commentary.

Graph 1 – **Overall findings** (discourse analysis averaged across the 20 country/regions)

Graphs 2 and 3 – **Country/region** (findings organized country/region)

Graph 4 – **Continental data** (findings organized by continent)

Graph 5 – **Income data** (findings organized by income/GNI per capita – World Bank source)

Graph 6 – **Educational data (**findings organized by education index – UN source)

HEADLINE FINDINGS

The final results showed all four discourses appeared in every chapter, which was a slightly unexpected outcome, as a question arose as to whether these dominant discourses from

[1]To arrive at the percentages, each country/region was scored with a percentage of each discourse revealing dominant and weaker leadership discourses as they appeared in the text. For each chapter, 20 allocations of 5%, totalling 100%, were made to account for the discourses. Therefore, if one discourse, e.g. the Messiah, was totally dominant without any of the others showing, the results would have been 100% Messiah; or if only three discourses were found in the chapter a result might show 70% Messiah, 20% Controller, 10% Therapist without any showing of Eco-leadership. The final results actually showed all four discourses in all chapters, which was not a foregone conclusion. There was also much leadership that did not fit into this insider-discourse analysis, and these gaps are accounted for in the next chapter.

the West would appear in all non-Western contexts. In Chapter 21 the methodology discusses how the discourses had an adaptive quality, arising from a different starting point in some non-Western contexts, yet retaining the overall leadership qualities of the discourse itself.

The collective results showed that the leading discourse across all countries/regions was Messiah leadership, with a strong showing of 31%. Therapist leadership 26% and Controller leadership 25% were very close together in second and third place, followed by the emerging discourse, Eco-leadership, on a healthy 18%.

GRAPH 1: OVERALL DISCOURSE ANALYSIS FINDINGS

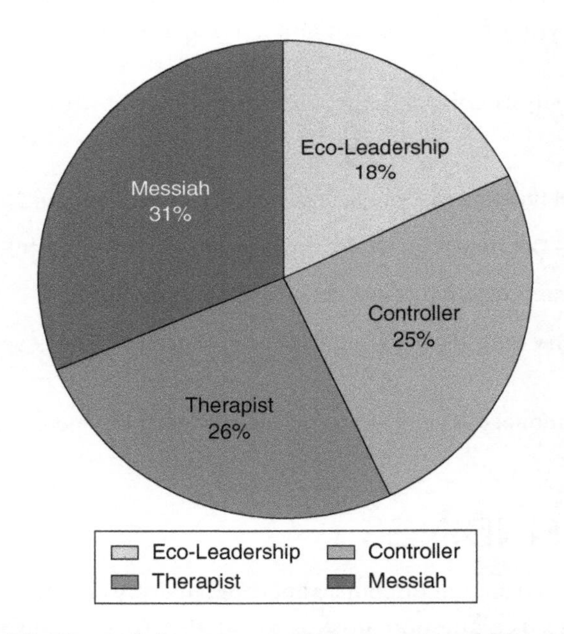

Figure 23.1 Overall findings of discourse analysis: average of 20 countries combined

1. Messiah leadership 31%
2. Therapist leadership 26%
3. Controller leadership 25%
4. Eco-leadership 18%

The findings show that Messiah leadership is the leading discourse across the chapters, which mirrors the dominant leadership literature that continues to represent the leader as a charismatic/powerful individual (a 'Messiah'). These findings may show that leadership is most commonly enacted in this way, and/or it may reflect that the Messiah discourse is so dominant that it limits perceptions so that people mainly look for this individualized leadership and interpret what they see in this way (if you only have a hammer, all you see is nails). An example of how a particular view of leadership discourses creates blind-spots is shown in a recent study of 'leaderless' new social movements (Western, 2014). The research showed how activists in the movements (and also those researching, observing and commentating on them), were both heavily invested in two things that limited their capacity to see leadership. First, they were invested in being 'leaderless' as this formed a strong part of their identity and egalitarian idealism. Second, they limited their perceptions of leadership to the Messiah and Controller discourses seeing leaders only as 'bad', i.e. as an authoritarian person holding a senior position in a hierarchy, and/or someone who used their charismatic personality, position and resources to wield power over others and control them. Their conscious and unconscious investments create blind-spots that missed the exciting new leadership developments taking place in their movements. Using new social media and virtual networks distributed leadership flourished throughout their movements, with activists taking up new forms of Autonomist leadership (Western, 2014). This meant leadership ebbed and flowed, with temporary support from others, but without fixed or hierarchical positions.

One of the questions that arises from these findings is whether the chapter authors were expressing leadership in a way that mirrors the global dominant discourses that are more familiar and individual (Messiah, Therapist, Controller) and misses lesser-known forms of leadership discourses such as Eco-leadership.

> We embody the discourses that exist in our culture, our very being is constituted by them, they are part of us, and thus we cannot simply throw them off. (Sullivan, 2003: 41)

The analysis findings show that leadership is primarily perceived as within the Messiah discourse, but only by a small margin across all countries and it did not dominate in each individual country/region. The findings also show that leadership is not primarily experienced as a dominant or a controlling figure with position power, or a relational leader or systemic and holistic thinker. However, these discourses of Controller, Therapist and Eco-leadership are all strongly represented and are influential across the whole.

A more granular look at each individual country/region reveals a richer and more diverse picture. Each chapter reveals how different aspects of the collective leading discourse, 'Messiah', plays out in each specific context. This is discussed further below.

In the overall findings, the Controller 25% and Therapist 26% discourses were very close, suggesting that when leading others motivation and relational means of influencing are balanced with the need to control resources and drive for efficiency (including human resources). Controller leadership may portray a leader acting in a coercive way, or that he/she is very focused on results and has excellent control systems and processes.

The more emergent and newest Eco-leadership discourse showed quite strongly with 18%. Eco-leadership is often less easy to notice as a form of leadership than the other discourses, because it is not located in an individual personality and is more distributed throughout an organization. The normative way of seeing leadership is via position power, or through charismatic leadership, so by its very nature Eco-leadership challenges the norms and will be less visible to contemporary ways of seeing leaders, although this is changing as Eco-leadership grows as a significant leadership discourse. This finding that Eco-leadership at 18% was more than 50% of the Messiah discourse score of 31%, is a real sign of change in leadership across the globe.

GRAPHS 2 AND 3: INDIVIDUAL COUNTRY/ REGION DISCOURSE ANALYSIS

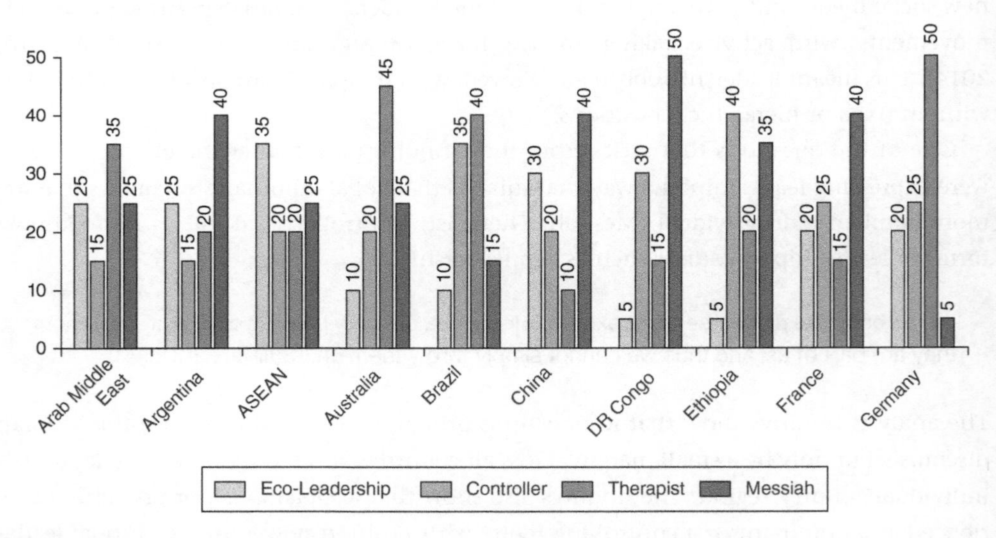

Figure 23.2 Leadership discourse analysis – by region/country (Part 1)

Individual country/region discussion

The short commentary below highlights key findings from the data in Figures 23.2 and 23.3.

The leadership discourse which dominated in most countries/regions was the Messiah discourse; it led in 7.5 countries/regions (it dominated in 7 countries, and was equally dominant in 1, Russia). The second most common discourse was the Therapist

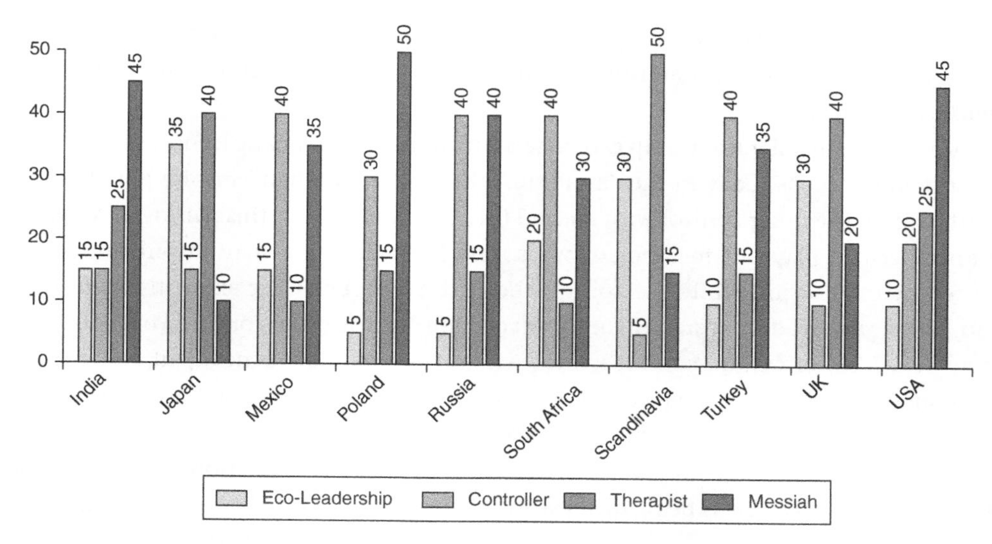

Figure 23.3 Leadership discourse analysis – by region/country (Part 2)

discourse, in 7 countries/regions. The Controller discourse dominated in 4.5 countries/regions (4 plus Russia as above) and Eco-leadership dominated in only one region.

We will now briefly look at each discourse and see what patterns and themes emerge.

Messiah discourse

Poland and DR Congo scored the highest in Messiah leadership with 50%, followed by the USA and India on 45%. In Poland and DR Congo the second discourse to the Messiah was the Controller, whereas in India and the USA the Therapist was ranked second. These pairings of discourses give quite a different feel to the leadership approaches in these countries. Messiah/Controller leadership indicates a classic all-powerful (typically paternalistic) leadership approach. It projects an individual's authority and charisma to a followership in order to produce a form of leadership that promotes the leader's power, which is accompanied by high levels of control. Together they produce a level of emotional or fearful dependency on the leader that leans towards authoritarianism.

Usually Messiah leadership splits follower support in a country or organization, carrying on the one hand populist support, those who regard the Messiah as a saviour leader and believe the authoritarian stance is necessary to lead the organization/nation out of trouble, while on the other hand, it creates resistance and resentment from those who see leadership as unnecessarily authoritarian, diminishing the autonomy and democratic voice of many and abusing its power. This is true in both organizational and political settings.

Messiah/Controller leadership can be seen in political charismatic leaders such as Fidel Castro and perhaps today in Russia's Putin, who on the one hand inspire populist support, and on the other control with an iron fist. In organizations, this pairing of Messiah/Controller can play out in different ways. The Messiah leader may inspire employees to follow their vision while the control they exert may be either explicitly authoritarian, when they lead by fear, bullying and coercion 'follow orders or lose your job', or it may be a form of culture control which, while it is seemingly benevolent and encourages autonomy is also critiqued as a totalizing form of culture control. Casey (1995) calls this a 'corporatized and capitulated self' when employees unknowingly capitulate to the rhetoric and culture of the organization. In these cultures, any questioning of the vision or the leadership is seen as being disloyal and the employee is side-lined from promotion, silenced or pushed out.

When Messiah/Therapist pairing dominate in the West, it usually reflects the individualistic cultural bias, as both Messiah and Therapist leaders are identified with individuality. The Messiah is identified as a charismatic individual and the Therapist as a caring leader focusing on motivating employees to self-actualize at work (Maslow, 1968), or as Rose (1990) puts it, 'we come to work to work on ourselves'.

When the Therapist is paired secondary to Messiah leadership in the West, it reveals how soft power is utilized. Aligning charismatic-individual leadership and building strong organizational cultures that focus on employee engagement, good reward systems and loyal followers. This combination that aims for 'happy workers to be more productive workers' creates a powerful leadership model. In non-Western contexts Messiah/Therapist leadership has a different emphasis due to the less individualistic culture that does not have such a strongly embedded 'therapy culture' (Furedi, 2003). It often points to a charismatic/strong leader being very skilled at working with traditional and cultural relational-network ties. This was apparent for example in the Indian context and other Asian contexts where the Therapist appears to be strong alongside the Messiah.

The Messiah discourse was also dominant in Argentina and China with Eco-leadership in second place. In France and Russia Messiah led with Controller as equal for Russia and second for France. There are different reasons behind these results which can be reviewed in each related chapter. Scandinavia, Japan, Germany and Brazil had the lowest Messiah discourses, reflecting a general dislike and distrust of a lot of power being given or taken by individual leaders. It is worth noting that when the Messiah leadership is dominant it never rises above 50%, therefore it is always partial and influenced by the other discourses.

Therapist discourse

Scandinavia and Germany with 50% had the most dominant Therapist outcomes, followed by Australia with 45%. These countries have relatively strong and stable economies. They are also recognized as highly valuing democracy. Interestingly, the second discourse behind Therapist was not consistent across these but varied in each country pointing to a diversity of leadership approaches even though they share the dominant focus.

Scandinavia's dominant pairing of Therapist/Eco-leadership reveals a leadership that is people-focused with a systemic, connected and networked view of the world. Germany's dominant discourse was Therapist/Controller leadership, which perhaps reflects their valuing of democratic and relational leadership approaches, expressed for example by their laws for workers to be represented at board level (Therapist), alongside a strong scientific-rationalist bias, which informs their strong engineering base and great success at efficient and high-quality organizational delivery (Controller). Interestingly in Germany, the chapter points to a lesser revealed shadow of this scientific rationalism, 'German romanticism', which is discussed later in the book. The Australian Therapist/Messiah leadership reveals a highly valued relational leadership, relating to its egalitarian, new world democratic culture, alongside the belief in individualist, heroic, even perhaps rebellious leadership.

Therapist leadership was also the leading discourse in the Arab Middle East, Brazil, Japan and the UK. Where Therapist leadership emerged in non-Western cultures, it revealed how regions like Japan and the Arab Middle East have very strong relational-network ties that are deeply embedded in their cultures, and which often strongly influence political and organizational leadership. To get things done one has to be very skilled at working within the particular expression of the indigenous relational-networks. This is different to Therapist leadership in the West, which is partly about relationships, especially in team dynamics, but is also focused on a more pervasive Therapeutic culture, i.e. motivating individuals, and leading with emotional intelligence.

The countries scoring lowest on Therapist leadership were China, South Africa and Mexico on 10% and Russia, France, DR Congo and Poland on 15%.

Controller discourse

Ethiopia, Mexico, Turkey, South Africa and Russia all had dominant Controller discourses, on 40% (for Russia, Controller was level with Messiah). Interestingly, all had Messiah in second place, pointing to powerful individual leadership and leaning towards controlling and authoritarian approaches, sharing similarities with Poland and DR Congo with the same two discourses in reverse order. All of these countries have been through turbulent times, post-communist, post-apartheid and economic turbulence which reveals a pattern of Controller–Messiah type political leadership which then impacts on how leadership is enacted in organizational life too. The lowest representation for Controller leadership was in Scandinavia at 5%, and the UK at 10%, both countries that led with the Therapist discourse. Unusual findings were Brazil, which had a high Therapist score and Controller in second place, indicating an unsettled and dynamic leadership situation.

Eco-leadership discourse

The Eco-leadership discourse was dominant in only one region, ASEAN at 35%. It was strongly represented in second place in Japan 35%, followed by China, Scandinavia and the UK, respectively, with 30% while both Arab Middle East and Argentina scored 25%. Eco-leadership usually scored low when Messiah was strong with the exception of China where it was second place to Messiah. This reflects the paradoxical nature of Chinese leadership, which is discussed in Chapter 24.

Eco-leadership is an emergent discourse in the West, becoming important as organizations struggle to come to terms with the increasingly networked society. Eco-leadership is emergent in the leadership literature and in practice as leaders and organizations try to become more adaptive and adjust to the fast-changing network society in which we now live.

Eco-leadership in the West is concerned with the pragmatic necessity of distributing leadership and also is focused on social responsibility and the environment. It is a growing but not yet dominant trend in European countries such as Scandinavia, UK, Germany and France, where it showed at 20% or more. In the East, Eco-leadership represents less of an emergent discourse and reflects a longer holistic tradition. It equates less to the theme of distributing leadership to adapt to the digital age, or to new ethical sensibilities in relation to social responsibility and the environment. In China, Japan and ASEAN regions, Eco-leadership had a strong showing that reflects much longer-held holistic and collective traditions and cultures, which are also enacted through the Eco-leadership discourse. Perhaps the strong showing of Eco-leadership in these regions reflect a very interesting trend where premodern sensibilities and wisdom are proving to be very useful in our postmodern era.

The ASEAN region produced an unusual result. The chapter pointed to strong Messiah and Controller leadership within many of the ASEAN individual countries, yet each with a capacity to act in a relational and collaborative way across the ASEAN region taking a more holistic, strategic and collective position. This unique position accounts for the high Eco-leadership discourse with Messiah in second place. The lowest scores on Eco-Leadership were Russia, Poland, Ethiopia and DR Congo, interestingly all countries with recent histories of totalitarian systems (communist) and/or recent wars.

GRAPH 4: CONTINENTAL DATA

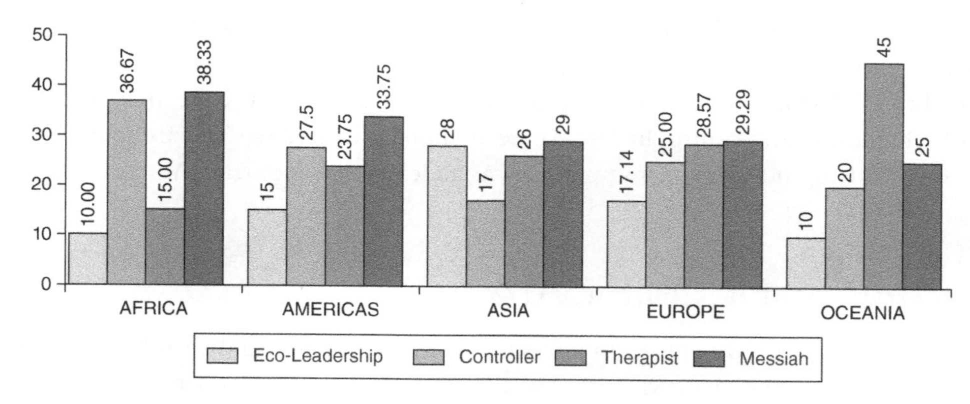

Figure 23.4 Leadership discourses by geographic region

Continental data discussion

Figure 23.4 shows the results of organizing the country/region data into continental groups. Messiah leadership dominates all continents but always with a very fine margin (with the exception of Oceania, which is represented only by a single country, Australia).

Africa has a very strong score for Controller as the second discourse, indicating a pattern of authoritarian leadership dominated by strong individual leaders. The Americas have the same pattern as Africa, with Controller in second but with more balance towards the Therapist in third place. Asia and Europe are more equally balanced across the leadership discourses. Europe's first and second discourses are Messiah and Therapist leadership, with Controller and Eco-leadership showing more strongly than other continents (excepting Asia). This reflects the strong individualism alongside the democratic traditions and therapy culture that exists in Europe.

A key difference between Europe and Asia is that Eco-leadership is only 1% behind Messiah leadership in Asia, which puts Eco-leadership over 10% higher than Europe. This reflects the more collective and holistic cultures and traditions that are translated into leadership practices in Asia. In Europe, the Controller scored higher in third place, reflecting the continuing influence for the demand for efficiency which is delivered by science and rationalism inspired by industrial leaders such as Henry Ford in the USA, Gottlieb Daimler in Germany, Henry Fayol in France.

These findings therefore reveal many similarities in shared leadership discourses but also culturally nuanced differences. The Westernized view that Controller leadership is more common in Asia than Europe is challenged in these findings, and this contrasting view is discussed within the Chinese chapter. Westernized assumptions of Controller leadership as being about 'power distance' (Hofstede, 2001) and inferring authoritarian control are contrasted with other assumptions from within Asian cultures (as written by the chapter authors) that reflect practices and traditions that demand a different view. Relational leadership and holistic thinking that infiltrates leadership practices (Therapist and Eco-Leadership), undermine a projected Westernized perspective that sees only authoritarianism and control in Asia. These are important findings for further reflection as they challenge normative assumptions of Asian leadership through a Westernized gaze.

GRAPH 5: INCOME DATA

The importance of economy and more specifically the income and wealth inequalities in this increasingly globalized world has become a major issue for a growing number of people across countries. The international interest shown in the research revealing this growing disparity published by Thomas Piketty (2014) reveals how important this issue has become, both in terms of social justice, but also in terms of social stability. It is therefore interesting to look for any correlation between the findings of the discourse analysis and the level of Gross National Income (GNI) per capita in each country/region represented. To this end, the discourse findings are organized into five 'income groups' based on the World Bank Atlas method and its 2016 data, as in Table 23.1.

Figure 23.5 shows the key findings that Messiah with Controller leadership are the highest discourses in the lower income groupings. In the high income groups, Therapist followed by Messiah leadership are the leading discourses. The data suggest a link between

Table 23.1 Countries/regions by income group

Income groups[a]	Countries[b]
Low	Ethiopia
	Congo DRC
Lower–Middle	ASEAN
	India
Upper–Middle	Brazil
	China
	Mexico
	South Africa
	Turkey
High non-OECD	Argentina
	Middle East
	Russia

Income groups[a]	Countries[b]
High OECD	Australia
	France
	Germany
	Japan
	Poland
	Scandinavia
	UK
	USA

[a] For the 2016 fiscal year, low income economies are defined as those with a GNI per capita, calculated using the following World Bank Atlas method: Low income economies are those with a GNI per capita of $1,045 or less; Lower middle income economies are those with a GNI per capita between $1,046 and $4.125; Upper middle income economies are those with a GNI per capita between $4.126 and $12,735; High income non-OECD and OECD economies are those with a GNI per capita of $12.736 or more.

[b] Note that between 2016 data and the 2018 fiscal year three countries changed groups: Congo DRC is now part of the Lower middle group and Argentina and Russia are now part of the High non-OECD group.

charismatic-authoritarian leadership in low income countries versus relational, humanistic and charismatic leadership in higher income countries. The question that arises here is how much is cause and how much effect, i.e. does a low-income economy produce a charismatic–authoritarian leadership, or does charismatic–authoritarian leadership produce a low-income economy? The answer to this will be local and specific rather than universal, and will be nuanced and reflexive, rather than polarized.

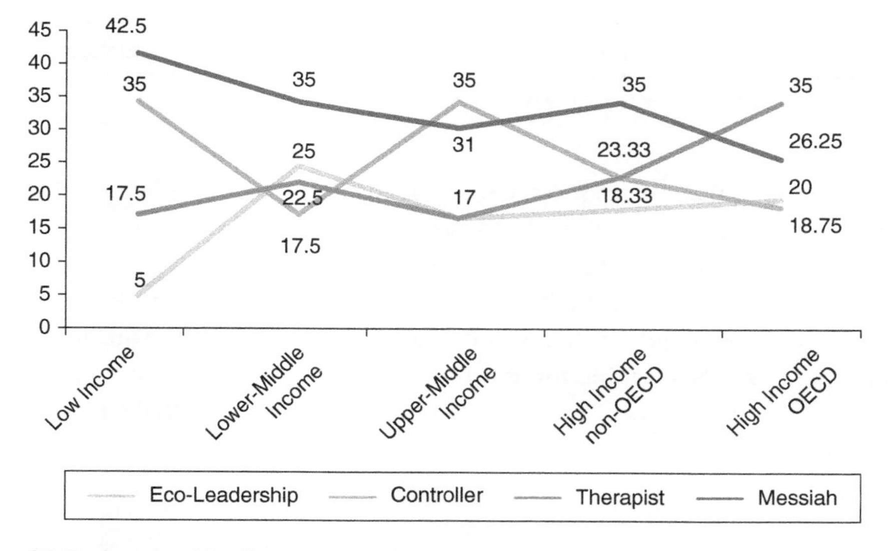

Figure 23.5 Leadership discourses by income group

GRAPH 6: EDUCATIONAL DATA

More than ever, education plays a central role in our growingly connected and networked societies. Yet, despite significant gains in human development levels in almost every country, millions of people have not benefited from this progress. According to the Human Development Report (2016), in every society certain groups are far more likely to suffer disadvantages than others and identifies deep-rooted, and often unmeasured, barriers to development.

It was therefore interesting to explore the relationship between the discourse analysis findings and the 'Education Index' provided by United Nations Development Programme. Based on this Index, Table 23.2 shows how the countries/regions are distributed.

Table 23.2

Education Index[a]	Country	Education Index	Country
Group 1 'High'	Scandinavia	Group 3 'Medium'	Russia
	Australia		ASEAN
	USA		Turkey
	Germany		Mexico
	UK		Brazil
Group 2 'Medium high'	Japan	Group 4 'Low'	China
	France		South Africa
	Poland		India
	Middle East		Congo
	Argentina		Ethiopia

[a] http://hdr.undp.org/en/content/education-index.

Figure 23.6 shows that Therapist leadership dominates the highest educational countries (Group 1), far above the other three discourses. Controller–Messiah discourses are strongly dominant in the lower two educational groupings.

Humanistic and relational leadership approaches therefore seem to be dominant in countries that score highly in terms of education, and in countries with lower educational scores, there is a leaning towards Controller–Messiah leadership that indicates a more authoritarian approach. This probably suggests a vicious circle that reproduces these outcomes.

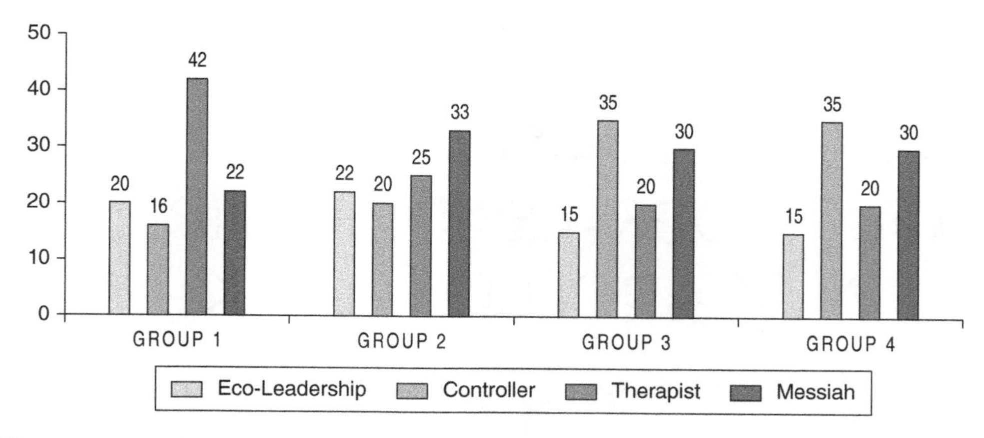

Figure 23.6 Leadership discourses by Education Index (Groups 1–4 in order of ranking, High to Low).

REFERENCES

Casey, Catherine (1995) *Work Self and Society after Industrialisation*. London: Routledge.

Furedi, Frank (2003) *Therapy Culture: Cultivating Vulnerability in an Uncertain Age*. London: Routledge.

Hofstede, G. (2001) *Culture's Consequences: Comparing Values, Behaviours, Institutions, and Organizations Across Nations*, 2nd edn. London: Sage.

Human Development Report (2016) UNDP Human Development Report 2016: Human Development for Everyone. http://report.hdr.undp.org (accessed 9 November 2017).

Maslow, Abraham (1968) *Toward a Psychology of Being*. New York: Van Nostrand.

Piketty, Thomas (2014) *Capital in the Twenty-First Century*. Boston: Belknap Press.

Rose, Nikolas (1990) *Governing the Soul: The Shaping of the Private Self*. London: Routledge.

Sullivan, N. (2003) *A Critical Introduction to Queer Theory*. New York: New York University Press.

Western, S. (2014) 'Autonomist leadership in leaderless movements: anarchists leading the way', *Ephemera: Theory & Politics in Organization*, 14 (4): 673–98.

24
OUTSIDER-LEADERSHIP: IN SEARCH OF LACK

Simon Western

INTRODUCTION: 'MINDING THE GAP' TO REVEAL EMERGENT LEADERSHIP

The previous chapter analysed the regional chapters for insider-leadership and now this chapter aims to 'mind the gap', that is, to identify leadership approaches that are found in the gaps that appear in the dominant leadership literature. The outsider-leadership themes inform and influence the way leadership is practised, usually in a way that goes unnoticed because they are outside of the normative leadership thinking, remnants left over from the previous discourse analysis. The aim is to reveal historically and culturally informed leadership themes and approaches found locally and which are specific to particular regions. These outsider-leadership influences are often unseen, hidden or simply unnoticed because they do not fit into mainstream leadership accounts.

This analysis of the 'lack' revealed the outsider-leadership approaches listed below. Each region or country had one outsider-leadership theme identified for the purposes of this book, although others were also present:

- Ambivalent leadership
- Authoritarian–Democratic leadership
- Collaborative–Controlling leadership
- Conformist leadership
- Disenchanted leadership
- Gaucho leadership
- Fusion leadership
- Paralysed Leadership
- Maverick leadership
- Melancholic leadership
- Negative–Knowledge leadership
- Networked leadership
- Paradoxical leadership
- Progressive leadership
- Racial leadership
- Romantic leadership
- Sacrificial leadership
- Silent–Avoidant leadership
- Transmission leadership
- Trickster leadership

Theoretical account of 'minding the gap'

This chapter draws on a Lacanian psychoanalytic formula of 'minding the gap' (Boxer, 2014). The Freudian unconscious is classically imagined as an ice-erg, with the conscious above the water and different levels of the unconscious beneath the water. Lacan reversed this and claimed that the unconscious was not hidden beneath the surface but was on the surface, there for everybody to see and yet we don't see it, like the 'Purloined Letter' (Lacan and Mehlman, 1972), hence it is unconscious. We can begin to partially see the unconscious by taking the stance of the 'Analyst' (one of Lacan's four discourses) to look for repetitions and also by taking a parallax view, to 'look awry' through a psychoanalytic lens (Žižek, 1992).

In relation to this book, this requires a reading of the regional chapters from a different perspective. Rather than undertaking a forensic-type analysis and looking for traces of the four discourses in each chapter, the task is to *look awry* and search for the gaps that exists. This means reading from different angles, letting go of our attachments to the normative forms of leadership that are familiar. It is to look beyond a linear gaze to search for what isn't there, what is lacking, also for repetitions and for the remainder that reveals what is surplus to the previous discourse analysis. This surplus covers the gap creating an imaginary whole that helps us manage our anxiety about not-knowing and about facing a lack. Lacan called the remainder the *object petit a* and this both covers the gap, hiding what Lacan calls the 'Real', and at the same time acts like a symptom that points us towards the Real. The Real is unnameable, it is beyond symbolization and language, and yet points to an unconscious truth. In this case the Real points to a subjective truth of how leadership is really practised, perceived and understood at a deeper level beyond rational knowledge. Lacan argues that at the very centre of any reality, there is an element that 'resists being symbolized absolutely' (Lacan, 1988 [1953–1954]: 66) and which he defines as the Real (Arnaud and Vidaillet, 2017).

In psychoanalytic clinical practice, the lack can be revealed to the patient on the couch as a symptom which points to the very essence of who they are becoming. In this book, each outsider-leadership theme discussed acts like a social symptom specific to the region or culture, a symptom that points to the Real of leadership practice. Such a symptom brings to light a subjective truth about leadership that captures an underlying and unconscious affective essence of leadership which cannot be seen or named in the mainstream, positivistic and knowledge-based accounts of leadership. These outsider and nuanced forms of leadership are the remnants that speak through the texts, being informed by the countries cultural and subjective relations to its unconscious truths.

Within this approach, the objective is to open a radical new space in the leadership literature, a space that allows local, regional and diverse contexts to produce their singularity of leadership, one that escapes the globalized leadership norms, and refuses to be conformed to fit into the dominant leadership language.

The themes/symptoms that arise are clearly alien to most leadership theory and development. For a start, they unmask a different idea of leadership, pointing to its cultural historical and affective nature and undoing the individualistic and behavioural bias that exists in the literature.

When a symptom of leadership is named, it (however partially) points to an unconscious truth about the singularity of leadership in that context. It also points to how a culture or country unconsciously enjoys its subjective relationship to leadership (i.e. how the country attains its *jouissance* in Lacan's terms). *Jouissance* is both a pure enjoyment we strive for, and also a form of painful enjoyment that arises from taking an unconscious 'pleasure in our displeasure' (Žižek, 2001; Western, 2016a).

As you read the outsider-leadership of each country, take this into account as it helps to understand and locate the leadership theme we discuss. For example, when *Melancholic leadership* is viewed from a normative perspective it presents a problem that requires a solution. For Melancholic leadership is not normally presented as a leadership ideal that people aspire to, or as a competency that can be used to develop people. Yet, if Melancholic leadership is viewed as a symptom, it reveals vital data in relation to understanding the perspective and challenges in its specific cultural environment; a symptom that reveals the unconscious attachments and investments to this way-of-being in the world. Attempting to cure or overcome this symptom (such as striving for Transformational and Messiah leadership) will only produce defensive responses and repression. This is particularly true as the country will have a particular relationship to the jouissance stimulated by Melancholic leadership. There will be both at the same time, a displeasure, discomfort or hatred of being stuck in melancholia and a perverse pleasure derived in this displeasure/hatred. The task is to understand this symptom, using it as subjective data, accepting it is part of an essence of leadership that points to the Real. By allowing the symptom to speak, and to guide the work of leadership in this specific setting, it will point to finding new leadership ways-of-becoming for this country/region. It may also point to wider leadership lessons and approaches that can be transferable to other countries and regions, or to our global understanding of leadership. For example, Melancholic leadership can challenge the overly positivist hyperbolic stance of leadership in the West, claiming the space for a different leadership. It can also reveal a hypocrisy that creates low morale when the rhetorical calls for authentic leadership clash with a reality that melancholia and sadness have to be masked and hidden.

In the descriptions below a remnant, an outsider-leadership approach, is identified within each chapter. This will reflect an undercurrent or social symptom of a cultural and social way-of-becoming that helps unravel leadership in the present and point towards the future. Further exploration, research and validation of these outsider-leadership approaches/themes are required to develop this work, and these findings will be further discussed in the Conclusion chapter.

AN OUTSIDER-LEADERSHIP ACCOUNT OF LEADERSHIP FOR EACH COUNTRY/REGION STUDIED

The analysis will now focus on the outsider-leadership approaches and themes that have been identified via the mind-the-gap analysis of each individual chapter. These new expressions of leadership offer new insights into the particularity of leadership in each country and region 'its leadership symptom'. Each leadership theme identified also offers a lens to look at leadership in other contexts, an opportunity to cross-wire, to see with new eyes what might be hidden within our own normative assumptions about leadership.

This is not a comprehensive account of these 20 outsider-leadership approaches. This is only the first tentative steps, a beginning of an exploration into peripheral and outsider accounts of leadership. Within these chapters there are many more themes and approaches that can be found. Seek them yourselves in the chapters.

The insights offered should help leadership to be recognized and developed on a one-by-one basis, with a local and specific lens, and not to reduce it to generic skills and universal competency frameworks as in Transformational leadership literature (Bass, 1985, 1998; Conger and Kanungo, 1987; Burns, 2003). The task is to take into account the particularity of each country/region, noting also that the specific nature of the leadership dynamic will also vary pending on its context, e.g. the political, business, social movement or service sector in which it operates. Below are the 20 symptoms of leadership identified in this mind-the-gap analysis.

THE SYMPTOMS OF LEADERSHIP: ONE BY ONE

1 Arab Middle East: Networked leadership

In this region *Networked leadership* is a dominant, if under-reported form of leadership. The author explains that wasta is a term used in the region for 'a social network of interpersonal connections rooted in family and kinship ties that surround and frame specific leadership situations. Wasta involves the exercise of power, influence and information-sharing through social and politico-business networks and is intrinsic to the operation of leadership, central to the transmission of knowledge and the creation of opportunity.' Previously, David Weir explains that wasta has changed over time and will continue changing; it has very positive attributes relating to loyalty, strong kinship ties and bonds, respecting elders and for conflict resolution. It also has negative overtones ranging from complaints about groups and networks that use wasta to protect their elite power, to claims of outright corruption. Networked leadership reflects the two leading discourses of Therapist and Eco-leadership in the Arab Middle East, but with a very particular and localized expression of these discourses. The Eco-leadership part of Networked leadership in

this region emerges mainly from the Islamic religious influences of the Ummah, the belief in the whole community of Muslims that creates a traditional and historical 'networked mindset' which transcends nation states and national borders, what the author calls 'a strongly integrative meme around the one-ness of all creation'. The Therapist influence in Network leadership reflects how wasta privileges networks of relationships and relatedness that are an essential part of the leadership and followership dynamic in this region.

Networked leadership in Western culture is usually associated with the digital age, the networked society (Castells, 2000) and the new forms of a-hierarchical and lateral forms of leadership emerging, such as Autonomist leadership, within new social movements (Melucci, 1989; Castells, 2000, 2012; Western, 2013). It is fascinating to think that Networked leadership is far from being a very recent postmodern and social-media or technology driven phenomenon, as it has particular resonance in premodern Western cultures, and diverse non-Western cultures as well. Perhaps it was this heady mixture of old and new Networked leadership that so radically changed the Middle East in the hopeful days of the Arab Spring revolutions that shook the world. A more sinister and perverse form of Networked leadership is the rhizomatic form of leadership (Deleuze and Guattari, 1987) enacted so effectively by Osama bin Laden, al-Quaeda and other terrorist networks such as Daesh in Syria.

How Networked leadership manifests within each region and across regions, utilizing virtual and real, human and non-human forms, will be a vital factor in the development and impact of leadership in the near future. Networked leadership is a symptom that is pervasive in the Arab Middle East, it informs every aspect of leadership and followership dynamics in a particular way. The next generation of leaders have the opportunity to utilize leadership qualities drawn from the traditional networking culture and infuse this into the new digital era.

2 Argentina: Gaucho leadership

The gaucho is a nomadic horseman adept at cattle work, famous in Argentina for bravery, independence and generosity. *Gaucho leadership* reflects the metaphorical influence of the gaucho in Argentinian culture, a powerful archetype which is still very present in both political and organizational leadership. Drawing on the writing of Martín Fierro, the imagery of the gaucho has 'had a profound contribution to the formation of Argentine national identity. In that sense, pride, strength, nobility, violence, loyalty, insubordination as well as friendliness and empathy define the gaucho' (Barrial et al. in Chapter 2). The itinerant gaucho 'is particularly known for his solitude and single mindedness. ... this idealized, predominantly insular, male leadership is where the essence of Argentine leadership resides' (Chapter 2).

Gaucho leadership merges with other outsider-leadership themes. e.g. Melancholic, Trickster and Maverick leadership come to mind, yet it has its own distinctive 'flavour'. In relation to countries beyond Argentina, the gaucho perhaps reflects back to us both the strength and weaknesses of the focus on radical individuality and leadership. At once heroic and independent, this form of leadership is seductive and attracts emotional projections from followers who either love or hate these leaders. The problem with this is two-fold; first, it creates a polemic leadership that splits a country or organization, and second it disempowers those followers who support the leader as they can give away their power depositing unrealistic hope of salvation in this messianic form of leadership. The Argentinian examples of Peronism followed by Military leadership shows this splitting and idealism and the damage it can do. Learning how to live with their symptom of Gaucho leadership is the key task for Argentinians. That is, how to celebrate and utilize the positive aspects of this essence of their culture, without turning it into the same destructive cycles of the past century that has undermined their political and organizational capacity to work together for economic and social success.

3 ASEAN region: Collaborative–Controlling leadership

The ASEAN (Association of Southeast Asian Nations) region is unusual as it represents 10 very diverse countries (Indonesia, Malaysia, Philippines, Singapore, Thailand, Brunei, Cambodia, Laos, Myanmar and Vietnam). This diversity is political, religious, cultural, historical and economic. What is interesting is that in many of these individual countries political leadership can be authoritarian and controlling, yet in the ASEAN framework they have managed collectively to work very collaboratively. In their chapter, Vaseehar Hassan Bin Abdul Razack and Firoz Abdul Hamid summarized the key factors in ASEAN leadership:

1. Asian-inspired leadership approaches do not fit Westernized individualistic trait models.
2. 'Good' ASEAN leadership is defined by its capacity to bridge differences.

3. Relational leadership is important: whether family, public, private or political.
4. Culture and religion are vital to understand ASEAN leadership styles.

The *Collaborative–Controlling leadership* model is very interesting and clearly does not fit easily in Westernized, individualistic and democratic leadership assumptions. Yet, there is much to learn for global leaders here. Sometimes controlling/authoritarian political systems and leaders are explicit, and sometimes implicit and act through culture control (Kunda, 1992; Casey, 1995). Either way, the capacity to bridge differences and to work more comfortably with what appears to be a paradox to the Westernized conception, seems an essential learning point for leaders across the globe. Balancing Controller leadership and collaborative leadership maybe vitally important to manage transitions. The radical idealism that political systems can move from authoritarian control to democracies, idealism that has been supported by Western governments in places like Syria, Iraq and Libya with disastrous effects may open the door to learning from other ways of leading such as seen in the ASEAN leadership model. *Collaborative–Controlling leadership* may also be very relevant for organizations in transition from hierarchical top-down models towards more networked and Eco-leadership approaches fit for the twenty-first century.

4 Australia: Maverick leadership

Australia has a deeply held maverick and egalitarian ethos, that emerged from its immigrant population and a 'give-it-a-go' attitude. There is a healthy regard for risk-taking leadership and an entrepreneurial spirit in organizational life, politics and sport;

a maverick 'outsider' leader is often a popular national figure. *Maverick leadership* is commonplace in countries and regions that can be tolerant and containing enough to allow the space for healthy dissent and risk-taking. Leadership from the edges (often the maverick) can often provide new insights and innovations in business, politics and social fields, as they offer unconventional 'outsider' views. These leaders have similar profiles to the Trickster leaders so admired in France. In today's fast-changing political and organizational fields, there is a great need for unconventional leaders to find the space to think outside of conventions, to take risks and to experiment. Successful Maverick leaders are early adopters of new technologies and invent or co-create new products and ideas that become mainstream later. Steve Jobs was a maverick, starting on the edge, working with a very focused vision of the future and his legacy is there for all to see. For Australia, the *jouissance* they gain from their attachments to Maverick leadership, like all *jouissance* is a bitter-sweet affair. Maverick leaders can bring something innovative and/or they can be leaders with an adolescent, often male acting-out tendency. Steve Jobs was both, but managed to overcome the latter which made him a great leader. Managing the tensions between being a maverick and managing mainstream expectations is the real skill of a Maverick leader. Without this, the Maverick leader remains an uninfluential outsider often with a small but loyal followership.

5 Brazil: Disenchanted leadership

In Brazil, a generic disenchantment with political and business leaders exists. For instance, leadership is spoken about synonymously with corruption. After many diverse influences that have shaped Brazilian leadership, it seems to privilege hierarchy, authoritarianism and machismo. Drawing on global universal modes of leadership models exported mainly from the USA, it seems that Brazilian leadership is still in search of its own unique identity. This probably contributes to corruption as these factors do not encourage a critical or engaged followership who will challenge upwards. Although there are other more positive influences in Brazil, it seems that in current times, *Disenchanted leadership* is a good descriptor. Brazilian political leaders use disenchantment as a mobilizing force, feeding off the disenchantment felt about their opponents, which creates a vicious circle of disenchantment and hopelessness.

Disenchanted leadership can operate in two directions. Followers are disenchanted in leadership, which reveals and perpetuates a lack of trust and engagement. This process effectively de-authorizes leaders in general, even the good ones, producing wider societal and organizational discontents. Leaders often turn further towards authoritarian control when confronted with disenchanted followers, as they do not feel authorized from below.

Disenchanted leadership in general is a widespread phenomenon in many parts of the world. Political leadership in Europe is under scrutiny and also in the USA. Among business employees, disenchantment with leadership is rife. The 2014 Edelman's Trust Barometer of public attitudes found that 'CEOs and government leaders remain at the bottom of the list of trusted figures'.[1] Disenchantment in leadership is a widespread global phenomenon. Disenchanted followers who desire and expect more ethical and thoughtful leadership can either use the disenchantment as a force for bottom-up change, or they can 'fall in love with their symptom'. This problem arises when the symptom 'Disenchanted leadership' is constantly complained about but in reality provides hidden benefits, for example as an excuse for followers not to take responsibility for change and always blame the bad leaders. A group-think and comfort zone is created whereby disenchantment is the glue that holds the in-group together. I have witnessed Disenchanted leadership in many public-sector and large bureaucratic companies, where the disenchanted followers take great pleasure in their complaining about the leader/ship and at the same time block any positive change. This surplus enjoyment or '*plus de jouir*', in Lacanian terms, points to how people become attached to a symptom and enjoy its destructive aspects too much. In psychoanalytic terms, this is an over-identification with the Thanatos, the death drive.

6 China: Paradoxical leadership

Paradoxical leadership refers to a leadership that can embrace paradoxical situations without trying to solve the paradoxical dilemma in a black-and-white or linear fashion. The Chinese capacity to work comfortably with paradox, stands out as one of its defining

[1]Edelman's Annual Survey 2014: p.6. www.edelman.com/insights/intellectual-property/2014-edelman-trust-barometer (accessed 24 November 2017).

features of leadership. In Part One Jeff de Kleijn, Nai-keung Lau, Jian Liang and Chao Chen state that 'Chinese culture has "the ability ... to hold different propositions simultaneously without distress"'(Cotterell, 2002: 30) (p. 54) and they contrast this approach with cultures that think in a more linear way and have a stronger tendency to remove paradoxes to reach a state of unambiguity. This, they say, makes Chinese leadership hard to comprehend.

The meta-picture of a communist party unleashing and managing a capitalist economy with results that are stunning, is an example of such Paradoxical leadership in practice. The chapter authors say that Chinese leaders 'are consciously balancing among many competing opposites, refusing to permanently settle on one side, preferring to leave themselves opportunities to fall back on a broad base of mental and cultural resources. For example, the Chinese executive continues to navigate between pragmatism and spirituality, socialism and capitalism, universalism and particularism (the rule of man and law) etc.' (p. 55).

Paradoxical leadership in the Chinese context, brings together aspects such as 'action is by not action; leader is the follower; change is not strategically planned but sudden enlightenment' (Lee, 1987: 31). The chapter authors explain Western misconceptions: 'Chinese leadership in the West is often still stereotypical and perceived through a lens of Western leadership practice. Consequently, a feature of Chinese leadership like paternalism is too often interpreted not only as a single dominate aspect but linked to an assumption of strong top-down authoritarianism, high power distance (Hofstede, 2001) and uniformity over diversity and creativity' (p. 53). The authors point to the Yin of Confucian paternalism and the Yang of Taoist holistic thinking, that does not see opposites but rather different aspects of the same system.

Applied beyond the Chinese context, Paradoxical leadership is also found in other non-Western cultures that have more paternalistic and holistic cultures and are less binary and linear than the West. Paradoxical leadership is also becoming increasingly important in Westernized cultures, as disruptive forces in today's globalized-networked society creates environments of volatility, complexity and ambiguity. In this scenario, leaders are constantly facing contradictory, complex and non-binary challenges.

Three common paradoxes faced by leaders across the globe are:

From vertical to lateral

Senior leaders can no longer control from the centre or from the top as they could before the network society unleashed its disruptive influences. Organizations need to distribute leadership and give more power to lateral forces in order to create adaptive organizations that maximize the potential of all employees, i.e. they need to embrace Eco-leadership. Yet to give more power to lateral forces and to distribute leadership is also to relinquish control. This can feel highly risky when their own futures are judged on short-term results, and when volatile environments traditionally require the opposite, i.e. strong leadership from the top. The paradox of letting go of control and distributing leadership when advisers, experience and gut instinct are telling a leader to take control in the face of disruptive forces is difficult to manage.

Messiah leadership before Eco-leadership

To address the disruptions created by the network society, CEOs and leaders grapple to deliver Eco-Leadership e.g. to distribute leadership, recruit and retain talent and create more adaptive, ethical, purposeful and creative organizations. Some organizations grow organically towards Eco-leadership which emerges from the edges and bottom up. However, and paradoxically, in traditional hierarchical organizations it can take Messiah leadership to deliver Eco-leadership. In this case, a CEO and leadership team mobilizes followers with a vision, purpose and strategy to deliver Eco-leadership and the new organizational forms required. The paradox of requiring individual charismatic leadership with influence and power (Messiah), to deliver the opposite, distributed leaders everywhere (Eco-leadership) creates challenges that require a way of transcending this paradox. I consult to many organizations whose CEOs realize the urgent need to change to an Eco-leadership way of working. Yet this desire for change is often undone by an inability to let go of being the Messiah, and/or Controller leader, which they rely on to deliver the change (see Western, 2018, for a book chapter that expands on this).

Leaders in leaderless social movement

Despite the claims of social movement activists and commentators that they are leaderless, they are actually filled with leaders, albeit leaders without position power. Research shows how 'leaderless' social movements such as Occupy are actually filled with Autonomist Leaders (Western, 2014) and this creates internal tensions in these movements. The inability of these movements to live in a world of Paradoxical leadership undermines their potential to move from protest movements to social change movements (Western, 2014: 694).

Paradoxical leadership is increasingly becoming a much required capability in mainstream organizations, as discussed in the *Harvard Business Review* and other mainstream literature (see Lewis et al., 2014; Smith et al., 2016).

7 Democratic Republic of Congo: Racial leadership

The DR Congo offers a few distinct outsider-leadership themes; clannish leadership and divine leadership arise, for example. But what stands out is the *Racial leadership* that runs throughout the chapter, with the story of colonization still unfolding in cultural, social, economic and racial terms. The chapter author Déo M. Nyamusenge discusses racial-based leadership that contradicts Congolese authenticity-based claims on leadership. I quote him:

> There is a real 'white' perception of leadership-power. The 'white' people are frequently perceived as rich and powerful or very close to the source of formal power. They access and utilize power more easily, e.g. getting bank loans or public contracts; and live in the most comfortable areas. Among them, European people and, especially the Belgians, are called 'maternal uncle' (*noko*) in Kinshasa. This wording is ambiguous. In matriarchal areas of DRC, maternal uncles have solid relationships with nephews because they are their inheritors. But uncles are also feared; accused of causing mysterious deaths of nephews.

Racial leadership points to a leadership that draws on race as a main influence as to how leaders gain and retain, position, power and authority. Sadly, I doubt if many countries could claim to be free from Racial-leadership influences, even in countries that assert themselves to be the most advanced and developed, or the most egalitarian. When Obama became the first black US President, the West was reminded of how much work on identity and racial issues is still needed to get beyond distorted advantage and privilege based on race, and the political reaction to his presidency (e.g. the election of Trump, and the rise of Black Lives Matter in the face of ongoing racism) is asking big questions again about race and the role of racial leadership in the USA. Racial leadership emerges in other chapters and is especially overt in those with diverse histories and cultures, e.g. South Africa. Looking at leadership through the lens of privilege gained via identity, ethnicity and gender remains a key task if we are to improve opportunity for all and to maximize the potential of hidden or repressed leadership in organizations. Racial leadership in the DR Congo needs to find reparative ways to engage with its own history and legacy in order to come to terms with this ongoing traumatic symptom.

8 Ethiopia: Negative-Knowledge leadership

Negative-Knowledge leadership is learning the art of 'what not to do' in order to get things done. This form of leadership is accentuated in Ethiopia due to historical and socio-cultural factors, but signifies a more common leadership phenomenon that is rarely acknowledged in other countries and cultures. The Ethiopian authors cite Kapuscinski's reconstructed interviews with former officials of Haile Selassie's imperial court:

> Whoever wanted to climb the steps of the Palace had first of all to master the negative knowledge: what was forbidden to him and his subalterns, what was not to be said or written, what should not be done, what should not be overlooked or neglected. Only from such negative knowledge could positive knowledge be born – but that positive knowledge always remained obscure and worrisome, because no matter how

> well they knew what *not* [italics original] to do, the Emperor's favourites ventured only with extreme caution and uncertainty into the area of propositions and postulates. (Kapuscinski, (1983 [1978]: 49)

In stark contrast to the popular idea of an action-orientated leadership, in Ethiopia it is only when negative-knowledge is mastered that positive action can take place. In authoritarian regimes and totalitarian cultures, particularly where it is dangerous to challenge hierarchies Negative-Knowledge leadership becomes essential for survival and also to get things done.

Such a leadership is a product of authoritarian cultures. At first it is underpinned by fear, which then becomes a culturally learned norm. It produces a coerced and passive followership which stifles economies such as the Soviet communist system (Fukuyama, 1992). Authoritarian cultures, however, are not always as explicit, as when led by dictatorships. They occur in different forms, and do not always have to be overtly brutal. Highly bureaucratic cultures, such as large public-sector bodies and the military, can produce a fear of challenging authority which turns into a learning about how to gain position power through mimicking the Negative-Knowledge leadership from above. Although things have changed in Ethiopia since Selassie's reign, in their chapter Fentahun Mengistu, Vachel Miller and Girma Shimelis point to a continuation of Negative-Knowledge leadership, in order to retain one's position or to attain favour to climb the hierarchical ladder:

> This notion of 'negative knowledge' remains salient in contemporary organizational life in Ethiopia. Often, staff members maintain a passive stance, cautious about making independent decisions for fear that mistakes or missteps will be sharply criticized. Safety is found in mastering the 'negative knowledge' of what not to do, and when taking action, only implementing explicit directives from above. (p. 000)

I have witnessed such stifling cultures in large public-sector bureaucracies such as the NHS in the UK, where the most committed clinicians who try to change things for the good of their patients can be marginalized or pushed out of the institution, often in a very brutal and harsh way.

However, Negative-Knowledge leadership also reveals something else, beyond the reaction to working in explicitly authoritarian regimes. Kapuscinski is identifying two things; first 'coercive passive-followership' which creates conformist and totalizing cultures. The other is the form of leadership whereby those who rise to power in the court are those who have best mastered how to get things done through Negative-Knowledge leadership. These leaders mentor and role-model to others showing how to work the system, how to behave as a leader–follower without threatening the hierarchy above. This is a real act of contextualized leadership. There is a difference between dependent leadership (and followership as these are fluid and interchangeable) and Negative-Knowledge leadership/followership. Dependent leadership indicates a dependency state of mind, that evokes a passivity whereby individuals and teams wait for others in the hierarchy to tell them what to do as they lack the confidence to act. Negative-Knowledge leadership is where the individual or team is actively participating in a culture that limits their autonomy, so they work very hard to perform having negative knowledge, in order to get things done. If such a culture is kept strong by its members (despite their awareness of overt dysfunctionalities) it is also because such bureaucracies protect their members and create sub-elites and sub-cultures where power is exercised to those lower in the pecking order.

From a culture such as Ethiopia where this leadership is quite explicit, Negative-Knowledge leadership may have much wider implications in unexpected places. Could the organizational disasters such as Enron and the financial collapse of 2008 be due in part to Negative-Knowledge leadership? Retrospectively, it was very clear that the failures were inevitable, yet so many employees and regulators just did not see what was happening. The culture control that occurs in large global corporations that on the surface demands creativity and autonomy, can also impose group-think and can silence critical voices, revealing another form of Negative-Knowledge leadership. Employees learn a performativity that looks from the outside like there is a dynamic and open culture. Yet in reality, there is conformity and silence taking place. In this case a hidden form of Negative-Knowledge leadership creates a culture where leaders and employees turn a blind-eye to bullying, sexism, unethical practices etc. all claiming to have negative-knowledge of what is really going on. Perhaps Negative-Knowledge leadership can be found in successful corporate companies as well as political dictatorships. Employees can become unaware of their own subjugation to an organizational culture (Casey, 1995). They can be active and successful leaders in their teams and departments, without being aware that they are also turning a blind-eye (Steiner, 1985) to how they are also practising Negative-Knowledge leadership (Willmott, 1993).

9 France: Trickster leadership

The French ideal vision for a leader is presented by the French author Valérie Petit as a charismatic leader who is 'charming, amoral and individualistic' following the French fondness for the ambivalent and roguish qualities of the *trickster* (Radin, 1987 [1956]). Petit makes the case for French particularism that separates religion and state, private and professional, claiming this undermines the call in many countries for moral leadership. The trickster is a mythical archetype character who plays tricks and subverts the establishment in unconventional ways. The trickster was usually a figure on the edges, sometimes an imaginary being, often an outsider who could say the unsayable with humour or magic, like in Molière's comedies such as *The Misanthrope, The School for Wives, Tartuffe,*

The Miser, The Imaginary Invalid and *The Bourgeois Gentleman.* Often a trickster would be brought into the court by a king or emperor to challenge the norms, bring humour and break tensions or to name the unnameable ensuring a safety valve for the court system.

The trickster would not usually be thought of as a leader, particularly a leader in a formal setting. So, the French connection between leaders and trickster qualities challenges this norm. Perhaps in times where technological disruption is the norm, there is growing place for disruptive and subversive Trickster leaders who can make disruptive interventions themselves. Emmanuel Macron, elected as President in 2017, may have a few of the trickster qualities discussed, in that he has an unconventional marriage (that may have been challenged moralistically in other countries), he is charming and he subverted the institutional power of the Socialist party he left and all the other political parties, starting alone with a new party called 'En Marche', meaning 'walking'/'on the move'. His election completely undid the normal political order; that took a courageous strategy and elements of being a charming trickster.

Trickster politicians have also appeared in other countries under the banner of populism; for example the charming, ponytailed subversive leader of Podemos in Spain, and perhaps the roguish amoralistic and disruptive politics of Donald Trump align him to this

Trickster leadership camp. The symptom presented by Trickster leadership links closely to Maverick and Gaucho leadership; they all have endearing qualities that delight and create affective attachments from admirers; yet at the same time they can be disruptive and dangerous. A symptom that requires careful attention!

In organizations, Trickster leadership is usually seen as leadership from the edges, that disrupts for both good and bad, but following politics trends perhaps we will see more Trickster leadership in organizations.

10 Germany: Romantic leadership

Within German leadership, tensions and dualities work alongside each other, as the German author Claudia Nagel says: 'The fundamental tension that characterizes the German approach to leadership is best shown in the most unusual and most important pair of opposites – the art of engineering, desiring perfection and rational thinking and, on the flip side, the philosophical mode of thinking of German Idealism (Kant, Fichte, Hegel, Schopenhauer, Schelling, among others) paired with the art of German Romanticism (e.g. Novalis, ETA Hoffmann, Goethe, Eichendorff, Wagner and also Karl May)' (p. 95).

Nagel points to a very present and particular form of *Romantic leadership*, that is hidden in most organizational leadership literature, yet is very much of the essence of the German soul. The author directs attentions to a 'hidden desire to achieve something greater, more beautiful, deeper and higher at the same time, which is essential to the German Romanticism and German Idealism, is probably the more unconscious part of this leadership-influencing pair of opposite notions' (p. 95).

The Romantics of the eighteenth and early nineteenth century in Europe (Goethe, Shelley, Burns etc.) provided an external form of cultural and critical leadership through poetry, art and literature. They critiqued the early modern, urbanizing and industrializing world in which they saw the seeds of natural destruction and dehumanizing factories. Looking at leadership in contemporary times through this lens of Romanticism, I see in my international coaching and consulting role a growing body of leaders who would identify with this description of Romantic leadership. They are desirous of seeking more beauty and something deeper and more purposeful and meaningful than exists in their current roles and organizations. The overuse of the superlatives such as 'being passionate' and the hyped-up grandiose vision statements are losing authentic leaders who are becoming disenchanted with rhetoric. Leaders in middle management positions who after a bright start in their careers look upwards and don't like what they see. I also coach CEOs and senior leaders later in their careers who have been very high achievers but having chased their career successes, they now feel an emptiness and lack in their lives that creates a desire to turn to higher ideals. Romantic leadership as a symptom produces a very important antidote to a harsher utilitarian and functionalism, ever more driven by short-term goals, excessive data and number crunching. Perhaps Romantic leadership needs to be included in mainstream executive education and will help develop leaders who are more balanced, creative, idealistic, sensitive and humane in their approaches to their work.

11 India: Transmission leadership

Transmission leadership reflects a particular dynamic in India, one where leadership is transmitted between leader and follower. This cultural assumption comes from the deeply embedded religious sensibilities in India. As the Indian authors Asha Bhandarker and Pritam Singh write:

> Evidence of religious and spiritual orientation was found in a recent study (Spencer et al., 2005) which concluded that Indian CEOs have reported greater spiritual and or religious sources of inner strength as compared to their global peers. (p. 101)

The Hindu religious practice of the Guru–disciple relationship cannot be detached from the belief in karma, rebirth and 'destiny':

> The concept of Guru – the remover of darkness, who leads one towards enlightenment – is embedded in Indian religion and philosophy. Faith in Gurus can be seen even today in the manner in which religious cults flourish in India and the complete faith and suspension of judgement which Gurus evoke among their acolytes. (p. 99)

Within the workplace, Transmission leadership is a hidden cultural norm that remains a largely unspoken and unrecognized assumption (a lack that is present as a remainder) and it can have different impacts. According to the insider-analysis, Indians are prone towards Messiah leadership (45%), which perhaps is partly due to these cultural beliefs, which have both positive and negative effects. At a positive level, it offers a particular mentoring relationship, a focus on continuity and embraces a longer-term even transcendental aspect of leadership that counters short-termism and informs a values-based and socially committed leadership. On the downside, Transmission leadership can lead to a misuse of power, and destiny can be used as an individual and cultural excuse for not achieving and for keeping people in their place. The belief in destiny has both positive and negative implications, as the Indian authors write:

> On the positive side, we have observed that those leaders who believe in destiny (karma) attribute their success to destiny rather than attributing it to self. This protects the person from hubris, generates humility and open-mindedness. This belief also provides a psychological placebo to those who are unable to cope with the terrible tragedies, which occur in life. However, continued negative interpretation of karma, blaming past life for one's non-performance rather than take responsibility for one's actions in the present life is one of the real dangers of a continued use of this approach. (p. 101)

Overall in India, the idea of Transmission emanates from the Hindu religion but is culturally pervasive in other ways. Using famous leaders like Mahatma Ghandi as role models to follow in the hope that their essence will transmit to the follower is commonplace. Transformational leadership theory (Bass, 1998; Burns, 1978) echoes this way of transmitting leadership in the modern world:

> Leaders are authentically transformational when they increase awareness of what is right, good, important and beautiful, when they help to elevate followers' needs for achievement and self-actualization, when they foster in followers higher moral maturity and when they move followers to go beyond their self-interests for the good of their group, organization or society. (Bass, 1998: 171)

This is why Transformational leadership fitted so well and was very popular in the Indian workplace (Singh et al., 2012). Beyond India, Transmission leadership seeps into our unconscious through the language and discourse of Messiah leadership:

> Transformational leaders exhibit charismatic behaviours, arouse inspirational motivation, provide intellectual stimulation and treat followers with individual consideration. These behaviours transform their followers helping them to reach their full potential and generate the highest levels in performance. (Dvir et al., 2002: 736)

It also seeps in via leadership development programmes that often fetishize Eastern exotic approaches and utilizing these for gaining loyal and committed even cult-like followership in corporations (Tourish and Pinnington, 2002). Lacan claims 'our desire is the desire of the other', meaning that what we desire is an unconscious expression of what our parents, partners, leaders (significant others) desire for us. Transmission leadership when understood in this context can be either beneficial or undermining. If our unconscious desires are inspired by those of a leader acting in good faith, she/he will transmit the desire also to act in good faith, which will be internalized by the follower. However, if the leader is egotistic, narcissistic or power-driven, the desire for selfish power will be transmitted at an unconscious level, whatever veneer of 'good leadership' they may show to the world.

The symptom of Transmission leadership has positive qualities when it is culturally aligned and used to drive an ethical, dynamic and humane leadership approach.

If the Indian context produces Transmission leadership as a cultural symptom, then the question for the next generation of Indian leaders (the youngest country in the world) is how they will adapt, embody, shape or reject this approach in their leadership. Bhandarker and Singh hint at a secularized and optimistic use of the symptom, whereby the Transmission takes place via mentoring and coaching, saying:

> Millennial Indians look for leaders who are mentors and coaches, who give them greater independence and autonomy. (p. 103)

This is a story to unfold!

12 Japan: Silent–Avoidant leadership

Two things stand out in the Japanese chapter, both are counter-cultural to mainstream Western views on leadership: the first is Silent leadership, the second Avoidant leadership.

Silent leadership

The first is counter-cultural to the commonly held idea that a good leader is an excellent orator and communicator, and are action-orientated, extrovert and charismatic. The Japanese essence of leadership suggests the opposite, a form of *Silent leadership* described as follows by chapter authors Yasuhiro Hattori and Daniel Arturo Heller:

> [A] Japanese leader is asked to show his or her attitude without using any words. It is partly about speaking through actions, but more importantly a leader or future leader is evaluated by how consistent his or her efforts have been over an extended period of time ... a silver tongue is generally not enough to win over others. The silent leader is often viewed as the best leader. (p. 109)

Avoidant leadership

The second counter-cultural idea is that leadership itself is not desirable. In Japan people are not constantly fighting to climb the ladder to leadership success, as other values override the desire for leadership. The Japanese chapter suggests that power, responsibilities and type of work that come under the banner of leadership are often viewed as unattractive and unwelcome. This judgement is based on: (a) quality of life decisions and (b) how leadership is valued less than a professional specialization or expertise. Taking a generic leadership role can be seen as an obstacle to develop the specialization expertise and the career it offers. This leads to '*Avoidant leadership*', which is a powerful emergent force in Japan, and perhaps is more widespread outside of Japan and in other areas of life than we realize. The accepted narrative that leadership is desirable and offers opportunities in terms of holding power, gaining personal respect, improving one's career and compensation, and being able to 'make a difference' is challenged by the symptom, Avoidant leadership.

Looking beyond Japan, the intense public scrutiny that public leaders now endure, and the growing lack of respect towards once-revered establishment leaders in many contexts, undermines the desire to lead. This change can mean a lowering standard of candidates for leadership positions both in public service and in organizational life. In the UK the once-revered position of being a head teacher in a school no longer seems attractive as thousands quit, and a shortage of applicants is creating a deficit problem (Woolcock, 2016) The challenges of leadership today in complex and bureaucratic systems is also a challenge that many avoid.

Another factor echoing the Japanese example is that people may find more stability or security through specializing in transferrable expert technical-professional skills, than mastering generic leadership skills which may leave them less protected in challenging labour markets.

Silent–Avoidant leadership in Japan reflects old and new culture coming together. Across the globe we can surely learn from the Japanese idea of the Silent leader which can bring a much greater balance to overvaluing the power of leadership rhetoric, charisma and hubris. There is a rising disenchantment with the grandiose vision statements, performative charisma and banal passionate rhetoric that gets peddled out in so many leadership 'Ted' talks, keynotes and publications.

While Silent leadership offers a vitally important counter-narrative to the normative Messiah leadership literature, Avoidance leadership offers a real warning about the undesirability of leadership in today's world. Perhaps the two are linked!

13 Mexico: Fusion leadership

Fusion leadership is a phenomenon that could describe aspects of leadership in all of our chapters. In Mexico, it has a particularly strong presence with a fusion that impacts on leadership dynamics drawing on so many influences, from indigenous, colonial, pre-modern, modern, social movement, emancipatory revolutionary, religious and autocratic leadership approaches and cultures. The authors list examples of leaders who symbolically represent just some of the different parts of the whole that makes up Fusion leadership today in Mexico.

- Miguel Hidalgo: national identity leadership
- Porfirio Diaz: authoritarian leadership
- Emiliano Zapata: revolutionary leadership
- Lázaro Cárdenas del Río: reforming leadership
- Don Eugenio Garza Sada; Rafael Rangel Sostmann: leading via education
- Elba Esther Gordillo: social justice and corrupt leadership
- El Subcomandante Marcos: social movement leadership
- Andrés Manuel López Obrador: contemporary leadership

Fusion leadership expresses a form of leadership that can be rich and integrative drawing on a multiplicity of influences. When leaders of organizations or countries have high levels of diverse influences and cannot embrace Fusion leadership, serious problems arise as different groups or influences get privileged at the expense of others who get marginalized, creating social and workplace tensions. Pragmatically, Fusion leaders always have to make choices and privilege particular influences, but at the same time a thoughtful and skilful Fusion leader remains aware and empathetic to the many influences that merge to make up cultural norms of their country or company.

Fusion leadership works well when it reflects a leadership that embodies an awareness of the cultural, social, religious, political and technical, generational influences that inform the organizational and/or national and regional culture. This does not impose a particular way of leadership, nor does it demand integration where it is impossible, but rather it shows 'leadership in relationship' to the wider cultural context. Fusion leadership when working well respects and honours the parts that make the whole.

In Mexico, the rich history of diverse native traditions and legends that fuse with modern culture are held together in sharing common values: 'a festive spirit, a strong spirituality, and common occurrences of kindness and hospitality' (p. 114).

Mexico faces many challenges, yet the authors state it is a 'young vibrant and dynamic society'. If it can enjoy the symptom of Fusion leadership in a positive way, it has a bright future. At a more general level, there is no escape from global influences in the network society; and Fusion leadership should be one of the essences of any leadership today.

14 Poland: Conformist leadership

Conformist leadership in Poland arises from both its recent and distant past. There is a long history of fighting for statehood and suffering many defeats that have left the nation wanting to embody 'being Polish', which has included striving for homogeneity in terms of ethnicity (diverse 'others' have been expelled, and new immigrants are not overly welcomed). A Eurostat news release in 2015 announced that Poland has the lowest proportion of foreigners in the European Union, with foreign citizens making up just 0.3% of the population.[3]

Recent influences are the fusion of a nationalist populist politics, an authoritarian Catholic church, a post-communist legacy that demanded conformity, and in the

[3]http://ec.europa.eu/eurostat/documents/2995521/7113991/3-18122015-BP-EN.pdf/d682df12-8a77-46a5-aaa9-58a00a8ee73e (accessed 8 November 2017).

workplace a passive attitude towards conforming to the dominant Messiah leadership rhetoric, espoused in books and training programmes imported from the USA. The Polish authors Beata Jałocha and Michał Zawadzk write: 'The functionalist approach, exalting conformism and treating organizational culture as a "social glue" (Alvesson, 2013) dominates Polish management sciences as well as university business schools' (p. 123).

Conformist leadership is identified by the Polish authors as one of the main challenges that limits their capacity for change. Conformism is never a totally dominant force, and there are always resistances. In Poland, there are rich strands of creativity and resistance to conformist leadership power. However, when Conformist leadership dominates many dynamic, skilled and ambitious people leave as they experience being stifled and shut down. Dube (2016) writes 'Poland ranks second in the world when it comes to the rise in outflow of qualified personnel, surpassed only by India, according to the World Bank (WB) report 'Global Talent Flows.' This is problematic for companies who need entrepreneurial and creative talent, and for the country as a whole where migration is a big issue, and where immigration that may import diversity and difference to challenge homogeneity and conformism is stifled. The current political situation as I write this in late 2017 is that there are great concerns that the government is undermining Polish democracy and becoming autocratic; *Guardian* columnist Tim Garton Ash, writing in January 2016, warns that 'The pillars of Poland's democracy are being destroyed.'[4]

Beyond Poland, I experience Conformist leadership as one of today's greatest challenges in many corporate companies and also in the large public sector and third sector organizations I work in internationally. Leaders engineer conformist cultures (Kunda, 1992) under other names to hide and consciously to deny the negative implications. Terms such as aligned cultures are used, and a particular favourite in global corporations is using the term 'one company'. At a pragmatic level this makes sense, to have alignment of functions and culture, but at another level it can produce conformity cultures that marginalize difference voices and cultures, and this problem (or hidden desire) is rarely acknowledged. Conformist leaders often hide behind the Messiah leadership rhetoric of creating strong loyal cultures (Deal and Kennedy, 1982; Axtel Ray, 1986; Tourish, 2008).

Conformist leaders create conformist cultures, and these are enacted in both organizational and political spheres. Two clear forms of conformity stand out. The first is a soft form of conformity, hidden underneath the rhetoric of freedom, innovation and creativity. Progressive hi-tech companies, for example, value creativity and dynamism and yet they also wish to forge conformist company cultures. They impose an unspoken and unseen conformity on employees, who often willingly sign up. Employees then become walking brands and corporate avatars. Google, for example, calls it workers Googlers, and

[4]www.theguardian.com/commentisfree/2016/jan/07/polish-democracy-destroyed-constitution-media-poland (accessed 9 November 2017)

employees conform willingly (mostly) to this branding and identification. The 2017 film *The Circle* (based on Eggers' novel of the same title, 2013) took a giant hi-tech company modelled on Google and Apple to show an extreme dramatic version of this conformity. The other form of conformity is a hard form imposed by leaders often working within the Messiah/Controller discourse. In Poland, it seems both hard and soft forms of Conformist leadership are at play. If Conformist leadership is a symptom of Polish culture arising from a traumatic past, then the task for Poland is to discover how it can celebrate and protect its Polish essence, without self-harming the nation and their organizations by shutting out diversity, creativity and the dynamics of difference within it.

15 Russia: Sacrificial leadership

Russia has a very particular context whereby over 50 million died in the past century, which brings *Sacrificial leadership* to the fore. The authors Ekaterina Belokoskova-Mikhaylova, Konstantin Korotov and Irena Izotova write, 'it is particularly focused on the past and on the indebtedness of the current generations to the previous ones for their sacrifice. ... The leader is expected to mobilize the troops for sacrifice. The cause of the sacrifice has to be positioned in noble terms' (p. 130).

Sacrificial leadership comes in many forms and is connected to a past trauma and/or linked to an ideology or religion such as Christianity, which has a sacrificial identity (e.g. Christ died on the cross to save the world). In Russia, it is closely associated with three things: past traumas, religion and military sacrifice.

Sacrificial leaders use the notion of sacrifice in two key ways. First, they utilize the idea of sacrifice as a vehicle to gain influence. They mobilize and gain followers on the basis of past 'chosen trauma's' for either 'reparative or destructive' ends (Volkan, 1991):

> The Turkish-American Psychoanalyst Vamik Volkan used the term 'chosen trauma' to describe the process of a group evoking the memory of a persecutory event and ascribing it an inordinate amount of emotional and historic significance. According to Volkan traumatized groups may evolve two kinds of leadership; the 'reparative' type uses the traumatic event to unite the group and solidify its identity without harming another group. The 'destructive type' uses the 'chosen trauma' to increase a sense of victimization, vilify a real or imagined enemy and to resurrect dormant ideologies. These ideologies typically claim exaggerated privilege and endorse revenge. (Tariq, 2016)

Second, Sacrificial leaders mobilize people to sacrifice themselves for a contemporary cause the leader is championing, which is often linked to a past 'chosen trauma' but is not always the case. Sacrificial leadership can take on moderate or extreme forms. An extreme example links the rise of the terrorist network ISIS to destructive forms of Sacrificial leadership that utilize chosen traumas from US and Shia attacks shown repeatedly in graphic details on videos as an ideological weapon (Tariq, 2016). More moderately, it is found in religious orders and monastic communities, where religious followers take on asceticism and sacrifice worldly pleasures to gain deeper spiritual experience with the altruistic aim 'to do good in the world'.

Sacrificial leadership evokes problematic psychosocial dynamics. Sacrifice and altruism are very rarely pure or without a shadow side, particularly when utilized in nationalist political arenas, or in organizations striving for success. Repressed unconscious attachments and investments require exploration in any case of Sacrificial leadership. A perverse egoistical pleasure is often taken from self-identifying as a being 'for others not for myself' or as an authentic leader without ego. The repressed shadow-side of the idea of sacrificing oneself, or of identifying with past traumas where others sacrificed themselves on behalf of the current generation, often erupts as violence against others, the sacrifice being utilized by leaders to justify aggression against others. Sacrificing oneself, whether as an aesthetic monk, or a warrior willing to die for a cause, can both be acts of aggression turned inwards.

Psychoanalysis refers to the 'return of the repressed' (Freud, 1961), which expresses how what we are unable to consciously acknowledge becomes repressed, but will always return to haunt us. The worst examples of recent Sacrificial leadership have been the scandals such as the institutional sexual and physical abuse in the Catholic church in Ireland and Boston, USA. The church preached a doctrine of personal and institutional Sacrificial leadership, while abusing power relations and unleashing terrible aggression and hurt on those unable to defend themselves.

I have personally experienced Sacrificial leadership in the nursing profession, particular in my early career as a nurse, where nurse leaders identified as sacrificing themselves for their vocation as caring 'angels'. They expected their teams to work tirelessly and unquestioningly for the cause and without questioning the leader's authority, or a bureaucratic system that often failed patients. The duty was to serve and not to ask questions. The symptom of Sacrificial leadership can be harnessed to produce motivated, loyal and caring teams. A leader can utilize personal or collective past traumas as a driver that demands reparation, and those attracted to caring professions such as nursing often have personal identifications with loss, or past traumas such as relatives who have been sick. However, I have experienced a hidden cruelty and harshness in the nursing and other caring professions that is shocking. This can be directed either towards patients/clients, or colleagues, and often directed towards the self as well.

Servant leadership (Greenleaf, 1977) is often espoused by altruistically minded leaders and is one example of how Sacrificial leadership plays out in the workplace. In an essay entitled 'The servant as leader' published in 1970, Greenleaf writes:

> The servant-leader is servant first ... It begins with the natural feeling that one wants to serve, to serve first. Then conscious choice brings one to aspire to lead. He or she is sharply different from the person who is leader first, perhaps because of the need to assuage an unusual power drive or to acquire material possessions.

In my experience of working in many sectors and across international borders and with my background in psychoanalysis, I have learned to distrust altruism as a pure intention in senior leaders, as it usually acts as a cover for another displaced emotional need. This is not to say that people do not have altruistic intentions or that they want to 'serve first'. Those who are most likely to be in the best position to become servant leaders are those who speak least about it, and those who have done a lot of personal reflective work to understand conscious and unconscious motives. Rarely do we find these Servant leaders in senior positions, far more often in quiet caring positions quietly doing amazing work, and showing leadership through being rather than performing. Those who cast themselves as Servant leaders when at senior levels have to contend with the usual unconscious projections that followers place on powerful leaders, which are difficult enough to manage. In addition they must deal with excess projections attached to being 'saintly', which can create a greater dependency in followers, as it encourages discipleship rather than active and autonomous followership. The histories of religious leaders who fail to live up to their espoused ethics are examples of the challenge this poses. In commercial or political life, where power and profit also come into play, claiming to be a Servant leader who is self-sacrificing is very problematic!

Thomas Merton, the world-famous author and monk, warns of the dangers of monastic novices idealizing him when he was their spiritual guide with very damaging results, as they lose their autonomy aiming only to please and mimic him. He talks of how he lost his bearings as their spiritual director for a while.

> Penitents (Novice Monks) seduce you into taking the role of omnipotence and omniscience and in this situation, you are self-deluding. (Merton, 1966: 55)

Sacrificial leadership can be hugely important if the leader creates an important link to past traumas and works towards reparation, finding ways to integrate the trauma in a positive way. Ignoring and repressing past traumas will always lead to a return of the repressed, often with devastating results. The task of the Sacrificial leader is clearly to avoid a repetition of the past, or to abuse the power that the Sacrificial object gives them. Russia has a symptom of sacrifice at the heart of its leadership and followership dynamic; its task is reparation not repetition of more trauma.

16 Scandinavia: Progressive leadership

Progressive leadership in Scandinavia may look like democratic and participative leadership (Lewin and Lippett, 1938) but it has an essence that goes beyond this. It is ideologically motivated rather than utilitarian motivated. Democratic leaders create participative structures that are organizationally embedded, such as voting systems for decision-making, gender quotas on boards and worker representation. The overall aim of democratic-participatory leadership is to work within the Therapeutic discourse to empower people. Progressive leadership embraces these participatory structures but goes further and embeds the organizational culture with the liberal-progressive politics of identity which are underpinned by forces of political correctness ('PC') (Schwartz, 1997, 2010; Western, 2016a).

The authors of the Scandinavia chapter claim that equality is 'the pinnacle of Western culture'. They link their ideological belief in equality to producing high-quality outputs as a by-product. In Scandinavia, and in liberal progressive areas of Western Europe and the USA, Progressive leadership is a very dominant force. This is particularly true in public and non-for-profit sectors where there is an ethos of providing a social service, and is also true in sections of the media.

Progressive leadership underpinned by liberal-progressive ideology can successfully support a values-based and engaged workforce. However, its shadow is that unwittingly it can lean towards a 'totally administered society' (Marcuse, 1964) underpinned by an unconscious desire to create a new (hidden) authoritarian settlement, policed by politically correct culture and activists. Political correctness began as a struggle for equality of opportunity for minority groups who were being oppressed or excluded, however it morphed into a different ideology:

> Political correctness now goes beyond fighting for an ideology of progressive politics, centred around human rights and values such as being anti-racist and anti-sexist. The PC tribe utilise this liberal-progressive ideology as their organising principle yet what they actually strive for (albeit unconsciously) is a more authoritarian settlement, based on their intolerance of others who think and speak differently to them. This 'illiberal liberalism' explicitly aims to limit free speech and free thinking to further their cause. (Western 2016a)

Many experience PC culture as rendering them silent and impotent, unable to master the nuances, language and ideology of the politically correct discourse, or simply not agreeing with many of its premises. PC is a form of soft power that mimics the creation of a 'total administered society' as it shuts down speech and in doing so shuts down thinking (Schwartz, 2010). It is divisive, rendering those who don't speak PC as guilty 'outsiders'. Watching the culture wars getting played out in the USA with the liberal-progressive media and talk show hosts relentlessly mocking Trump and his supporters, and likewise Trump and his followers relentlessly attacking the PC tribe, one again sees *'plus de jouir'* (surplus enjoyment) taking place. Excess enjoyment of mocking the other rather than focusing on bridging differences and winning hearts and minds to create real change, indicates the enjoyment of power abuse on both sides. The impact is an impasse, whereby the concerns of many go unheard until they reach breaking point, and vote for nationalistic populist leaders who they feel at least gives them a voice and attacks those they experience as unaccountable elites pushing unwanted agendas upon them.

Progressive leadership is commonplace in organizational settings as well as political environments. When it is attached to the values of supporting gender equality and minorities it can lead to improvements in employee engagement and participation, which usually improves output and organizational success as well. However, I have witnessed in large organizations diversity policies that are little more than 'rainbow wash' (Western, 2013). Diversity propaganda symbolically portrays the firm in a progressive way but employees know it is window dressing which creates a resentment that cannot be spoken. The 'return of the repressed' in these situations gets played out elsewhere in the organization through dysfunctional behaviours such as hidden bullying, for example.

Another example of Progressive leadership leading to dysfunction is when a Western-owned global company pushes PC ideas into a global company to align its culture. Illiberal liberalism is the outcome. I recall talking to a senior woman, a Middle Eastern HR representative of a global bank, after attending a session promoting gender and sexual equality and she said quietly to me after the session in private, '*When with the others, I publicly agree because I have to, but when I return home to work this will not be discussed publicly as it challenges too many local and cultural norms. It puts me in a very, very difficult position.*'

Diversity is preached but in reality, a top-down Westernized ideology is pushed through a global corporate company, without space for listening or adaption to think about what Progressive leadership means in different contexts.

A step back is needed with more open dialogue and examination of 'what-is-really-going-on' when we see Progressive leadership. We need to ask what hidden power agendas are getting played out? This would reveal the need for accommodating differences, whilst maintaining ethical positions. It would also mean separating progressive and emancipatory ideas from hidden forms of soft-authoritarianism that appear when Progressive leadership adopts a radical politically correct ideology. Scandinavia is a hugely successful example of social democratic governance and culture. Yet, it now finds itself being stretched at the margins, as alternative voices who have felt marginalized by a dominant elite rebel against the long-held public 'liberal' consensus. It is not only the tensions between a rising individualism versus social 'collectivism' that Scandinavia and many 'progressive leaders' face. It is also to re-imagine what Progressive leadership looks like in a world that becomes ever-more divided between polarizing ideologies such as PC culture and populist reactionary responses. The Progressive leadership symptom runs deep in Scandinavia; it has strong affective attachments derived from a pride in identifying with social justice that has been linked to economic and social success. Today's Progressive leaders now need to harness that symptom to produce the next generation of success.

17 South Africa: Paralysed leadership

Paralysed leadership reflects how leadership in many areas of South African life has become very stuck due to both recent and past history. Peliwe Mnguni and Jeremias De Klerk write in their chapter that '[t]he dilemmas that seem to paralyse leadership practice in South Africa are as baffling as they are to be expected' (p. 150). They point to racialized, politicized and genderized issues that limit the personal authorization an individual requires to take up their leadership with full confidence. Another agenda always seems to exist that undermines leaders and creates the stuck position of Paralysed leadership. When this state of mind becomes the norm, as it appears now in South Africa, demoralization and decline set in. While Paralysed leadership is starkly described in South Africa, many people throughout the world would recognize this leadership–followership experience. In organizations that experience Paralysed leadership a low-level depressive culture exists which produces disengagement and self-interested behaviour, as collectively acting to make improvements seems futile. Like Racial and Conformist leadership, low-level depression can also turn into despair. Naming the symptom of Paralysed leadership openly, would be the starting place to address the underlying causes, which will be unique in each local context.

Paralysed leadership can only be resolved by a change in the leadership–followership dynamic. It will rarely change solely through a top-down leadership initiative; the old adage 'we get the leaders we deserve' has some merit here. There are usually hidden investments and attachments that maintain the paralysis. Sometimes these are conscious and manipulative as the paralysis keeps a status quo that offers secondary gains to particular individuals or groups. Or even when the status quo feels miserable and stuck, the fear that any change would make things even worse can also keep the paralysis in place. In South Africa, as in other places where there is Paralysed leadership, the task is to identify these underlying attachments and investments (some conscious and some unconscious) that keep producing and reproducing this situation. Quite often a repetition from history will occur in each generation, repeating the same patterns but in new ways. This is why it is important to look at the Paralysed leadership as symptom of a cultural way-of-being in the world. The history of colonialism, racism, tribalism and more recently apartheid and revolutionary resistance has taken its toll. The authors explain that to understand leadership today, looking closely at apartheid leadership and the ANC leadership can offer insights:

> This includes interrogating both the apartheid and the ANC exile authority systems. These two systems continue to influence how authority and leadership are understood and enacted across various institutions in the country. While the two systems might be expected to be different, they actually had much in common. Both were characterized by heightened anxiety, of a persecutory kind. Mutual hatred and suspicion meant that both systems put authoritarian and oppressive authority structures in place. Totalitarian forms of control emerged within both groups as fear of the 'other' was actively propagated and used as a rationale for demanding complete submission to authority. As the struggle against apartheid gained momentum, traditional leadership within black communities was gradually joined and at times overtaken by revolutionary political leadership. Within the white society, persecutory and paranoiac leadership emerged to fend off (prevent the occurrence) the '*swart gevaar*' (black threat). (p. 146)

When talking about leadership in South Africa, the name Nelson Mandela ('Madiba') comes to the fore. Recognized as one of the world's great leaders of the past century, Mandela's brilliance and success were always going to be a difficult act to follow. The world's projections of 'Messiah' onto Mandela's leadership leave those following him in a very difficult situation. Following a Messiah is not easy!

The splitting between black and white, is also reproduced in male and female dynamics in South Africa and the authors point to how the genderized culture adds to the overall paralysis. When 50% of a population is disempowered, this always has a huge impact on the whole. It does not make men stronger, it just reveals the weaknesses and insecurities that get covered over, often with acts of aggression.

To work with the symptom of Paralysed leadership means working at a meta-level on the conscious and unconscious psychosocial dynamics. Like with Sacrificial leadership, the symptomatic trauma that causes the Paralysis needs addressing to create a long-term strategy for change. At micro-levels, the task for individuals and small groups is to subvert the structures that maintain the Paralysed leadership. Where there is a dominant negative culture, a counter-culture must be created. To achieve this requires a grass-roots engagement with Eco-leadership that can subvert the dominant discourses of Controller-Messiah in South African politics and organizational settings. Taking a networked and distributed leadership approach means connecting people who have energy and skills to create small changes that can lead to bigger changes in the wider eco-system. Creating dynamic nodes and clusters of individuals/groups with libido and drive in connected informal networks, can work together to begin to undo the Gordian knots that maintain the Paralysed leadership systems and cultures.

18 Turkey: Authoritarian–Democratic leadership

Turkey struggles today with its symptom of *Authoritarian–Democratic leadership*. The state of Turkey has moved between these two positions since its founding in 1926 by Kemal Atatürk. The authors point to the ongoing tension between the Secularists and Islamists that has *'become a national obsession'* over the past 90 years, and this tension has produced authoritarianism on both sides, alongside a secular struggle to become fully democratic. In recent decades Turkey moved towards the European model of liberal democracy, with an aim to join the EU. This was being achieved under a moderate Islamic party that was hailed as a model for other Islamic political parties. It appeared able to embrace an economic and political liberal ideology within an Islamic culture, and do so very successfully. However, in recent years under Recep Tayyip Erdoğan Turkey has swung back towards authoritarianism and has used the mandate of democracy to gain legitimacy for this position.[5]

The authors Serdar Karabatı and Beyza Oba claim that authoritarianism seeps into organizational leadership as well, writing 'This dominant leadership model is characterized by a belief in the role of an authoritarian, typically male leader with full command to organize the private and the public, a model that can be articulated as a form of "paternalistic leadership" (Aycan, 2006; Pellegrini and Scandura, 2008)' (p. 153).

---

[5]www.theatlantic.com/international/archive/2017/04/turkey-referendum-erdogan-kurds/522894 (accessed 9 November).

Turkey is not alone in the move towards Authoritarian–Democratic leadership in recent times. This echoes similar moves that are causing concern elsewhere in Europe, e.g. Hungary, Poland and with political parties such as the Front National in France as well as Donald Trump accused of wanting to move the USA in this direction, as he has overtly supported Authoritarian–Democratic leaders in Poland and Russia, and Marine Le-Pen in France.[6] Those who support Authoritarian–Democratic leadership claim it offers stability when a country (or company) is in crisis or transition, while others always see it as leading to dangerous outcomes.

Authoritarian–Democratic leadership in the West is identified with nationalist and populist politics. This trend follows other examples of Authoritarian–Democratic leadership that have emerged elsewhere, such as Iran, Singapore and Russia, all of which

[6]www.theguardian.com/us-news/2017/apr/21/donald-trump-marine-le-pen-french-presidential-election (accessed 9 November 2017).

offer very different examples. In the past, totalitarianism has emerged from democratic countries that moved towards Authoritarian–Democratic leadership, so there are reasons for concerns.

Authoritarian–Democratic leadership goes beyond political leadership and is enacted in organizations too. This is seen where the context of organizations are set in liberal democracies and whereby organizations espouse a rhetoric of democratic-participatory employee relations, yet they act in authoritarian ways. This can be enacted explicitly by a bullying leadership that creates a fearful culture; taxi-hailing company Uber is a recent example, which led to their innovative and dynamic CEO resigning for such behaviour.[7] It can also happen in hidden implicit ways via particular forms of culture control (Axtel Ray, 1986).

Turkey seems evenly split between secularists and Islamists. There are splits between authoritarians and democrats on both sides of this Secular-Islamist divide. Those who support authoritarianism believe it is the only way to protect the 'pure state' from the 'toxic other' who will bring about destruction. The current leadership utilizes democracy to legitimize an increasingly authoritarian position to 'defend the nation', while the opposition point to the state corrupting and distorting democracy to create a dangerous authoritarianism. Maybe Turkey's obsession between the polemic positions of Secularist versus Islamist is partly a cover that masks the deeper challenge of moving beyond its repetitive symptom of Authoritarian-Democratic leadership. To do this is to address the attachments to authoritarianism and the surplus enjoyment – *'plus de jouir'* that is derived from their heroic leaders. A long history from the Sultans of the Ottoman Empire to the secularist Ataturk, and now Erdoğan the Islamist represent different expressions of the same symptom. Social obsessions are usually connected to too much affective investment, and when people enjoy their symptom too much (Žižek, 2001) these social problems become entrenched in each generation.

19 UK: Ambivalent leadership

The UK offers a good example of the ambivalence that many people and cultures have towards leadership. *Ambivalent leadership* plays out as a symptom of the nation emerging from a historical struggle between rich and poor, powerful elites and the disempowered, a desire for great leaders and a counter-desire for egalitarian social movements to lead grass roots change.

Leaders in the UK are both praised and admired and at the same time they are envied and denigrated. A leader may be heralded and celebrated and then quickly fall from grace. A once-admiring public and media take great pleasure in a leader's fall, revealing the

---

[7]www.nytimes.com/2017/02/22/technology/uber-workplace-culture.html (accessed 9 November 2017).

ambivalence towards the individual leader and to leadership itself. An anecdotal story by Jacques Lacan about a client in analysis captures this ambivalence towards leadership and authority figures:

> *Psychoanalyst*: What do you desire?
>
> *Client*: I desire a master.
>
> *Psychoanalyst*: What kind of master?
>
> *Client*: A master I can dominate.

The UK's ambivalence towards leadership is often expressed via soccer coaches who are welcomed and celebrated as a new 'Messiah' when appointed, then trashed very quickly and with a surplus of pleasure being expressed when they don't live up to the messianic expectations. The excess pleasure that is seen when a leader fails reveals a displacement of a more generic ambivalence towards both organizational and political leaders. The UK has a specific identification with its symptom of Ambivalent leadership. It is very proud of a long history of modern democratic governance since the late 1600s. The UK lectures other nations on the merits of democracy, and fights foreign wars claiming to promote democratic states, while it has a constitutional monarchy and an unelected second chamber, 'the House of Lords', consisting of birthright lords, Church of England bishops and individuals selected by the governing party in power, who give patronage to donors who support their party. When there is an attempt to modernize and reform, there is usually general agreement that this necessary, then always a gap appears, and a lack of will to make this happen – again revealing Ambivalent leadership.

The authors of the UK chapter, Richard Bolden and Morgen Witzel, reveal a further tension that emerges within the UK. They write: 'individuals and organizations demonstrate both an appetite for clear and inspiring leadership and a healthy scepticism of bureaucracy and power, with a preference for participative decision-making and teamwork' (p. 163). This exposes another facet of Ambivalent leadership revealing a dual desire.

First is the desire to be led by a competent and/or visionary leader. This desire is for a leadership that offers inspiration, hope and salvation, and the comfort of feeling secure and safe due to a competent leader taking control. This first desire emerges from an unconscious regressed hope for a 'good mummy or daddy' to care for and look after us, and/or a Messiah leader to save us from our anxieties and fears and lead us to 'the promised land'.

Second, a competing desire exists for equality and fairness, for participatory and egalitarian engagement that does not require a top-down or heroic leadership. The history of the UK plays out these contrasting yet often co-habiting desires, which are fuelled by the tensions between individualism and collectivism in the UK.

These competing desires can be represented by different groups or they can be held and acted out within the same group or even within the same individual. Psychoanalysis reveals how ambivalent and contradictory positions are commonly held by individuals and groups in organizations (Hirschhorn, 1990). These tensions become problematic when unconscious identification to one of these contradictory positions distorts perceptions and behaviours in practice. For example, individuals/groups may identify as being as egalitarian, valuing participation, and espouse being anti-leadership and yet unconsciously they crave heroic leaders. The miners' strike in the UK in the 1980s enacted this through the socialist, collectivist and egalitarian ethos held by those who supported the striking miners, yet at the same time they followed Arthur Scargill, a charismatic Messiah leader who was criticized by many for blocking a national ballot (i.e. a democratic vote on the strike), which further split the mining community and contributed to their defeat (Macintyre, 2014). Another excellent example is Jeremy Corbyn, the left-wing leader of the British Labour Party. His collectivist and egalitarian approach has led to a 'mass' grass roots movement joining and supporting the Labour Party.[8] Yet he has also acquired Messiah leadership status as these collectivist-egalitarian supporters treat him like a rock star.[9] UK Ambivalent leadership personified!

---

[8]www.theguardian.com/politics/2016/sep/27/jeremy-corbyns-team-targets-labour-membership-one-million (accessed 9 November 2017).

[9]http://news.sky.com/story/jeremy-corbyn-gets-rapturous-reception-at-glastonbury-10926081 (accessed 9 November 2017).

Conversely groups and individuals can be consciously pro-leadership, while also unconsciously resenting a leader's power and feeling guilty about their own dependency on the Messiah leader. This often leads to an unconscious undermining of the leader they consciously revere and support. Social movements that claim to be leaderless are also excellent examples of this ambivalence. Researching and observing 'leaderless movements', it became very clear that leadership exists under different names – 'activists', for example. Leadership happens (mostly) outside of a formal hierarchy and takes on a form of leadership I call 'Autonomist' leadership (Western, 2014). This ambivalence/denial of the leadership undermines their potential to shift from protest movements, and to engage more fully as social change agents (Western, 2014).

In workplaces across the world this ambivalence towards leadership is projected by followers onto leaders, who may introject (take in) these powerful projections and become 'Ambivalent leaders'. This plays out in two main ways. First, there are Ambivalent leaders who understand this ambivalence towards leadership, and the tensions it creates. They often experience this ambivalence themselves, and are insightful as to how it can become polarized and dangerous when anxiety rises due to external pressures such as economic decline. These aware leaders utilize this knowledge of ambivalence to ensure they try to create healthy, successful and balanced organizational dynamics. They are not fearful of 'being a leader' and making difficult decisions when necessary. However, they balance this by being sensitive to the desire for participation and they maximize the widest engagement possible. Second, if the ambivalence is repressed and denied, it is then acted out unconsciously and often destructively. It can then produce polarized leadership, some siding with the desire for Messiah leadership others siding with collectivist-egalitarian desire, this producing paralysis or conflictual and dysfunctional dynamics.

Ambivalent leadership is a symptom that points to a healthy scepticism towards power abuse by individuals or elites, while recognizing the power of the collective. How it plays out is determined by the awareness of the individual and collective actors involved.

20 United States of America: Melancholic leadership

The title of the United States chapter, 'Mourning in America', points to what I refer to as *Melancholic leadership*. Drawing on Freud's *Mourning and Melancholia* (1917), melancholia represents a failure to fully mourn a loss: 'the melancholic does not consciously know what he or she has lost in losing the object'.

In the USA, Messiah leadership has long been a dominant force; individualism plus heroic struggle and courage underpins the American Dream, yet when this dream fades Messiah leadership becomes infused with melancholy. The election of Donald Trump in 2016 represents this Melancholic leadership in the USA (Western, 2016b). Trump acknowledged the great loss of the American Dream in his successful presidential campaign,

saying 'America is broken'. However, what is *'lost in losing the object'* is not acknowledged by Trump. Trump's Messiah leadership approach in his campaign created the ideal of him alone as the saviour of America. The lone-hero riding in on the white horse to 'make America great again' and 'drain the swamp' of the corrupt elites, and be 'the greatest jobs President ever'. This is a refusal to mourn the loss of the American Dream, and perhaps to mourn the demise of its recent empire too. Without mourning a loss, and then rebuilding a life that recognizes and embraces the loss, melancholia will set in. This means that an unconscious attachment to the lost object cannot be let go. While consciously the loss is known, unconsciously the loss is not acknowledged.

Freud's famous paper also observed that melancholia can have a manic side to it, which is another way to avoid facing the reality of what has been lost. This mania was very present at Trump's rallies and in his excess in language and tweeting. To renew and regenerate, the reality principle must be faced: the loss of the American Dream and the empire it once had needs to be mourned. In 1979 President Jimmy Carter made his famous 'Crisis of Confidence' speech, which stated the cultural crisis the USA was facing.

> I want to talk to you right now about a fundamental threat to American democracy ... It is a crisis of confidence. It is a crisis that strikes at the very heart and soul and spirit of our national will. We can see this crisis in the growing doubt about the meaning of our own lives and in the loss of a unity of purpose for our nation ...
>
> In a nation that was proud of hard work, strong families, close-knit communities, and our faith in God, too many of us now tend to worship self-indulgence and consumption.

> Human identity is no longer defined by what one does, but by what one owns. But we've discovered that owning things and consuming things does not satisfy our longing for meaning ... (Carter, 1979)

This crisis of confidence was not addressed and denial set in, leading to decades of demise leading to the so-called un-electable Donald Trump being elected. As Devega writes (2016), Donald Trump's popularity is driven by a culture of greed and consumerism. Although his wealth and financial success are greatly exaggerated, he is an inspirational figure for a public that confuses money with wisdom and civic virtue.

The Democrats led by Hillary Clinton at this time also engaged in this melancholia, claiming things were not so bad, ignoring the voice of the marginalized, claiming more of the same would mean a brighter future. Together they both engaged in Melancholic leadership in different ways and both were in denial. Melancholic leadership represents a symptom that leaves the USA in an unresolved place today, and we are witnessing the challenges that are arising from this position of denial.

Melancholic leadership beyond the USA

Looking at all 20 of these chapters and drawing on experience in the field, I believe that Melancholic leadership is a very common, yet hidden leadership theme. I am not referring to a leader's personal melancholy, but a melancholy that reflects cultural situations where collective and social loss takes place and where a leader galvanizes support and influences others on the basis of the melancholic dynamic. The unconscious repression that 'protects' the individual's conscious ego from facing the impact of a deep loss is fairly common in organizations as well as nation-states. For example, leaders of family businesses or firms with charismatic founders can be caught in a mesmerized trap of over-identifying with the founding idea or founding individual. If the current leadership galvanizes support on the basis of this founding idea/individual, yet does not face new realities that demand change, they end up running the company on nostalgia with Melancholic leadership. There is a further danger that Melancholic leadership turns its nostalgia for a utopian past into a paranoia that blames a 'bad other' for preventing the recovery of the lost object. Immigrants or the hidden forces within are then identified as hate objects that are stealing the pleasure (Stavrakakis, 2007) of those who are failing to mourn loss. In the USA, this narrative is unfolding as the symptom of Melancholic leadership underpins the presidency of Trump and his followers.

When Melancholic leadership is identified, the work can then commence to build the emotional containers in which the mourning process can begin, thereby liberating the leaders and others to imagine and create new futures. New futures that recognize and accommodate the loss after a period of grieving.

REFLECTIONS ON OUTSIDER-LEADERSHIP

The 20 regional chapters revealed many gaps in the dominant literature on leadership. These gaps reveal a lack in the leadership literature that is reflected in perceived and expected leadership practices. The outsider-leadership undercurrents picked up in this analysis are just some of many more themes that could be explored. These chapters with their limited word counts were necessarily restrictive. A deeper and broader exploration of the local and specific regional leadership dynamics that account for cultural, social, historical and economic factors would reveal more. The outsider-leadership themes and symptoms identified in this chapter need further research to develop a greater understanding of how they inform leadership thinking and practice both locally and globally. The outsider-leadership themes are listed in Table 24.1 and they have been grouped where there is overlap and potential merging. The following conclusion chapter will offer further reflections on these pairings and groupings.

Table 24.1 Outsider-leadership themes from 20 countries/regions

Outsider-Leadership groupings	Country/region
1. **Reclaiming the Negative**	
Silent-Avoidant leadership	Japan
Negative-Knowledge leadership	Ethiopia
Ambivalent leadership	United Kingdom
2. **Edgy and Disruptive**	
Trickster leadership	France
Maverick leadership	Australia
Gaucho leadership	Argentina
3. **Symptoms of Despair**	
Conformist leadership	Poland
Paralysed leadership	South Africa
Racial leadership	DR Congo
4. **Trauma and Disenchantment**	
Melancholic leadership	USA
Sacrificial leadership	Russia
Disenchanted leadership	Brazil
5. **Co-existing Differences**	
Authoritarian–Democratic leadership	Turkey
Collaborative–Controlling leadership	ASEAN region
Paradoxical leadership	China
6. **Hopeful**	
Progressive leadership	Scandinavia
Networked leadership	Arab Middle East
Romantic leadership	Germany
Fusion leadership	Mexico
Transmission leadership	India

REFERENCES

Alvesson, Matt (2013) *Understanding Organizational Culture*, 2nd edn. London: Sage.

Arnaud, G. and Vidaillet, B. (2017) 'Clinical *and* critical: the Lacanian contribution to management and organization studies', *Organization*, [online first] DOI 1350508417720021.

Axtel Ray, C. (1986) 'Corporate culture: the last frontier of control', *Journal of Management Studies*, 23 (3): 286–95.

Aycan, Z. (2006) 'Paternalism: towards conceptual refinement and operationalization', in Uichol Kim, Kuo-Shu Yang and Kwang-Kuo Hwang (eds), *Scientific Advances in Indigenous Psychologies: Empirical, Philosophical, and Cultural Contributions*. London: Sage. pp. 445–66.

Bass, Bernard M. (1985) *Leadership and Performance beyond Expectations*. London: Collier Macmillan.

Bass, Bernard M. (1998) *Transformational Leadership: Industrial, Military, and Educational Impact*. Mahwah, NJ: Lawrence Erlbaum Associates.

Boxer P.J. (2014) 'Minding the gap – three moments of time'. Blog post 19 March. www.asymmetricleadership.com/2014/03/minding-the-gap/ (accessed 24 November 2017).

Burns, James MacGregor (1978) *Leadership*. New York: Harper & Row.

Burns, James MacGregor (2003) *Transforming Leadership: A New Pursuit of Happiness*. New York: Grove/Atlantic.

Carter, J. (1979) 'Energy and the national goals – a crisis of confidence', speech delivered 15 July 1979. Available at www.americanrhetoric.com/speeches/jimmycartercrisisofconfidence.htm (accessed 23 November 2017).

Casey, Catherine (1995) *Work, Self and Society after Industrialism*. London: Routledge.

Castells, Manuel (2000) *The Rise of the Network Society: The Information Age: Economy, Society and Culture, I*. Oxford: Blackwell

Castells, Manuel (2012) *Networks of Outrage and Hope: Social Movements in the Internet Age*. Cambridge: Polity Press

Conger, J.A. and Kanungo, R.N. (1987) 'Toward a behavioural theory of charismatic leadership in organizational settings', *Academy of Management Review*, 12: 637–47.

Deal, Terry and Kennedy, Allan (1982) *Corporate Cultures*. Reading, MA: Addison–Wesley.

Deleuze, Gilles and Guattari, Felix (1987) *A Thousand Plateaus: Capitalism and Schizophrenia*. Minneapolis, MN: University of Minnesota Press.

Devega, C. (2016) 'The "malaise" has metastasized as Donald Trump: Jimmy Carter presciently diagnosed the cancer in our body politic in 1979', salon, 8 November 2016. https://tinyurl.com/ybcjanza (accessed 23 November 2017).

Dube, N. (2016) 'World Bank: Brain drain from Poland second-highest in the world', *World Bank Journal*, 24 October.

Dvir, T., Eden, D., Avolio, B.J. and Shamir, B. (2002) 'Impact of transformational leadership on follower development and performance: a field experiment', *Academy of Management Journal*, 45 (4): 735–44.

Freud, Sigmund (1917) *Mourning and Melancholia*. The Standard Edition of the Complete Psychological Works of Sigmund Freud, Volume XIV (1914–1916): On the History of the PsychoAnalytic Movement, Papers on Metapsychology and Other Works. London: Hogarth Press. pp. 237–58.

Freud, Sigmund (1961) *The Standard Edition of the Complete Psychological Works of Sigmund Freud*, 24 vols (ed. and trans. J. Strachey). London: Hogarth Press.

Fukuyama, Francis (1992) *The End of History and the Last Man*. New York: Free Press.

Greenleaf, Robert K. (1970) *The Servant as Leader*. Atlanta, GA: Center for Servant Leadership.

Greenleaf, Robert K. (1977) *Servant Leadership: A Journey into the Nature of Legitimate Power and Greatness*. New York: Paulist Press.

Hirschhorn, Larry (1990) *The Workplace Within: Psychodynamics of Organizational Life*. Cambridge: MIT Press.

Kapuscinski, R. (1983 [1978]) *The Emperor: Downfall of an Autocrat* (trans. W.R. Brand and K. Mroczkowska-Brand). San Diego, CA: Harcourt Brace Jovanovich.

Kunda, Gideon (1992) *Engineering Culture: Control Commitment in a High Tech Corporation*. Philadelphia, PA: Temple University Press.

Lacan, J. (1988 [1953–1954]) *Freud's Papers on Technique: The Seminar I*. London: W.W. Norton & Co.

Lacan, J. and Mehlman, J. (1972) 'Seminar on "The Purloined Letter"', *Yale French Studies*, (48): 39–72.

Lee, S.K. (1987) 'A Chinese conception of "management": an interpretive approach'. Doctoral dissertation, School of Education, University of Massachusetts, Amherst.

Lewin, K. and Lippett, R. (1938) 'An experimental approach to the study of autocracy and democratic leadership', *Sociometry*, 1: 292–300.

Lewis, M.W., Smith, W.K. and Andriopoulos, C. (2014) 'Paradoxical leadership to enable strategic agility', *California Management Review*, 56 (3).

Macintyre, D. (2014) 'How the miners' strike of 1984–85 changed Britain for ever', *New Statesman*, 11 June. www.newstatesman.com/politics/2014/06/how-miners-strike-1984-85-changed-britain-ever (9 November 2017).

Marcuse, Herbert (1964) *One-Dimensional Man: Studies in the Ideology of Advanced Industrial Society*. Boston, MA: Beacon Press.

Melucci, Alberto (1989) *Nomads of the Present: Social Movements and Individual Needs in Contemporary Society*. London: Hutchinson.

Merton, Thomas (1966) *A Search for Solitude: The Journals of Thomas Merton*, Volume 3, 1952–1960 (ed. Lawrence Cunningham). San Francisco, CA: HarperCollins.

Pellegrini, E.K. and Scandura, T.A. (2008) 'Paternalistic leadership: a review and agenda for future research', *Journal of Management*, 34 (3): 566–93.

Radin, P. (1987 [1956]) *The Trickster: A Study in American Indian Mythology*. New York: Schocken Books.

Schwartz, H. (1997) 'Psychodynamics of political correctness', *Journal of Applied Behavioral Science*, 33 (2): 133–49.

Schwartz, Howard (2010) *Society against Itself: Political Correctness and Organizational Self Destruction*. London: Karnac.

Singh, Pritam, Bhandarker, Asha and Rai, Singdha (2012) *Millennials and the Workplace: Challenges for Architecting the Organizations of Tomorrow*. New Delhi: Sage.

Smith, W.K., Lewis, M.W. and Tushman, M.L. (2016) '"Both/And" Leadership', *Harvard Business Review*, May.

Stavrakakis, Yannis (2007) *The Lacanian Left*. Edinburgh: Edinburgh University Press.

Steiner, J. (1985) 'Turning a blind eye: the cover up for Oedipus', *International Journal of Psychoanalysis*, 12 : 161–71.

Tariq, K. (2016) 'ISIS and the chosen trauma narrative'. www.huffingtonpost.com/khwaja-khusro-tariq/isis-and-the-chosen-traum_b_8223950.html (accessed 9 November 2017).

Tourish, D. (2008) 'Challenging the transformational agenda: leadership theory in transition?', *Management Communication Quarterly*, 21 (4): 522–28.

Tourish, D. and Pinnington, A. (2002) 'Transformational leadership, corporate cultism and the spirituality paradigm: an unholy trinity in the workplace?', *Human Relations*, 55 (2): 147–72.

Volkan, V.D. (1991) 'On "chosen trauma"', *Mind and Human Interaction*, 3: 13.

Western, Simon (2013) *Leadership: A Critical Text*, 2nd edn. London: Sage.

Western, S. (2014) 'Autonomist leadership in leaderless movements: anarchists leading the way', *Ephemera: Theory & Politics in Organization*, 14 (4): 673–98.

Western S. (2016a) 'Political correctness and political in-correctness: a psychoanalytic study of the new authoritarians', *Organisational and Social Dynamics*, 16 (1): 68–84.

Western, S. (2016b) 'The meaning of Trump'. www.academia.edu/30105520/The_Meaning_of_Trump (accessed 9 November 2017).

Western, S. (2018) 'The Eco-leadership paradox', in Benjamin W. Redekop, Deborah R. Gallagher and Rian Satterwhite (eds), *Innovation in Environmental Leadership: Critical Perspectives*. New York and London: Routledge.

Willmott, H. (1993) 'Strength is ignorance; slavery is freedom: managing culture in modern organizations', *Journal of Management Studies*, 30 (4): 515–52.

Woolcock, Nicola (2016) 'Schools struggle to find head teachers as thousands quit', *The Times* [online], 11 November 2016. www.thetimes.co.uk/article/schools-struggle-to-find-head-teachers-as-thousands-quit-d7zz5fxbl (accessed 23 November 2017).

Žižek, Slavoj S. (1992) *Looking Awry: An Introduction to Jacques Lacan through Popular Culture*. London: Verso.

Žižek, Slavoj (2001) *Enjoy your Symptom! Jacques Lacan in Hollywood and Out*. London: Routledge.

CONCLUSION

Simon Western and Éric-Jean Garcia

CONCLUDING DISCUSSION

Overview

The book set out with two clear aims, which in conclusion we have achieved to some degree. We invited our authors to write their chapters and to focus on:

1. 'Allowing leadership to speak with different voices ...'
2. 'To open up a new space for leadership to speak, reflecting historical, cultural, economic and sociocultural influences'

Achieving these aims is, of course, only partial, and we will say more about this later. We have been delighted by the responses, and the 20 chapters produced such rich material that it was a very difficult task to undertake an analysis worthy of the chapters' rich content. There is much more to be done and we invite each reader to bring their own insights and analysis to the texts that interest them.

IN SEARCH OF A SYMPTOM

The 20 chapters speak for themselves, and the analysis undertaken by Simon is in addition to these independent voices. The findings of this analysis will be briefly discussed below. We recognize that 20 chapters was the maximum number for this book and yet they could only produce partial findings. Partial, because there are many other countries and regions we had to leave out that would offer other competing rich and diverse accounts of leadership which would further inform our research on regional leadership. Also, partial because the word count we allowed for each chapter meant that both we and the authors had to heavily edit each chapter and omit many other parts of the leadership story, ensuring we only received restricted accounts of how leadership emerges and is practised today. Our imperative to the authors that they addressed and applied historical, economic and sociocultural influences to contemporary leadership, ensured this was an impossible task to fulfil comprehensively. Finally, partial because all the authors we selected have their own particular experience and knowledge. Therefore, if we had selected another set of authors, the emphasis and findings would have also been different.

Partiality as a methodology

In the methodology designed for this book, 'partiality' is used to subvert the normative scientific dogma that views gaps and omissions in research as a deficit and weakness. In this research analysis, partiality is used as a strength, as a way to discover more. All research is always partial, in particular the social sciences and qualitative research that operate in open systems. Whether you are funded with vast resources and undertake a huge project, or whether it is a smaller project, there is always something left out, a lack, a remainder that is not accounted for. The methodology designed by Simon for the analysis took this into account. Drawing on Lacanian theory, the idea of partiality, looking awry, lack and the remainder that is left over, enabled a methodology that did not place a pressure on ensuring that each chapter produced full results, or to discover a particular form of leadership that emerged with universal meaning and could be replicated. It worked with the premise that there is always a lack and identifying the gaps can open us to discover something new. In this case, the gaps identified in the insider-analysis allowed us to look for what was left out, what was the remainder that was left over from the discourse analysis. Lack leads to desire, and desire points to the symptom, which in turn points to the Lacanian 'Real'. The 'Real' in this case is the leadership that cannot be spoken, the leadership that cannot be captured by empirical research or by knowledge, that sits outside of language and the symbolic, yet resonates in mysterious and unidentifiable ways. This research analysis approach aimed not only to define knowledge but also to gain a glimpse of the Real; to loosely name symptoms that emerged from the chapters, and to use these symptoms to get a sense of the unobtainable 'Real' of leadership that exists in each chapter and in each context.

The conclusions from this search will be discussed under 'Outsider-leadership' below. First, we turn to the discussion of insider-leadership.

Insider-leadership discussion

The discourse analysis methodology aimed to discover how the insider-leadership discourses did or did not appear in each chapter, and in what ways they appeared. Also, to discover the leadership commonalities that existed across chapters. To Simon's surprise, all four discourses appeared (utilizing this discourse analysis in many different international settings he was not convinced this would be the case, and expected some discourses not to appear). Another discovery was that the discourses appeared in diverse and locally inscribed ways, that made him rethink how the discourses work outside the West in regional and global settings.

Diversity within commonality

The dominance of the mainstream 'insider-leadership' discourses that emerged in the twentieth century in the West, Controller, Therapist, Messiah (the Eco-leadership discourse emerged later) have been exported by global power centres of leadership, creating

Western-centric perceptions of leadership both at 'high and low' culture levels. The repetition of theory and rhetoric present distorted and culturally biased views of leadership, that privilege an individual actor whether Therapist, Controller or Messiah. The Messiah leadership is the most powerful and pervasive discourse ideology that leaps directly out of the American Dream and Westernized sensibilities, and has become a globally pervasive discourse. What this book finds, however, is that a dual reality exists.

At one level, the Messiah discourse is the leading discourse across the 20 chapters and continues to dominate leadership perceptions, development and practices. This limits the development of other diverse and imaginative leadership theories and practices that exist. Yet at another level the hegemony and global dominance of this approach is not as all-pervasive as it first appears. Our research analysis shows that although Messiah leadership is the highest-scoring discourse across the whole, this is not true of each individual country or region. Other Insider-leadership discourses are also strongly present and are in close proximity in terms of weighting across the 20 chapters:

- Messiah leadership 31%
- Therapist leadership 26%
- Controller leadership 25%
- Eco-leadership 18%

The Eco-leadership discourse emerged at the beginning of the twenty-first century in the West, in response to the need for new distributed and ethical leadership in the fast-changing network society, and it is not yet fully assimilated into Westernized sensibilities or exported, as with the other three discourses. It also differs as it is not embedded within the constructs of individuality as are the other three discourses; it signifies distributed and dispersed forms of collective leadership.

What became very interesting and surprised us in our research was how Eco-leadership approaches were strongly represented in unexpected places, and paired alongside other discourses that were paradoxical to the practice of Eco-leadership (note these paradoxes have been explored in more depth in Western, 2018). The Eco-leadership discourse was strongly represented in ASEAN region and Japan at 35% and China, Scandinavia and UK at 30%, with the Arab Middle East and Argentina on 25%. The paradox of Eco-leadership occurring in countries that also had Controlling even authoritarian tendencies (China and ASEAN) alongside others with strong democratic traditions (UK and Scandinavia) reveals just how important the Eco-leadership discourse may be as a meta-discourse, for guiding and offering a containing framework for future leadership development and practice.

The research revealed how Eco-leadership is not only a Westernized construct of leadership that emerged to deal with new complexities within the fast-changing network society, or to bring new ethics to the challenges presented by the environment and social responsibility. Eco-leadership has other deeper roots in the East and other non-Western countries, that draw from holistic ideologies linked to different relationships to the cosmos, to nature and to science and linear thinking. Eco-leadership also resonated with traditions that work comfortably with paradoxes rather than those who try to solve binary dilemmas. Eco-leadership emerges from this research analysis as having great potential to help us theorize and develop leadership in diverse regions in and beyond the West for the following reasons:

1. Eco-leadership is able to embrace paradox as in the Eastern tradition.
2. It has a holistic tradition linked to nature that fits with many non-Western cultures.
3. It aims to distribute leadership and conceptualize leadership beyond the individual, therefore paving the way to work within the network society that demands distributed leadership at the edges and throughout organizations. This challenges the twentieth century hegemony of the top-down individual CEO (and a small elite of senior leaders) holding centralized power. Eco-leadership embraces that his shift is towards leadership decentralization and lateral dynamics and away from centralized vertical leadership dynamics.
4. It takes account of the external eco-systems, looking outwards to identify social, technical and natural changes.
5. It takes an ethical stance, placing the environment and social justice as a central concern. This shifts the leadership focus from the sole purpose of exploiting natural and human resources for profit, and engages rethinking how value is measured; accounting for the value of a healthy natural environment, for breathing clean air and for valuing the quality of human life (see Western, 2013 for further discussion).

What is also revealed in this book is the diversity that exists within the other insider-leadership discourses. No leadership approach is pure or 100% dominant, and each country revealed all four discourses interacting with each other in different balanced weightings. When Messiah–Therapist is a dominant pairing, this creates a very different leadership approach than when the dominant pairing is Messiah–Controller for example. We knew this prior to the research analysis, yet what became very clear during the analysis was how each individual region or country infused each insider-leadership discourse with their history, social traditions, culture, religious influences and economic experiences, creating diversity within commonality.

As previously stated, the four dominant discourses of leadership researched and found in the West are also found and practised in all the chapters in this book.

This may have different meanings:

1. Globalization is truly a powerful force that impacts in all regions, i.e. when leadership discourses emerge and are consistently supported, transmitted by dominant actors they become globalized, pervasive and 'sticky'.

2. It could also mean that a gap exists between the espoused leadership and the reality of leadership in practice, i.e. if perceptions of leadership are defined within the limits of the four discourses, then leadership will be explained in this way.
3. Finally, it could mean that the four discourses emerge beyond the Westernized literature in their own forms. They are both shaped by the overt global influences, and also by indigenous variations, local nuances and traditions that form leadership in ways that are similar and different to Westernized developments.

We conclude that globalization is truly is a powerful force and that at the same time indigenous forms of the four discourses emerge from traditions and blend with the globalized leadership norms that pervade the literature. The global and local interactions between the key carriers of leadership identified before might form what Thrift (1999) calls a 'creolized body of knowledge' about leadership. The concept of creolization is defined by Hannerz (2000) as a dynamic process involving a creative cultural mix of knowledge forms originating from both global and local dominant cultural forces.

Through this process, leadership is culturally determined but not simply by a given set of national characteristics such as language, history, educational system, and corporate values. It is also determined by exogenous cultural influences that blend with endogenous ones (Garcia, 2008).

Also, we discovered a gap that exists between the insider-discourses and alternative leadership approaches and themes that the research uncovered. This is described in the outsider-leadership chapter (Chapter 24) and is commented on below.

OUTSIDER-LEADERSHIP DISCUSSION

The analysis undertaken in Chapter 24 produced an unexpectedly rich source of findings called 'outsider-leadership' by Simon. What the analysis process discovered was that while all four discourses were present, the outsider-leadership themes and approaches emerged in parallel rather than in place of them. These themes and approaches undoubtedly have a huge impact on leadership and followership dynamics in their specific country and region. They are more akin to culturally infused essences that speak of the deep cultural traces that cannot be wiped out by imposing homogeneous leadership ideologies and discourses from centres of power. They are the symptom that hints at the unspoken 'Real' of leadership in each country or region. Each outsider-leadership approach and theme emerged from reading the texts and looking awry at leadership.

Each one is discussed fully in Chapter 24, and here in the Conclusion Simon grouped them and made a few suggestions as to the wider understandings beyond the regional or national contexts. The table below shows them in their groupings.

Outsider-leadership groupings

Outsider-Leadership Groupings	Country, Region	Comments
1. **Reclaiming the Negative** Silent-Avoidant Leadership Negative-Knowledge Leadership Ambivalent Leadership	Japan Ethiopia United Kingdom	Mainstream leadership texts would identify these leadership 'symptoms' as negative attributes. Yet there is learning here, and new potentially for positive use
2. **Edgy and Disruptive** Trickster leadership Maverick Leadership Gaucho Leadership	France Australia Argentina	Edgy and disruptive leadership is much needed in our post-industrial post-modern world. It can be a force for innovation, or a disruptive force in a negative way.
3. **Symptoms of Despair** Conformist Leadership Paralysed Leadership Racial Leadership	Poland South Africa D R of Congo	Identifying symptoms of leadership despair is to 'name the unnameable'. A first step to creating new potential openings that allow the symptom to be assimilated into a process of reparation that unleashes new potential.
4. **Trauma and Disenchantment** Melancholic Leadership Sacrificial Leadership Disenchanted Leadership	USA Russia Brazil	These leadership symptoms point us to a Lacanian 'Real' that is hidden in leadership texts. These leadership symptoms associated with loss & trauma and its effects, provide rich data to work with, and should not be ignored or repressed.
5. **Co-existing Differences** Authoritarian-Democratic Leadership Collaborative-Controlling Leadership Paradoxical leadership	Turkey ASEAN Region China	Living with co-existing differences and working with paradox, is emerging as an important leadership approach as an increasingly complex 21st century unfolds.
6. **Hopeful** Progressive Leadership Networked Leadership Romantic Leadership Fusion Leadership Transmission Leadership	Scandinavia Arab Middle East Germany Mexico India	These leadership symptoms signpost hopeful leadership potential when used for the common good. They also have a shadow side that requires acknowledging and working with.

Looking holistically at the individual outsider-leadership themes, these six groupings emerged. Local leadership themes/symptoms are grouped here to stimulate new thinking and learning that can be applied to broader leadership issues faced in other contexts.

Group 1: Reclaiming the negative

This group identifies what are usually considered negative leadership traits or approaches by the mainstream literature, yet each one in different ways challenges the norm, and offers new ways to think about leadership. Japan's example is very interesting and informative raising questions that challenge charismatic and action-orientated approaches, and also challenges the viability of leadership itself in its current state. Ethiopia's Negative-knowledge leadership can seem bleak and a reactive way of leading in an oppressive situation, but it also highlights hidden oppression in corporate cultures that are totalizing. Paying attention to hidden Negative-knowledge leadership, can indicate that a hidden culture of silence and conformity exists that urgently needs challenging. Negative-knowledge leadership can also offer lessons in how to work with difficult leaders or in a very stuck culture, and still get things done whilst trying to promote a new culture at the same time.

Group 2: Edgy and disruptive

This group highlights three countries with symptoms that point to disruptive and edgy leadership. Each example reveals the tension between outsider creatives and insider conformists. Many bureaucratic organizations cannot tolerate the outsider-creatives and marginalize or lose them. Start-up and entrepreneurial companies need them to thrive. Edgy and disruptive influencers have not usually been seen as good leadership candidates, yet in these countries there is something in their symptom and culture that demands this of their leaders. In today's disruptive fast-changing world, it is very likely that some companies will only survive if they learn how to tolerate and use distributed leaders throughout the organization, many who will need to be edgy and disruptive in order to continually re-invent and adapt to fast-changing environments. Perhaps it is enough to say that one of the world's leading companies, Apple, was founded by Steve Jobs .... an edgy and disruptive leader!

Group 3: Symptoms of despair

This grouping represents a place that is part of human experience but largely ignored in the leadership literature which focuses on the upbeat, charismatic influencing approaches of a leader. If leadership is to be humanized, it has to take account of all human experience, including despair. When the leadership in a country or company is paralysed or becomes conformist or is entrapped in racial dynamics that stifle creativity and movement, despair sets in. This can trigger other behaviours and emotions, from violence, bullying and aggression in blame cultures to deep depressive cultures that become intolerable. The first step in moving beyond despair is to name its underlying cause, the social symptom that binds the attachments and investments of leaders and followers together. Working with the symptom (rather than denying it or trying to eradicate it which causes repression and displacement) allows recognition and insights that enable leaders to begin to do reparative work in place of destructive acting out.

Group 4: Trauma and disenchantment

There is a special place for trauma and disenchantment in the leadership literature, that currently presents a vast gap and lack. Trauma and loss are probably two of the most common drivers of leadership–followership behaviour in organizational and national cultures. As discussed previously, lack creates desire, and any symptom of trauma and loss requires the leaders to face this loss and lack, to enable a mourning, grieving and reparation to take place. If this is not done it leads to disenchantment, despair and often worse. If the loss is only partially acknowledged but not worked through, then melancholia sets in with very damaging results (see Chapter 20: USA). Sacrificial leadership provides a similar situation, usually linked to a trauma but with context-specific data that require context-specific leadership to work with it. Identifying trauma, sacrifice and loss as symptoms, and facing disenchantment opens up a nation or organization to undertake reparation and begin creative processes of renewal.

A final note on group 3 and 4 is that when dealing with trauma, despair, loss and disenchantment we must account for the unconscious part of this process. There is the common view that the unconscious (individually and collectively) often acts to deny, repress or displace the pain that is involved in facing these emotionally charged symptoms. Another less well-known view is the Lacanian idea of *jouissance*, which helps us to understand how people become over-identified with loss and trauma and this can lead them to take a perverse 'pleasure in the displeasure' they experience. Sacrificial leadership can be a form of leadership that harnesses the trauma to the leader's ends, utilizing the unconscious pleasure a collective group gains when identifying themselves with a particular loss or trauma. To undertake reparation work and to move beyond the loss and create new possibilities then means to relinquish the unconscious pleasure we gain from our collective identification to the trauma that bind us together. The 'chosen trauma' (Volkan, 1991) then becomes a barrier to potential positive change.

Group 5: Coexisting differences

Westernized sensibilities emanating from the Enlightenment that championed rationality and reason, find the idea of paradox and working with coexisting differences counter-cultural to the linear logic of scientific-reductionism that strives to find a pure solution. The Eastern traditions and culture embrace paradox in very different ways by working with coexisting differences rather than attempting to overcome them. This approach can teach Western leadership a lot about how to lead in today's complex world, which consistently presents leaders with unresolvable paradoxes. The coexisting positions that link Authoritarian–Democratic and Collaborative–Controlling leadership are examples of how this kind of leadership works in the countries and regions discussed.

Group 6: Hopeful

This grouping of Progressive, Networked, Romantic, Fusion and Transmission leadership present different themes and symptoms from each particular context, but collectively they resonated as having the potential to offer hope. This hope points to a leadership 'Real' that is underpinned by the pleasure derived from working creatively with others. Each has a shadow side which requires transparent acknowledgement to enable leaders and followers to work with it, but each points in its own way to how leadership may positively unfold in the future.

Further gaps to mind

This book and its partial analysis of the chapters has led to many insights and also left many other gaps which require further research and exploration.

The leadership gender gap

Gender is mentioned in many of the chapters and we chose not to address it as a main piece of our analysis because there are many other texts that undertake this task, and in our limited space we decided that this literature was more complete than what we could present, so we chose to look at less well-documented leadership issues. It is sufficient here to say that from these chapters it is clear that the gender gap remains an absolutely key issue in leadership across the globe. The representation of women leaders in national politics and in senior organizational life remains an issue that is both oppressive to women and denies the workplace of a wealth of talent. Some countries are making good progress, such as Scandinavian countries with their equality agenda, and Germany where male leadership is being challenged:

> The traditional role model of the genders, which is strongly based on the long successful male society and old boys' network, is now opposed by a new female pragmatic leadership style that is embodied by Chancellor Angela Merkel. (Claudia Nagel, p. 94)

In other countries, some progressive movement is reported, e.g. from Russia where gender diversity in leadership also has its own peculiarities. Leadership discourse uses primarily masculine forms of the language, and many leadership practices are dominated by explicit demonstration of machismo and patriarchal values. Still, female leadership is increasingly present in Russian organizational and societal lives.

> According to a 2016 report by Grant Thornton entitled 'Women in Business', Russia now boasts the highest proportion of women in senior management roles worldwide (45% versus 23% in the USA, 21% in the UK, Japan ranking lowest with only 7% of

> senior positions held by women). Despite the generally sexist environment in Russia, women can be successful enough in their movement forward. (Ekaterina Belokoskova-Mikhaylova, Konstantin Korotov and Irena Izotova, p. 134).

There is also a palpable gender dynamic in South African leadership. While South Africa prides itself as having one of the most gender-transformed parliaments and government institutions, women continue to be under-represented in senior corporate leadership. Anecdotal evidence also suggests that men appoint women, or allow women to be appointed in leadership positions, to maintain the fantasy of gender equality, but silently still lead from behind. The fact that women 'allow' this to happen is a matter for further leadership research and ongoing conversations. (Peliwe Mnguni and Jeremias De Klerk, p. 149)

Other countries report very serious problems as discussed in Mexican and the Ethiopian chapters:

> In terms of gender hierarchies, women leaders are almost non-existent in decision-making roles in Ethiopian institutions. Hora (2014) observed several barriers to women's positional leadership, including limited educational opportunity, patriarchal cultural attitudes, burdensome domestic responsibilities and the lack of role models. Women's access to leadership posts is largely determined by powerful male gatekeepers, as patriarchic culture still dominates organizational life. Overall, the conditions and expectations of leadership in Ethiopia are shaped by larger systems of social power and gender inequality. (Fentahun Mengistu, Vachel Miller and Girma Shimelis, p. 72)
>
> The stereotype of masculine supremacy, social oppression, and authoritarian politics pervade the arena of leadership and politics. Mexican men (almost exclusively in positions of power) often have very archaic beliefs about women in leadership roles, suggesting that motherhood is the supreme duty of a woman, and that it is an obstacle to a women's career rather than a motivation to succeed. (Maria Fonseca Paredes and Fernando Sandoval Arzaga, p. 114)

One of the challenges particular to leadership in relation to gender is the issue highlighted in Nirmal Puwar's book *Space Invaders: Race Gender and Bodies out of Place* (2004). Puwar describes this process that marks establishment spaces, and excludes those bodies that are not a part of this space. She cites Winston Churchill's reaction to Nancy Astor, the first woman MP to enter the House of Parliament:

> I find a woman's intrusion into the House of Commons as embarrassing as if she burst into my bathroom when I had nothing with which to defend myself, not even a sponge. (Winston Churchill cited in Vallance, *Women in the House*). (Puwar, 2004: 13)

Leadership spaces are often spaces of elite power and establishment. The experience of being a space invader highlights the often-unconscious processes of gender dynamics where normative assumptions expect men to be in that space, making it difficult for both genders to accommodate change.

The prominent issues that stand out from these chapters in relation to gender are, first, identifying the cultural, economic, social and religious forces that maintain the status quo of gender inequality at work and in leadership in particular.

The second issue is the connections between gender essentialism and leadership essentialism. What we are referring to is the way leadership gets identified with 'essentialized male attributes' such as active rather than passive qualities for example. This is particularly true of the Messiah leadership discourse. When leadership is reduced and essentialized to individuals with charisma and influence, this can be a shorthand way of saying leaders with alpha male attributes. This raises another problem for those who campaign for more women leaders on a female essentialist platform, such as Professor Lynda Gratton who took up a new role as head of the Lehman Brothers Centre for Women in Business in 2006, the first research centre dedicated to this issue in Europe. When interviewed she said:

> The sort of things women are good at – innovation, getting work done at the same time as getting on with people – are increasingly valuable as we move into a world in which flexibility and knowledge-sharing are a key ... women are good at networking, they just tend to network with people they like, men tend to network with more powerful people ... if we make organizations more humane guess what? They suit women. (*Guardian*, 3 November 2006)

This essentializes genders in an unhelpful way, and in a world where binary notions of gender and sexuality are fast blurring, the essentialist and reductionist generalizations that box men into Mars and women into Venus, seem outdated. Contemporary feminist theorists claim that 'essentialism' hinders the progress toward liberation (Rich, 1980; Butler, 2004).

Sexuality and leadership

The gap that appears around sexuality and leadership remains largely unspoken; it was mentioned in the USA chapter connecting sexuality, gender and race as key issues in leadership and pointing to the CEO of the world's most successful company, Apple, as being openly gay. It is noteworthy that Ireland, Simon's home country, has recently elected a gay man as the country's prime minister. Sexuality and identity politics are becoming more transparent and discussed, causing progressive breakthroughs alongside reactionary backlashes (Zachary Gabriel Green and Cheryl Getz in Part One, p. 174). In leadership, this is interesting as the blurring of gender and sexuality binaries that 'undoes gender' (Butler, 2004) hopefully will also work to undo the reductionism and essentialism of leadership as well, opening new spaces for individual leaders to emerge from a plurality of identities, and for leadership to emerge in a plurality of ways.

For further reading on gender, sexuality and leadership see Butler (2004, 2011), Walby (1997), Werhane and Painter-Morland (2013).

Religion and leadership

Another gap we have not addressed in depth but was very present in the chapters is religion and its impact on culture and leadership. There is a whole book to be written on this issue, how religion affirms, shapes and limits the roles and perceptions of how leadership plays out in each given context. In this book, it became clear that religion *per se* could not be separated from wider societal, cultural and historical factors, we therefore chose to leave the chapters to speak for themselves on leadership and religion, and we invite the reader to draw their own conclusions and encourage further research and development in this domain. Below are a few selected statements drawn from the country/region chapters in Part One that express the relationship between religion, culture and leadership

ASEAN

> It can be said, leadership in the ASEAN region has been shaped by many endogenous and exogenous factors over the last 50 years alone ... Diverse religions including Islam, Buddhism, Confucianism, Christianity and Hinduism ... have diverse leadership impacts across the region.

China

> Traditional Chinese philosophies, Taoism and Buddhism in particular, make people view management tasks or situations as a holistic process with particular characteristics. Effective Chinese leaders thus conduct their organizing role by 'following the nature' and understand their tasks as the 'combination of conditions' (Alves et al., 2005). ...
>
> Traditionally, the Chinese have 'the ability ... to hold different propositions simultaneously without distress' (Cotterell, 2002: 30). The mindset derived from the Yin of Confucian paternalism and the Yang of Taoist holistic thinking does not see opposites but rather different aspects of the same system (Li, 2012). ...
>
> The hierarchy of Confucian paternalism is extensively described. This hierarchical paternalism is a prerequisite of maintaining social harmony, where each actor should behave strictly in accordance with the hierarchical position that specifies the individual to a prescribed role (Yang, 1993).

France

> For the French, morality, like religion, belongs to the private sphere and can be separated from the exercise of leadership in the professional sphere.

Germany

They are closely tied to the religious-based ideas of life and work that are found in the Protestant-based ethics of Weber (Weber, 1905/2015) as well as in the Catholic Social Doctrine and the resulting Rhine Capitalism. ...

Religious aspects also influence the understanding of leadership in Germany. At this religious level, we find Weber's Protestant Ethic opposed and connected with the Catholic Social Doctrine – depicted in the first social encyclical Rerum Novarum by Pope Leo XIII. Both of these created the ethical framework for the leadership culture in Germany. ...

The guiding maxims of his Protestant Ethic for successful entrepreneurs are: proficiency, systematic ascetic way of life, deliberate modesty as well as joy in the obligatory fulfilment in the secular occupation as the highest content of moral self-exertion. The special role that the occupation has as a calling and place of inner-worldly fulfilment, is described by the idea that the occupation is a God-given task.

Mexico

Leadership in Mexico has been impacted by various elements from its culture such as: (1) Machismo and sexism; (2) Paternalism and male dominance; (3) Rigidity and hierarchy, all of which are expressed and reinforced in the social structures of Education, Family Dynamics, and Religion.

India

Evidence of religious and spiritual orientation was found in a recent study (Spector et al., 2005) which concluded that Indian CEOs have reported greater spiritual and or religious sources of inner strength as compared to their global peers. ...

The concept of Guru – the remover of darkness, who leads one towards enlightenment – is embedded in Indian religion and philosophy.

Arab Middle East

This is not the place for a theological discourse but it is impossible to understand the concepts of Tawhid or of Ummah, for example, without comprehending that in Islam there is a strongly integrative meme around the one-ness of all creation. 'Tawhid is the realization that God is One, is the Creator and Master of creation. He alone is the ultimate cause of all that is, as well as the ultimate end of all that was, is or will be' (Al Faruqui, 1985). A good leader is one who creates the condition for collective unity.

USA

> These early pilgrims believed God's favour was afforded and revealed through those who acted with individual initiative and effort. With the fervour of a chosen people, they believed that they were God's instruments in this 'promised land'.

Religion and culture are entwined in these and other countries; Poland cannot be separated from Catholicism, Russia with the Orthodox Church; and these influences have to be engaged with if we are to understand and re-imagine how we can makes sense of, shape and develop leadership.

Architecture, space and leadership

Architecture, space and leadership are rarely discussed but the importance is beautifully captured in these brief quoted passages from Part One, first from the Arab Middle East chapter, and second from the Ethiopian chapter.

> [In the Arab Middle East] the diwan is a room with low seats around the walls, circumscribing a space that is empty of furniture, uncluttered and available for the movement of people within it; and is found in one guise or other in every Arab home and office. For it is a place of decision as well as of social intercourse (Weir, 2008). In the diwan, decisions are the outcome of processes of information exchange, practised listening, questioning and the interpretation and confirmation of informal as well as formal meanings. Decisions of the diwan may be enacted by the shaykh, but they are owned by all (Weir, 2011). This ensures commitment based on respect for both position and process. ....
>
> In the swirl of the diwan, leaders are visible and available and they have the opportunity to listen attentively to information including soft signals as well as formal data and financial summaries: leaders who lose the ability to read the informal temper of the times also stand to lose legitimacy and become vulnerable. The use of decision-making space in this way is therefore distinctly different from the barrier of the executive desk or the rigidity of the boardroom table.

> In Ethiopian universities, it is common to see a sign that says 'Use next door' on the closed office doors of upper administrators. This sign directs clients to pass through an outer office guarded by an executive secretary who has the power to withhold access to the inner office of her boss. If admitted inside the leader's office, a client will sit at a long conference table placed perpendicular to the administrator's desk, in a T-shape. This spatial configuration centres the administrator at the 'head' of any meeting and makes the conference table an extension of the administrator's own desk. It reinforces vertical relations of power and the patriarchal authority of the positional leader.

Physical environments matter hugely: architectures, natural habitats, rooms shapes and décor, furniture choices and the use of space are key issues for leadership to engage with. Beauty and aesthetics matter. Working in corporate environments and staying in business hotels internationally Simon is constantly reminded of the stark, coldness and minimalist conformity of these places. His soul is desperate to walk in the forests, by the sea or in an art gallery after his excursions on a business trip in order to re-ignite his soul and creativity. Leadership is not simply about the human interactions, the constructed and natural environments in which leadership and followership dynamics are enacted play a huge part in how leadership is embodied, performed and engaged with. The recent interest in the new offices built by Apple, Amazon and Google are indicators of the importance of space.

There are many other gaps, far too many to identify in this short conclusion, but we acknowledge the limitations of this book, and encourage each person to identify their own gaps and use them to stir their desire and seek new insights into leadership for themselves.

THE FUTURE OF LEADERSHIP

There are two generic conclusions from this book, that relate to the future of leadership and also relate to these two aims of the book, restated here:

1. Allowing leadership to speak with different voices
2. To open up a new space for leadership to speak, reflecting historical, cultural, economic and sociocultural influences

New research methods to develop theory and practice that is local and specific

The first generic conclusion that emerges from the book is the need for more research in the two areas stated above. This is imperative if leadership scholars and developers wish to support developing 'new leadership for new times' and to enable new leadership approaches to emerge that are local and specific, and applicable to the contexts in which they are practised. Finding ways to allow leadership to speak with different voices, implies inviting marginalized and unheard voices to speak about leadership, and inviting them to speak about leadership in new ways by 'looking awry' through different lenses. To allow leadership to speak with different voices implies not only a change in the speaker, but also a change in the listener. Listening differently as well as expecting the speaker to speak differently. This is the biggest barrier to change, as the current situation in leadership studies and academia produces conformist and elitist work that is self-referential, and if it does challenge the normative studies via the critical theorist leadership literature, it is very limited in its applied impact to practice. Martin Parker declares that Critical Management Studies (CMS) have very little impact on what happens in reality:

> CMS has had little or no impact on what organisations actually do ... there are some serious and fascinating issues being discussed within CMS, but they tend to stay within the cloistered boundaries of academic work and find little echo outside those who are already converted. (Parker, 2002: 115–16)

In short, the current situation does not invite new voices to speak from the edges and margins, nor is it able to listen to them when they do speak.

Beyond behaviourism, individualism and organizationalism

The study of leaders and leadership is predominantly set within their organizational settings via undertaking reductionist empirical studies such as testing leaders' behaviours, or writing leadership case studies. This produces a certain form of inward-focused 'scientific' positivist knowledge, predominantly targeted at individual leaders as change agents who make a difference via their behaviours and activities. What this omits is an outward wider and more nuanced view, that can account for the technical, natural and social eco-systems that inform, shape and distort leadership practice. These psycho-social and technical eco-systems are influenced by histories, cultures, technologies, landscapes and traditions that speak through leaders and followers, organizations and politicians. This omission produces a 'lack' that creates an unresolved dissonance in the practice of leadership in regions across the globe. Working with global HR and OD leaders in some of the world's largest companies, Simon sees this dissonance at play all the time. Local and regional leaders are expected to fit into global and universalized norms of leadership as espoused from a Westernized centric ideology. An ideology that is so pervasive and normative, that those engaged with it do not question or challenge it. It is just the way things are. This form of ideology is most popularly captured in succinct soundbite articles in the *Harvard Business Review* and other such journals and populist business books, and is translated into leadership development and leadership practices by global consulting companies. What occurs is a particular type of 'performative leadership' that gets measured and rewarded by organizations in a performance review, in the same way that academia measures and rewards theorists who get published in the right journals by producing conformist texts.

This book revealed beyond our expectations the depths and riches of leadership practices and underlying themes and symptoms that go unnoticed, unrecognized, unsupported and unrewarded. Yet in reality, it is these unseen leadership themes, symptoms and practices that shape leadership that delivers or undermines success. When these local leadership approaches are not worked with, the hidden strengths of leadership that deliver success are not developed, and the hidden practices that undermine success are never addressed. Globally the loss of productivity, morale and overall success due to this 'lack' must be absolutely huge!

The second generic conclusion is that the type of research and the methods used to study leadership also need revisiting. If we are to discover new, emergent or different leadership approaches and practices outside of the dominant and normative, we have to design research methodologies that are also diverse, experimental and outside of normative research practices. How we observe, how we look and how we undertake research analysis has to become more diverse and experimental.

Leadership development

The conclusions to this book point to a different emphasis on leadership development that is required to complement the mainstream approaches that focus on knowledge, the individual and behaviour change, as set out in Figure 1.

The findings of this research show how important it is to take on board the following issues:

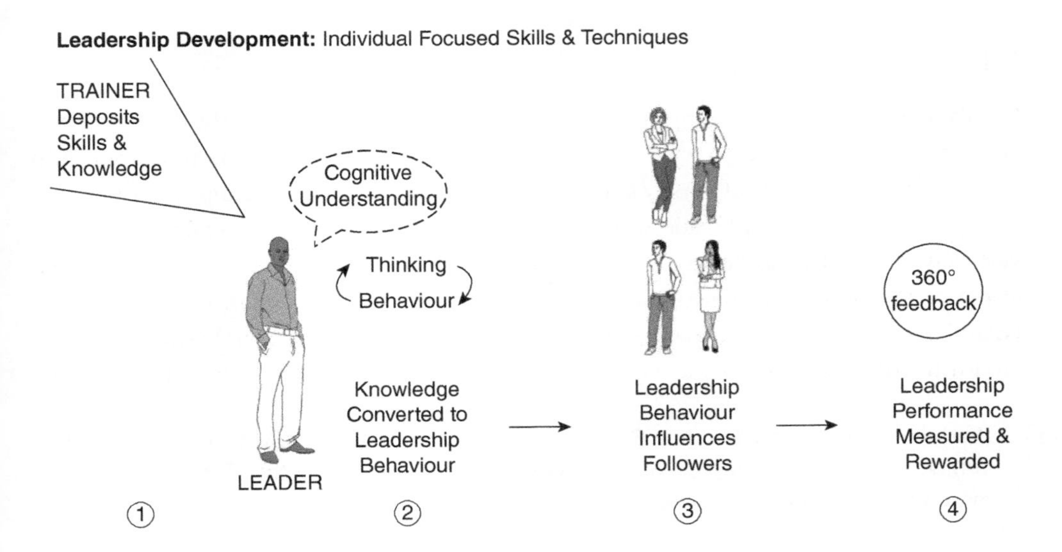

1. Leadership development should be tailored for local and specific consumption. Universal approaches utilizing generic leadership competencies and skills belong to the last century.
2. Leadership development is a collective as well as individual endeavour. No personal development without organizational development.
3. Historical, social and cultural awareness needs to be integrated into leadership developmental activities. Working without these insights is denying all of the outsider-leadership practices that emerged in this book.
4. Seeking the leadership symptom via 'minding-the-gap' research methods is a radical departure from the normative positivist leadership research that seeks to discover empirical and replicable knowledge. This approach also changes how leadership is conceptualized, and practised. The leadership symptom describes an affective and cultural essence of leadership that points to the Lacanian 'unknowable' Real of leadership. Leadership slips away from being the property of an individual, to being deeply embedded in culture and society. It also positions leadership as partially unknowable, which perhaps is the beginning of discovering radical and new leadership insights and practices.
5. Eco-leadership can act as a meta-theory for seeking new leadership approaches that address the networked society, which demands radical change in workplaces. Coaching leaders to develop their capacity to think and work as Eco-leaders requires new coaching and organizational development approaches that go beyond coaching individual-behaviour change. Leadership developers need to embrace new networked approaches that reframes leadership as a distributed phenomenon (for case studies and examples see Western, 2012; Western, 2017; Gosling and Western, 2018; and see www.analyticnetwork.com).

Digital native leadership

Finally, many of the chapters pointed to the next generation of leaders, the digital natives and millennials who are growing up in a world very different from the past leadership generation. The chapters of Turkey and Poland best express this, linking digital native leadership to social movement leadership, working more democratically, laterally rather than vertically, and with the notion of distributed leadership rather than a single individual leader or elite groups at the top of organizations functioning with position power. Both Poland and Turkey are experiencing turbulent times, with a polarization between authoritarianism and progressive democratic movements. The authors of the Polish chapter write:

> [Party] Razem, as opposed to PiS, has no single leader; leadership lies in the hands of democratically elected representatives and aligns its ideals with other European social movements and activist groups. (p. 126)

And the Turkish authors write about the protest social movement Gezi:

> The Gezi protests as with other leaderless, anti-hierarchical social movements, organize by consensus-based decision-making mechanisms and through cooperation rather than the iron hand of a single, powerful, heroic leader. (p. 157)

Both these examples are referring to emergent and new forms of Autonomist leadership, which emerges from anarchist, peace movement and social movement practices. Autonomist leadership operates within the five principles set out in the box below. We share this here because social movements have always been at the forefront of social and economic change, and Simon sees increasingly in his work in large corporate organizations the merger between ideas of distributing leadership and new social movement leadership.

The five principles that differentiate Autonomist leadership from other forms of leadership

Spontaneity, Autonomy, Mutualism, Networks and Affect

These principles are arrived at through participative observation in anarchist and other 'leaderless' groups over many years, combined with reviews of contemporary literature, texts and activist websites as well as through informal interviews with activists participating in new social movements (NSMs), such as the Occupy movement. Simon is not claiming these principles offer a fixed definition of Autonomist leadership, but they offer a heuristic device and he encourages dialogue and further research. This definition has been developed and expanded from an earlier version (Western, 2013: 80), with the addition of two principles: Affect and Networks.

Spontaneity

Leadership arises spontaneously, is temporary, without fixed roles and does not stabilize in any key actors or form of governance. It emerges and falls away as contexts arise, and actors take up leadership in diverse ways (both as individuals and collectively). A strength of this spontaneity is that it perpetuates unstable networks of individualized-collective action, thereby keeping movements agile and potentially able to utilize the leadership talents of all activists, rather than be limited to the talent of small elites.

(Continued)

Autonomy

The principle of autonomy applies to leaders, followers and all participating actors. Anybody and everybody can take up leadership, there is no ranking or hierarchy and there is a heightened awareness and commitment to the autonomy of all, guarding against coercion and the manipulation of power. The principle of autonomy reflects many anarchists' belief in individual freedom as a cornerstone of social justice, in contrast to socialist/communist privileging of collective allegiances over individual autonomy. Leaders or followers are interchangeable and both participate autonomously to co-create the enactment of leadership.

Mutualism

Leadership is enacted with mutual consent, mutual responsibility and for the mutual benefit of the movement/group. When functioning well, Autonomist leaders are upheld and supported to act in the best interests of the movement. Mutualism is the counter-balance to overzealous individual autonomy (found in some anarchist groups that can become narcissistic, and end up promoting self-interest). Any enactment of Autonomist leadership always works between the two tensions and forces of mutualism and collaboration, on the one hand, and competing individual and group interests on the other.

Networks

Autonomist leadership is embedded within networks as an active leadership dynamic that is fluid, changing and dispersed throughout the network. This differs from traditional leaders who may engage with and utilize networks; for example, when political leaders engage with and mobilize networks to gain support or fundraise. This is not Autonomist leadership. Autonomist leadership is a multiplicity and is rhizomatic (Deleuze and Guattari, 1987); it pops up, disappears, reappears, is beyond any single individual or elite group and is potentially within all individuals. Networked Autonomist leadership can make these movements appear 'leaderless' to those looking for orthodox leadership structures. While social movements have always used social networks to organize, the digital age has created new virtual platforms enabling a mobilization of Autonomist leadership in ways that were inconceivable before. The connectivity between virtual and physical networks has been one of the key innovations of NSMs and is transforming how social movements organize.

Affect

The importance of affect is amplified in NSMs in contrast to mainstream organizations. This is due to the strong personal affective investments that draw individuals to these emancipatory movements. Activists have personalized self narratives and emotional attachments that draw them to ideals such as freedom and to fight against oppression and abuse of power. Reciprocally, these movements generate powerful collective affects:

feelings such as hope, solidarity and love that arise from the idealism, camaraderie and unity expressed within them. An individual's personal affective attachments are reinforced and shaped through the networked conversations and exchanges that take place. Within NSMs, sub-groups are formed that appeal to diverse individual needs, desires and passions. Autonomist leaders act upon their personal affective investments and are mobilized by others into taking courageous or utilitarian acts of leadership. NSMs are charged with libidinal energy that arises from these affective investments and when attached to the emancipatory object, this produces and sustains pluralist and fluid forms of Autonomist leadership. However, when affective attachments become disinvested from the emancipatory object and become attached to fantasy objects such as being leaderless, the movements are weakened as activists' energies become displaced and Autonomist leadership is curtailed.

Taken from Western, 2014: 680–81.

The hope is that this millennial generation will feel more comfortable working adaptively and creatively in the networked society, utilizing new technologies and working more laterally peer-to-peer, rather than vertically within hierarchies. The greater hope is that this new generation adopts a humane and ethical leadership that counters many of the leadership traumas of the past century.

FINAL WORDS

We hope this book achieves for readers what it achieved for us as authors. Firstly, the regional chapters brought us exciting new perspectives into how leadership has developed, formed and is practiced across the globe. Secondly, it enabled us to get a glimpse of how the mainstream leadership discourses (researched from Western literature and practice) were found, reshaped and enacted in diverse regions globally. Thirdly and unexpectedly, it opened up a completely new way of thinking about leadership.

Taking a position that looked awry at leadership, rather than attempt to add to the existing mountain of 'empirical' leadership knowledge, we were freed to explore leadership from different perspectives. Whilst leadership in popular and academic texts is described in a variety of flavours, its key ingredients remain the same. It is underpinned and determined by a particular ideology (Zizek, 1989) made up of unspoken and unconscious, assumptions that reduces leadership to an individual actor whose behaviour influences others.

Being freed from this ideology 'individual-behaviourism', the book took up a third position. The insider-analysis reviewed how four key leadership discourses (Western, 2013) interplay with each other in each region/nation to help explain how leadership is thought about, embodied and enacted. The outsider-analysis then focused on what's lacking, and what leadership exists outside these discourses of normative leadership assumptions. The book revealed an essence of leadership in each region, which Simon calls 'the leadership symptom'. This offers us a tentative new way of making sense of how local 'symptoms of leadership' impact and shape leadership practices differently across the globe.

The 'leadership symptom' suggests how 'ways-of-being' and 'ways-of-becoming' leaders and followers are culturally, socially and historically inscribed. And that each situation is unique and particular and has to be worked with on a one-by-one basis. Without acknowledging or responding to these 'symptoms of leadership' researchers, teachers, trainers and practitioners ignore the 'libidinal economies' that define and shape how the Lacanian 'Real' of leadership is enacted.

Drucker reportedly said, 'culture eats strategy for breakfast' and he was right. To paraphrase this in relation to leadership, I (Simon) would say 'the libidinal economy eats empirical research for breakfast'. Producing and reproducing vast amounts of evidence-based data and knowledge about leadership that circles around the leadership ideology 'individual-behaviourism' has failed to produce tangible results that have improved political or organizational leadership. McCarthy (2017) reports that trust in CEOs across the globe has imploded, which alerts us that the old ways are not working. Without understanding the Sacrificial leadership symptom of Russia or the Melancholic leadership symptom of the USA, attempts to understand or develop leadership in these contexts will fall short, and miss the point. Ignoring the leadership symptom and the culturally inscribed 'libidinal economies' that shape leadership-followership dynamics is a futile act. It's like trying to cook a variety of cakes to reflect regional tastes, but being limited to using just one recipe.

To understand and develop leaders and leadership, we must firstly privilege and pay close attention to local and specific narratives; their histories, cultures, contexts and conditions that are inscribed into leadership and followership thinking, emotions and practices. It is time to look for new ways to conceptualize and understand leadership, beyond our 20th century frameworks. This means not undertaking another repetition, of creating new rhetoric, fads and fetishizing leadership to produce commercial commodities i.e. books, magazine articles, videos, training courses, consultancy processes, psychometrics, apps and the rest of the products that feed the insatiable, vast leadership industry. It means unfashionably looking at the past to engage with our embodied histories, as well as striving for a bright new future. It means paying attention to the social that speaks through individual and collective leadership actors. To account for our affects and collective traumas, to the historical, economic and political events that are inscribed into our ways-of-being, and to pay attention to culturally remembered emotions, embodied experience and the unconscious repetitions that inform our 'ways-of-becoming' leaders. Leadership cannot and should not be separated from the culturally inscribed world it inhabits.

This book took as a starting point nations and regions, but within nations and regions other local and specific conditions need to be accounted for. Each organization has its own specific history, product, peoples, technologies, nature and culture. These are not produced by the current CEO or leadership team, but the very opposite is true. The leadership team and CEO are selected and inscribed by the social and cultural contexts in which they exist, at both meta and micro levels. This is not to deny the influence of a skilled talented leader or leadership team, but it is to situate them in a context that both limits and opens up new possibilities. The initial work in this book was to invite authors to write subjective chapters courageously, to try and ignite a spark of understanding of what the libidinal economies are that underpin leadership in their country/region. The follow-up work was to analyse these chapters, firstly with commonly held leadership discourses and then to explore them to reveal gaps that suggested 'leadership symptoms'. In this Lacanian approach, these symptoms are a unique construction of leadership looking through a subjective, affective and cultural lens. The purpose is not a medical one, of treating the symptom or using it to diagnose a disease. The task is to help the leader/leadership to gain some insights into the meaning of the symptom for them and their team and organization. It is to preserve the uniqueness of the leadership symptom, finding creative ways of harnessing it and leveraging it for creative ends, whilst minimizing its negative and destructive capacity. The leadership symptom can never be pinned down or fixed, as we never quite get to its pure essence, we always miss something, there is always a lack which in turn creates further desire. Yet in the very act of seeking the 'leadership symptom', of looking for gaps and lack in the dominant leadership narratives, we begin the vital work of exploring leadership from new perspectives. It is only by acknowledging the importance of history, memory, culture and our collective subjectivities that make up particular leadership symptoms, will we develop new concepts, understandings and leadership practices for the 21st century.

REFERENCES

Butler, Judith (2011) *Bodies That Matter: On the Discursive Limits of Sex*. London and New York: Routledge.

Butler, Judith (2004) *Undoing Gender*. New York: Routledge.

Deleuze, Gilles and Guattari, Felix (1987) *A Thousand Plateaus: Capitalism and Schizophrenia*. Minneapolis, MN: University of Minnesota Press.

Garcia, E-J. (2008) 'Leadership in MBA programmes: an inquiry into lecturers' curriculum interests.' PhD thesis, UCL Institute of Education, London, UK.

Gosling, J. and Western, S. (2018) 'Leadership exchange: contextualized learning about how leadership is accomplished and personalized leadership development', in S. Kempster, A. Turner and G. Edwards (eds), *Leadership Development Field Guide*. Cheltenham: Edward Elgar.

Hannerz, U. (2000) *Transnational Connections*. London: Routledge.

Hora, E. (2014) 'Factors that affect women participation in leadership and decision-making positions', *Asian Journal of Humanity, Art and Literature*, 1 (2): 97–117.

McCarthy, Niall (2017) 'Global Trust in CEOs Has Imploded [Infographic]'. Available at: https://www.forbes.com/sites/niallmccarthy/2017/01/18/global-trust-in-ceos-has-imploded-infographic/#a5ec98f60a5c (Accessed 2 February 2018).

Parker, Martin (2002) *Against Management: Organization in the Age of Managerialism*. Cambridge: Polity Press.

Puwar, Nirmal (2004) *Space Invaders: Race Gender and Bodies out of Place*. New York: Berg Publishers.

Rich, A. (1980) 'Compulsory heterosexuality and lesbian experience', Signs: *Journal of Women in Culture and Society*, 5(4): 631–660.

Thrift, N. (1999) 'The place of complexity', *Theory, Culture & Society*, 16: 31–9.

Volkan, V.D. (1991) 'On "chosen trauma"', *Mind and Human Interaction*, 3: 13.

Walby, Yilvia (1997) *Gender Transformations*. London and New York: Routledge.

Werhane, Patricia and Painter-Morland, Mollie (2013) *Leadership, Gender, and Organization*. London: Springer.

Western, Simon (2012) *Coaching and Mentoring: A Critical Text*. London: Sage.

Western, Simon (2013) *Leadership: A Critical Text*, 2nd edn. London: Sage.

Western, S. (2014) 'Autonomist leadership in leaderless movements: anarchists leading the way', *Ephemera: Theory & Politics in Organization*, 14 (4): 673–98.

Western S. (2017) 'The key discourses of coaching', in Tatiana Bachkirova, Gordon Spence and David Drake (eds), *The Sage Handbook of Coaching*. London and Los Angeles: Sage. pp. 42–62.

Western, S. (2018) 'The Eco-leadership paradox', in B. Redekop, D.R. Gallagher and R. Satterwhite (eds), *Innovation in Environmental Leadership: Critical Perspectives*. New York and London: Routledge.

Zizek, Slavoj (1989) *The Sublime Object of Ideology*. London; New York: Verso, pp. 28–30.

APPENDIX

AUTHOR GUIDELINES

THE AIM: ALLOWING LEADERSHIP TO SPEAK WITH DIFFERENT VOICES

The originality and the challenge of this book are to highlight the complex interplay and evolution between global and regional influences impacting the understanding and the practice of leadership in organizations around the world.

To this end, the approach is essentially qualitative, open-ended and non-normative. It will draw upon the work of carefully selected regional authors from 20 highly contrasted regions.

The expected outcome will be a thought-provoking piece of work that transcends traditional academic boundaries as well as dominant discourses of leadership. The aim is to open up a new space for leadership to speak, reflecting historical, cultural, economic and socio-cultural influences.

Regional authors are selected by the editorial team (Simon Western and Éric-Jean Garcia) on the basis of their capacity to highlight the dominant discourses of leadership in their region and then critique it in its wider context.

Objectives for the regional authors

1. Your main task is to unravel leadership!
2. We are looking for accounts that offer insights, examples and explanations as to why leadership (and followership) in your particular country/region has a particular flavour, feeling, and way of being perceived and enacted.
3. Your task is not to write about your personal leadership identifications, but to try to be the voice that speaks for 'your' country/region. This means identifying the normative discourse (even if you don't agree with it), but then explaining the tensions within this. Is this just a rhetorical device, a mask for what lies below the surface?
4. What is really going on is usually much more diverse and often more complex, so it is important to consider:

- *The tensions between the global and the local:* It is important to clarify the extent to which competing discourses of leadership are influenced by different sources and are marginalized in some places but not others. The reader should get a sense of how this new wave of globalization impacts on local traditions and culturally embedded leadership, e.g. both how it is resisted and also how it changes leadership thinking and practice.
- *The sociocultural and historical influences:* Consideration must be given to historic, social, political and economic influences that shape leadership perceptions and practices. For example, monarchies and religion have a particular influence, as do democratizing revolutions and dictatorships, the question is how do these influences continue to shape contemporary leadership today? Are key individuals symbolic to leadership thinking in the past or present?
- *Writing style and approach:* We are keenly aware of the challenging task of writing a regional chapter, particularly in such a short word count. What we request is that you take a courageous stance, try to convey an essence of the leadership in your region. You will not be able to cover everything so don't be afraid to make cuts and edits that strengthen the overall clarity of your message. The house style will be to champion creativity, readability and accessibility. This book should appeal to academic scholars but also practitioners, it should be thoughtful and challenging, but please refrain from using academic language that excludes others. Write with the freedom to make the chapters come to life and speak to the readership.

THE THREE GUIDING QUESTIONS

The three following questions are purposefully open-ended so that a wide range of insights can be gained. We strongly encourage you to locate your answers in your regional context and illustrate them with specific examples where possible.

Each question is followed by some further leads to guide your thinking. But please, feel free to follow your own path on this journey.

[1] How is 'leadership' generally understood in your region?

- Try to engage in this question from an emotional and cultural as well as rational and pragmatic perspective, e.g. is leadership admired, feared or perhaps denigrated?
- What are the normative ways of thinking about leadership? e.g. via leaders in hierarchical position power? Or is this idea an unwelcome import that challenges local and traditional ways leadership is understood and experienced?
- Is leadership gendered or defined/constrained by age or race? Does it have military, tribal or religious connotations?
- What are the key competing narratives about leadership in your region?

[2] What are the main influences on how leadership has developed in your region?

- To what extent has this development been driven or constrained by ideological concerns such as a dominant religious influence, a particular political influence (e.g. fascism, socialism, democracy) or local ideology/cultures such as normative tribal organizing functions?
- Is there a conflict or a continuity between past and present influences?
- Are there key individuals who symbolically represent a particular leadership narrative that has taken hold? (this may be positive or negative or both)
- What are the emerging themes influencing change in leadership thinking and practice today?
- To what extent is globalization, normalization, digitalization, influencing the way leadership is conceived and practiced in your region? Can you identify one or two events that might symbolize the general tendency in this matter? Do you see serious changes in a near future?

WHAT ADDITIONAL FACTORS, THEMES OR IDEAS ARE IMPORTANT TO UNDERSTAND 'LEADERSHIP' IN YOUR REGION?

- Please add anything that you feel will add to our understanding of leadership in your region.
- Feel free to share questions you are left with having reflected on leadership in your region. The gaps that are left in our understanding are as important as the knowledge, as they point to new possibilities that require further development and research.

INDEX

NOTE: page numbers in *italic* type refer to figures.